CONSTITUTIONAL CONVENTIONS

D1579437

CONSTITUTIONAL CONVENTIONS

The Rules and Forms
of Political Accountability

Geoffrey Marshall

CLARENDON PRESS · OXFORD

*This book has been printed digitally and produced in a standard design
in order to ensure its continuing availability*

OXFORD
UNIVERSITY PRESS

Great Clarendon Street, Oxford OX2 6DP

Oxford University Press is a department of the University of Oxford.
It furthers the University's objective of excellence in research, scholarship,
and education by publishing worldwide in

Oxford New York

Athens Auckland Bangkok Bogotá Buenos Aires Cape Town
Chennai Dar es Salaam Delhi Florence Hong Kong Istanbul Karachi
Kolkata Kuala Lumpur Madrid Melbourne Mexico City Mumbai Nairobi
Paris São Paulo Shanghai Singapore Taipei Tokyo Toronto Warsaw

with associated companies in Berlin Ibadan

Oxford is a registered trade mark of Oxford University Press
in the UK and in certain other countries

Published in the United States
by Oxford University Press Inc., New York

© Geofrey Marshall 1984

ISBN 0-19-876202-X

We now have a whole system of public morality, a whole code of precepts for the guidance of public men which will not be found in any page of either the Statute or the Common Law but which are in practice held hardly less sacred than any principle embodied in the Great Charter or in the Petition of Right.

Edward Freeman
The Growth of the English Constitution (1872)

Preface

Two major themes of Dicey's *Law of the Constitution* that first appeared in 1885 were the sovereignty of Parliament and the role of the conventions of the Constitution. Some years ago in *Parliamentary Sovereignty and the Commonwealth* I tried to set out some developments in the post-Dicey career of the sovereignty principle. The present work is a stab in a similar direction taking Dicey's other thesis about the conventions as its starting-point. Both sovereignty and convention are similar in that, besides having a tangled history, they are difficult ideas whose general character has been, and still is, in dispute. Oddly they are also similar in that in recent times questions about their character have been provoked largely by constitutional developments occurring in Commonwealth countries as much as in Britain. In the 1950s a crisis in South Africa caused a revision of ideas about sovereignty. Thirty years later events in Canada have stirred up new questions about convention.

Parts of Chapter V originally appeared in *Public Law* and I am grateful for permission to reproduce the relevant material. Similar acknowledgements are due to the Inter University Seminar on Armed Forces and Society in respect of Chapter IX, most of which appeared in *Armed Forces and Society*, vol. 5 (1979). Some sections of Chapter XII are also adapted from a memorandum prepared for the House of Commons Foreign Affairs Committee in 1981. They were published as minutes of evidence to HC 42 (1980-1) and are reproduced by permission. Part of Chapter VIII is a revised version of an essay originally published in *Policy and Politics* (ed. D. E. Butler and A. H. Halsey (1978)).

A number of friends and colleagues have helped me both by their own writing and by their criticism. My thanks are particularly due to Stephen Scott, Robert Summers, Vernon Bogdanor, John Lloyd Edwards, Peter Hogg, Anne Bayefsky, and Yves de Montigny, all of whom I hasten to dissociate from anything here alleged whether as to law, fact, or opinion.

April 1983   GM

Preface to paperback edition

I have taken advantage of this reprinting to add an additional chapter on developments since 1984 that bear on the theme of governmental accountability. Amongst them are the nature of ministerial advice to the Queen as Head of the Commonwealth; the debate about conventions that should regulate the choice of governments and Prime Ministers in a 'Hung Parliament' situation; the Ponting and Westland affairs and a number of ministerial resignations. All these episodes raised questions about the rules of cabinet government, including questions about the relations of Ministers, civil servants, and Parliament and the roles of particular ministers, and the Law Officers of the Crown.

I have also added a short appendix on Dicey and Sir Ivor Jennings, whose views on constitutional conventions are not, I think, as far apart as they have been thought to be. In 1985, the centenary year of the publication of the *Introduction to the Study of the Law of the Constitution*, Dicey's work was widely discussed. He has been much misrepresented, but there is now every sign that his contribution to the study of both convention and law is better understood and appreciated.

April 1986   GM

Contents

Table of Cases

Table of Statutes

Introduction

One of the things that every schoolboy is supposed to know
(at least if he has taken the trouble to read Dicey's *Law of
the Constitution* and similar works) is that the Constitution
is unwritten, or to put it more accurately, it includes a large
number of non-legal conventional rules. Most of them deal
with the responsibilities of the major organs and officers of
government and with the relations between them. It could be
said that in general they are rules of non-legal accountability.
The rule or rules of ministerial responsibility provide an
obvious example. Since Dicey, many writers — such as Low,
Lowell, Laski, Jennings, and Wheare — have described the
conventions. Sir Ivor Jennings and Sir Kenneth Wheare in
particular analysed (and in Jennings's case rejected) Dicey's
analysis of the general nature of convention. Wheare's examination of convention drew particularly on his studies
of Commonwealth constitutional practice and of the relationships between Britain and the member nations of
the Commonweath. Since the basic principles of cabinet and
parliamentary government are not now peculiar to Westminster, it is not surprising that light has often been shed
on British constitutional doctrine by events occurring in
Commonwealth countries that share the parliamentary
tradition.

Within the United Kingdom, recent changes in the machinery of government, and developments in party and
electoral politics, have raised questions about the working
of particular conventions. If we examine the present rules
that are held to govern the responsibilities of the Crown, of
Ministers, of the Civil Service, and of other officers of government, we see a good deal of uncertainty. Some of it derives
from the fact that conventions are of more than one kind so
that the accountability of different branches and organs of
government may assume different forms. New institutions
and occurrences also exert a pressure on old rules. In some
cases the rules may need to be dispensed with. In other cases

they may be mistakenly or heedlessly changed. Sometimes they may be misunderstood or misapplied.

Given these uncertainties it is not surprising that the application of conventions in particular cases has often been a matter of sharp political controversy. In addition their general nature and their relationship to the ordinary law of the land has always been a matter of dispute amongst lawyers and political scientists. Within the United Kingdom the conventions provide a framework of political accountability. Externally, rules of a similar character regulate the relationship of the United Kingdom's political processes to those of other Commonwealth member countries focusing responsibility at the appropriate points regardless of the legal forms. In the following chapters we shall look at both types of convention and consider their character as rules of governmental morality.

I
The Theory of Convention Since Dicey

Constitutional conventions play a central part in the theory of British Government. A variety of names has been given to these non-legal rules of constitutional behaviour. 'Maxims', 'practices', 'customs', 'usages', 'precepts' and 'conventions' are some of them.[1] A concise enumeration of such rules is not easy to make since they shade off into what might be called 'traditions', 'principles' and 'doctrines'. (We might speak, for example, of the traditions of toleration and the rule of law; the principles of judicial independence and freedom of speech; or the doctrines of representative government and the electoral mandate.) There is also a problem of knowing which of a great many non-legal rules of political or official behaviour to treat as relating strictly to the Constitution. Should we, for example, include the rules for electing the leaders of the political parties, or the Standing Orders of the House of Commons, or the Judges' Rules for questioning suspected persons?

In his *Introduction to the Study of the Law of the Constitution* A. V. Dicey picked out a number of rules as being constitutional conventions. They included the rules that the King must assent to any Bill passed by the two Houses of Parliament; that Ministers must resign office when they cease to command the confidence of the House of Commons; and that a Bill must be read a certain number of times before passing. He also mentioned various questions that raise issues of conventional (rather than legal) propriety. What, he asked, are the conventions under which a Ministry may dissolve Parliament? May a large number of Peers be created for the purpose of overruling the Upper House? On what principle may a Cabinet allow of open questions? These last examples

---

[1] John Stuart Mill wrote of 'the unwritten maxims of the constitution' (*Representative Government* (1861)); E. A. Freeman of 'a whole book of precepts'; Sir William Anson of 'Custom' (*The Law and Custom of the Constitution*); and A. V. Dicey of 'the conventions of the Constitution' (*Introduction to the Study of the Law of the Constitution* 10th edn.).

appear to be cases in which it cannot be clearly stated what the conventions are, or cases in which the relevant conventions are conflicting or controversial.

Dicey's discussion implied that the conventions of the Constitution relate mainly to the exercise of the Crown's prerogatives and he suggested that their purpose was to ensure that these legal powers, formally in the hands of the Crown, were in practice exercised by Ministers in accordance with the principles of responsible and representative government. But though the conventions do provide the framework of cabinet government and political accountability, and often modify rules of law, they spread more widely than Dicey's description suggests. Besides the conventional rules that govern the powers of the Crown there are many other constitutional relationships between governmental persons or institutions that illustrate the existence of rules of a conventional character. Examples are:

- Relations between the Cabinet and the Prime Minister
- Relations between the Government as a whole and Parliament
- Relations between the two Houses of Parliament
- Relations between Ministers and the Civil Service
- Relations between Ministers and the machinery of justice
- Relations between the United Kingdom and the member countries of the Commonwealth.

Many of these relationships are in part governed by law and in part by convention. The relations between the House of Commons and the House of Lords, for example, are determined partly by the provisions of the Parliament Acts of 1911 and 1949 and partly by conventional usage. Equally, the relationships of the member countries of the Commonwealth are in a number of fundamental ways regulated by the Statute of Westminster, but in other ways rest upon agreements or conventions (some of which are mentioned in the preamble to the Statute).

Amongst the conventions of the Constitution there are some whose formulation is reasonably precise and specific, and others whose formulation is in more general terms. An example of the first kind is the rule that the Queen must assent to Bills that have received the approval of both Houses. An example of the second kind is that the House of Lords should not obstruct the policy of an elected government with a majority in the House of Commons. Many conventions fall into the second category. This, perhaps, explains why so many questions of constitutional propriety remain unsettled. Might a British Government ever be dismissed by the Crown (comparably with what happened in Australia in 1975)? Is a Prime Minister entitled to dissolve Parliament and hold a General Election whenever he wishes? Can a Government continue in office if its major legislation is defeated in the House of Commons? May a Minister blame his civil servants if mistakes are made in the work of his Department? The answers to all these questions are uncertain because in each case there is a general rule whose limits have not been fully explored; or possibly there may be two rules which are potentially in conflict.

Obedience to Conventions

This may in part account for a certain amount of confusion in the application of the terms 'usage' and 'convention'. In the opening chapter of the *Law of the Constitution* Dicey, in discussing 'the rules that belong to the conventions of the Constitution', remarks that 'some of these maxims are never violated and are universally admitted to be inviolable. Others on the other hand have nothing but a slight amount of custom in their favour and are of disputable validity.'[2] Confusingly, he goes on to explain this difference as one that rests upon the distinction between rules that bring their violators into conflict with the law of the land, and rules 'that may be violated without any other consequence than that of exposing the Minister or other person by whom they were broken to blame or unpopularity'.[3] This does not chime very easily with the thesis that the reason for obedience to all conventions is that breach of the conventions leads more or less directly to a breach of law. Dicey has often been criticized for holding this view, but it seems clear that he did not hold it in relation to *all* conventions. Indeed, it seems an explanation confined to a single contingency, namely

---

[2] *Law of the Constitution* (10th edn.), at p. 26 n.   [3] Ibid.

the possibility that a Government might try to remain in office and raise taxes after losing the confidence of the House of Commons. But Dicey mentions a number of examples in which no illegal consequences would follow a breach of conventional principles. A Government that persuaded the House of Commons to suspend the Habeas Corpus Acts after one reading, or induced the House to alter the rules as to the number of times a Bill should be read would not, he said, come into conflict with the law of the land. Nor indeed would the House of Lords if it rejected a series of Bills passed by the Commons.

Some who have criticized Dicey's supposed explanation for obedience to conventions have suggested alternative reasons. Sir Ivor Jennings argued, for example, that conventions are obeyed 'because of the political difficulties which follow if they are not'.[4] Others[5] have suggested that they are obeyed not because of the probability of a consequential breach of law, but because disregard of convention is likely to induce a change in the law or in the constitutional structure. But it could be objected that in the case of many infringements of convention, legal or structural change would be an unlikely outcome. It may be more illuminating first to remember that widespread breach of political (as of linguistic) convention may itself sometimes lead to a change of convention and secondly that conventions are *not* always obeyed. So although we can sensibly ask what the uses or purposes of conventions are, it may be unnecessary to ask why they are obeyed when they are obeyed, since we pick out and identify as conventions precisely those rules that *are* generally obeyed and generally thought to be obligatory. Those who obey moral or other non-legal rules they believe to be obligatory, characteristically do it because of their belief that they are obligatory, or else from some motive of prudence or expected advantage. Those who disobey them do so because they do not regard them as obligatory, or wish to evade them, or wish to change them. In other words we do not need any special or characteristic explanation for obedience to the rules of govern-

---

[4]   *The Law and the Constitution* (5th edn. 1959), p. 134.
[5]   e.g. G. Marshall and G. C. Moodie, *Some Problems of the Constitution* (4th edn.), p. 36.

mental morality. Whatever we know about compliance with moral rules generally, will suffice.

Two Types of Conventions

Sir Kenneth Wheare in *Modern Constitutions* wrote that:

> By convention is meant a binding rule, a rule of behaviour accepted as obligatory by those concerned in the working of the constitution[.] [6]

If this is to serve as a definition it may need some expansion and explanation for the following reason. In recent times a number of practices have been termed conventions of the Constitution, and politicians are sometimes charged with breaking them. The emphasis on *obligatory* behaviour in Sir Kenneth Wheare's definition may obscure the point that the conventions, as a body of constitutional morality, deal not just with obligations but also with rights, powers, and duties. Some familiar and important conventions do not in fact impose obligations or duties but confer rights or entitlements. One such example may be the rule or practice of cabinet secrecy. This is often called a convention, but it is not clear that the maintenance of secrecy about cabinet proceedings is a duty-imposing convention, or that any corresponding right exists (in say Parliament or the Opposition) to have cabinet secrecy maintained. Would there be any violation of such rights if the Cabinet were to make a practice of publishing all cabinet proceedings in full? Of course individual members may have a duty to each other, and the Prime Minister may have a right against them to have confidentiality maintained. But the question is whether the Cabinet collectively owes a duty of secrecy to anybody else. If the foundation of cabinet secrecy rested, as used to be asserted, in a duty to the Crown to maintain the secrecy of the Privy Councillors' oath then it could on that ground be treated as an obligation. But few Cabinet Ministers or Prime Ministers now seem to suppose that they are in breach of any such duty when individually or

---

[6] *Modern Constitutions* (1951), p. 179.

collectively leaking the results of cabinet deliberations to the press.[7]

Similar considerations apply to the convention of collective ministerial responsibility, in so far as it relates not to resignation or dissolution after defeat, but to the maintenance of solidarity in speaking and voting by members of the Cabinet or administration as a whole. This is certainly a firmly maintained usage and it might be politically foolish or imprudent of any Prime Minister to dispense with it. But would it represent a breach of any constitutional duty to the House of Commons if freedom to speak or vote against cabinet policy were willingly conceded by the Cabinet to individual Cabinet Ministers? On several occasions (in 1932 and 1975, for example) the rule of collective solidarity has been suspended. In 1975 Mr Harold Wilson's abandonment of the rule in relation to the referendum decision on EEC membership was widely criticized by his opponents as a breach of constitutional convention. But that criticism was misconceived if collective cabinet solidarity is not a constitutional obligation or the object of a duty-imposing rule.

It is useful therefore to separate duty-imposing conventions from entitlement-conferring conventions. That the Queen is (in some circumstances) entitled to refuse a Prime Ministerial request to dissolve Parliament is a further example of the second type of conventional rule. There is of course a well-established usage of compliance with requests for dissolutions and such usages often accompany entitlement-conferring conventions.

Establishing Conventions

It seems to be agreed that conventions may be established in several ways. Frequently they arise from a series of precedents that are agreed to have given rise to a binding rule of behaviour. On the other hand 'a convention may arise

---

[7] In view of the frequency of this habit it may well be asked what has become of the rule that 'Disclosures of Cabinet discussions are now made only with the permission of the Sovereign; and it is the practice that this permission should be obtained through the intervention of the Prime Minister'? Anson, *Law and Custom of the Constitution* (4th edn., ed. Keith), vol. ii, pt. i, p. 121.

much more quickly than this. There may be an agreement among the people concerned to work in a particular way and to adopt a particular rule of conduct. This rule has not arisen from custom; it has no previous history as a usage.'[8] The conventions that the United Kingdom would not legislate for Commonwealth countries except upon their request and consent, and that any change in the Royal style and titles should require the consent of all the member countries were recorded, for example, in the Balfour Declaration of 1926 and in the preamble to the Statute of Westminster as agreed rules (though against a background of usage).

Thirdly, however, a convention may be formulated on the basis of some acknowledged principle of government which provides a reason or justification for it. Though it is rarely formulated as a conventional rule the most obvious and undisputed convention of the British constitutional system is that Parliament does not use its unlimited sovereign power of legislation in an oppressive or tyrannical way. That is a vague but clearly accepted conventional rule resting on the principle of constitutionalism and the rule of law. (It illustrates incidentally the fact that many conventions are negative in form and rest upon a practice of refraining from some course of action.)

Each of these grounds for asserting the existence of a convention was illustrated in the disagreement that surrounded the patriation of the Canadian Constitution in 1980-1. The dispute turned (apart from its legal aspect) on the question whether there existed a constitutional convention that required the consent of the Canadian provinces before the Federal Government could properly request the British Parliament to amend the British North America Act in ways that would affect the powers of the provinces and the federal structure of Canada. By an unusual turn of events the question was resolved by a decision of the Canadian Supreme Court[9] which held that such a convention existed in Canada. It was based on precedent, on specific agreement (the practice having been set out in a White Paper on constitutional amendment in 1965) and on principle (the convention

---

[8]   Sir Kenneth Wheare, *Modern Constitutions* (1951), p. 180.
[9]   *Reference re Amendment of the Constitution of Canada (Nos. 1, 2, and 3)* (1982), 125 D.L.R. (3d) 1. (See chap. XI below and App. B.)

being necessary to maintain the balance of the federal division of powers in Canada).

This episode, however, illustrates precisely why arguments about the existence of conventions are so often unresolved. Each of the possible constituent elements is contentious. Precedents may be read in different ways. In this case it was argued on one side that in relation to the British convention no previous request for a British amending enactment had been rejected — thus establishing a precedent for action. On the other hand it was said that none of the previous enactments had been similar to the one in dispute or had affected provincial powers — thus establishing a precedent for inaction. In relation to specific agreement it was argued that the terms of the Canadian White Paper of 1965 were unclear or that they were in general terms. In relation to any alleged reason or justifying principle there may also be (and was here) the possibility of different and opposite inferences. In 1981 the Canadian Provinces (and the Supreme Court) thought that the Canadian federal principle clearly implied the existence of a convention requiring provincial consent to change the existing federal-provincial balance of powers. The Federal Government, however, asserted that the Canadian federal system did not contain any such implied protection against federal action.

In 1981 the Canadian courts accepted Sir Ivor Jennings's account of the establishment of conventions. Their existence, Sir Ivor wrote, turned on the answer to three questions, namely, Are there any precedents? Did the actors in the precedents believe that they were bound by a rule? Is there a reason for the rule?[10]

Sir Ivor Jennings's tripartite specification suggests, however, that there are some unresolved problems about conventions. These arise partly from the existence of rival tests for their establishment and partly from the disputed connections between convention and law.

Positive or Critical Morality

Most British writers, following Dicey, have emphasized

---

[10] See *The Law and the Constitution* (5th edn. 1959), chapter III.

the separation of law and convention, and accepted his characterization of conventional rules as 'maxims or practices regulating the ordinary conduct of the Crown, of Ministers and of other persons under the Constitution'. They have, however, gone on to define such rules as being those *believed* by the persons concerned to govern their conduct. So, Sir Kenneth Wheare defined convention as 'a rule of behaviour *accepted as obligatory* by those concerned in the working of the Constitution'.[11] Similarly Professor O. Hood Phillips suggests as a working definition 'rules of political practice *which are regarded as binding* by those to whom they apply'.[12]

This suggests that the primary evidence as to the existence of a convention lies in the beliefs of the persons concerned. This, we remember, was the point to which Jennings's second question relates. 'Did the actors *believe* they were bound by a rule?' But the implication of the other questions ('Are there precedents?' and 'Is there a reason?') is that such beliefs may not be conclusive. Jennings indeed allots some importance to reasons since he says that precedents may not decide the matter and that whilst a number of precedents may not establish a rule, a single precedent with a good reason *can* establish a rule. Equally, he suggests, the conviction of the participants without a good reason may fail to create a convention. When George V appointed Mr Baldwin as Prime Minister in 1923 instead of Lord Curzon he did not, Jennings says, establish a convention against the appointment of Peers as Prime Ministers, since even if the King had thought himself bound to appoint Baldwin 'it might be that he was mistaken in thinking himself so bound'.[13]

We are here faced with two possibilities. One is that conventions are what we might call the positive morality of the Constitution — the beliefs that the major participants in the political process as a matter of fact have about what is required of them. On this view the existence of a convention is a question of historical and sociological fact.

[11] *Modern Constitutions* (1966), p. 122. (Italics added.)
[12] *Constitutional and Administrative Law* (6th edn. 1978), pp. 104-5. (Italics added.)
[13] *The Law and the Constitution* (5th edn.), p. 136.

The alternative possibility is that conventions are the rules that the political actors *ought* to feel obliged by, if they have considered the precedents and reasons correctly. This permits us to think of conventions as the critical morality of the Constitution.

Though either view is possible, the second seems better. It allows critics and commentators to say that although a rule may appear to be widely or even universally accepted as a convention, the conclusions generally drawn from earlier precedents, or the reasons advanced in justification, are mistaken. This, on some occasions, is what political or academic critics do wish to say. But if the existence of convention were only a question requiring empirical investigations of politicians' beliefs, it would be impossible to say that they wrongly believed a convention to exist.

Conventions and the Courts

Some, including Sir Ivor Jennings, have disputed Dicey's separation of convention and law, holding that 'conventions are rules whose nature does not differ fundamentally from that of the positive law of England'.[14] What Jennings's arguments amount to is that many propositions that are true of law are also true of convention, and that convention is as important and sometimes more important than law. But that need not persuade us that the two are fundamentally the same. What the issue comes to in practice is whether law may be derived from conventions and whether conventions may be applied in courts of law. In the Canadian controversy already referred to, it was argued by some of the Canadian Provinces that the conventions governing amendment of the Constitution should be declared and affirmed by the courts as being basic conventions of the Constitution that had hardened or crystallized into law. If such a claim were admitted by a court, it would make nonsense of Dicey's claim that conventions are distinguishable from law precisely by their non-enforcement in courts of law. In fact in the *Law of the Constitution* Dicey is somewhat unclear. In his opening

---

[14] *The Law and the Constitution* (5th edn. 1959), p. 74.

chapter he speaks of conventions as 'understandings, habits or practices . . . not *enforced* by the courts'. But in his later discussion he says that they are 'not enforced or *recognised* by the courts'[15] Some later writers seem, moreover, to have treated these two assertions as identical. Professor Berriedale Keith, for example, spoke of 'conventions, which in themselves are without legal force and of which the law courts *can take no notice*'[16] Nevertheless the way in which courts do take notice of conventions and in certain senses give legal effect to, or derive legal consequences from, conventions needs some analysis. 'Convention-recognition' may be classified under several separate heads.

First, there are cases in which it may be recognized or noted by a court that a convention has been enacted, in more or less the same terms, into law, and that the law is in that sense based on a convention. The United Kingdom Parliament Act of 1911, for example, formalized relations between the two Houses of Parliament that had formerly been matters of convention. The Statute of Westminster gave legislative force to a number of conventions that had previously governed the behaviour of the member countries of the Commonwealth. The conventions were stated in the preamble, though it may be noted that not all were embodied in the Statute (for example the convention about common assent to a change in the succession to the throne, or the changing of the Royal Style and Titles). These facts may be noted in decisions and used in various ways. For example in *Copyright Owners Reproduction Society Ltd.* v. *E.M.I. (Australia) Pty. Ltd.*[17] the convention that was embodied in s. 4 of the Statute of Westminster was identified as the source of a rule of construction to be applied in the Australian courts.

Secondly, some conventions (especially those of responsible government) may be incorporated by name or reference into a constitutional instrument, as British conventions or the rules of British Parliamentary privilege were in some Commonwealth constitutions. The British North America

---

[15] *Law of the Constitution* (10th edn.), p. 417.
[16] *The Governments of the British Empire* (1935), p. 6.
[17] (1958) 100 C.L.R. 597.

Act, for example, declared that Canada should be federally united 'with a Constitution similar in principle to that of the United Kingdom,' thus importing by reference a number of Parliamentary conventions. In Nigeria the convention governing the holding of office by the Prime Minister and its relation to the confidence of the legislature was incorporated in the Constitution. Its meaning had to be elucidated by the Privy Council in *Adegbenro* v. *Akintola*.[18]

Thirdly, conventions may be the subject of enquiry in the course of statutory construction. The consideration of convention in *British Coal Corporation* v. *the King*[19] could be considered in this light. It led to the conclusion that in passing the Judicial Committee Act of 1833, Parliament had had a particular intention, namely to treat the Committee as being a judicial body because of the firmly established convention as to the way in which its advice was accepted by the Crown.

Many cases in administrative law illustrate this derivation of legal consequences indirectly from constitutional practice. The convention of ministerial responsibility to Parliament has frequently been relied upon as evidence for the assertion that Parliament had intended a particular result in enacting provisions about Ministers' powers — for example that it had not intended them to be subject to judicial review. Cases such as *Robinson* v. *Minister of Town and Country Planning*[20] or *Liversidge* v. *Anderson*[21] provide instances.

Fourthly, an occasion on which particular weight and lengthy consideration was given to the doctrine of collective responsibility of Ministers and the confidentiality of cabinet proceedings was *Attorney-General* v. *Jonathan Cape Ltd.*[22] An indirect legal effect was given to those conventional principles in that the confidentiality of cabinet proceedings

---

[18] [1963] A.C. 614. Reference to United Kingdom conventions was also inserted in the constitutional instruments of Ceylon, Ghana, and the Central African Federation.
[19] [1935] A.C. 500.   [20] [1947] K.B. 702 at 717, 723.
[21] [1942] A.C. 206. Cf. *R.* v. *Secretary of State ex parte Hosenball*, [1977] 1 W.L.R. 776. This point and connections between law and convention generally are discussed in S. A. de Smith, *Constitutional and Administrative Law* (4th edn., eds. Harry Street and Rodney Brazier), at pp. 41, 48-50.
[22] [1976] Q.B. 752. (See App. A.)

was held to fall within the ambit of the existing law restraining breaches of confidence in general.

Nevertheless all the above cases, with the possible exception of the Australian *Copyright Owners'*[23] case, might be said to be instances in which the courts did not apply or enforce conventions in the sense of treating them as direct sources of law distinct from legislative enactment or previous common law decisions. It might be said here that the courts were applying law not convention and that the notice taken of the conventions merely helped to clarify what the existing law was in various ways. For example:

1. By being a part of the material that was enacted into law.
2. By helping to elucidate the background against which legislation took place, thus providing guidance as to the intention of the legislature where the meaning of a statute had come into question.
3. By constituting a practice or set of facts that fell under an existing legal doctrine.

A distinction can be seen, therefore, between using conventions in this way and directly applying them or enforcing them as law. What would constitute a clear case of the direct application of convention would be a recognition that rules that were clearly conventional had changed or congealed or hardened into rules of law.

There is no doubt that in times past the common law has incorporated into itself rules of constitutional propriety. Many of the cases in which the limits of the Crown's prerogative powers were set, remain as evidence of this process and quite modern cases often hark back to these principles.[24] But modern examples of direct conversion or acknowledgement of non-legal rules as enforceable rules of law are hard to find.

The nearest approaches to what might be called judicial recognition and enforcement of conventions may be observed from time to time at a high constitutional level. One such instance occurred in South Africa in 1937 when the convention that the United Kingdom Parliament could not legislate

[23] (1958) 100 C.L.R. 597.
[24] e.g. *A.-G.* v. *De Keyser's Royal Hotel Ltd.* [1920] A.C. 508; *Burmah Oil Co.* v. *Lord Advocate* [1965] A.C. 85; and *Malone* v. *Metropolitan Police Commissioner (No. 2)* [1979] 2 W.L.R. 700.

so as to repeal the Status of the Union Act or the Statute of Westminster, appeared to be treated as an established rule of law in *Ndlwana* v. *Hofmeyr.*[25] ('Freedom once conferred', it was held, 'cannot be revoked.') It may also happen if ever the British courts accept the practice of not legislating inconsistently with the rules of the European Declaration of Human Rights as having created a rule of law to which they will give effect in litigation.

In *Madzimbamuto* v. *Lardner-Burke* however, the Privy Council drew as firm a line as Dicey ever did between law and convention. In considering Rhodesia's self-proclaimed independence they showed no inclination to recognize established conventional relationships or conventions as capable of creating or modifying law. They were not entitled, they said, to take account of the conventions that might have regulated the relations of the British and Rhodesian legislatures. ('Their Lordships in declaring the law are not concerned with these matters. They are only concerned with the legal powers of Parliament.'[26])

In Canada also the Supreme Court has firmly rejected the thesis that constitutional conventions may be directly enforced or may harden into law.

The proposition was advanced . . . that a convention may crystallise into law. In our view this is not so. No instance of an explicit recognition of a convention as having matured into a rule of law was produced. The very nature of a convention as political in inception and as depending on a consistent course of political recognition . . . is inconsistent with its legal enforcement.[27]

Since a majority of the court found as a matter of fact that a disputed constitutional convention existed, some have seen in this decision an acknowledgement that conventions may in principle merit judicial recognition.[28] That perhaps goes too far. The Canadian courts only felt able to declare the existence of the convention because under widely drawn

---

[25] (1937) A.D. 229 at 237. Such a conclusion may however be derived independently from law rather than convention. See Chapter XII below and cf. P. W. Hogg, *Constitutional Law of Canada* (1977), p. 8 and 60 *Canadian Bar Rev.* 307 at 329–30.

[26] [1969] A.C. 645 at 723.

[27] *Reference re Amendment of the Constitution of Canada (Nos. 1, 2 and 3)* (1982), 125 D.L.R. (3d)1 at 22.

[28] R. Brazier and St. John Robilliard, 'Constitutional Conventions: The Canadian Supreme Court's Views Reviewed', (1982) *Public Law* 28.

provincial and federal statutes providing for the furnishing of advisory opinions, they were specifically authorized to give such opinions on questions either of law or fact. The power to recognize the conventions derived therefore from statute. Where such statutes exist the law will treat the existence of a convention as simply a question of fact — though not a simple question of fact — since the conclusion may need to be established by a complex process involving both argument and historical exegesis (with politicians providing expert factual evidence). It may occur in some jurisdictions and not in others.

Force and Purpose of Conventions

But what then, one might ask (remembering Dicey's definition of convention), is the status of a non-legal rule that has been declared to exist by a court of law? Does that declaration in any sense change the character or increase the obligation or binding nature of the convention? The answer would seem to be that it does not. In so far as a convention defines duties or obligations they remain morally and politically, but not legally, binding. Nevertheless in one way a court decision may decisively change the situation since politicians' doubts about what ought to be done may stem not from uncertainty about whether duty-imposing conventions are morally binding but from disagreement as to whether a particular convention does or does not exist. Since opposed politicians are rarely likely to convince each other on this point an advisory jurisdiction, selectively used, seems a useful device in any political system where important constitutional rules are conventional and uncodified. The decision of a court may be accepted as decisively settling a political argument about the existence of a conventional rule.

The establishment of such a judicial arbitration may complicate but it does not controvert Dicey's separation of law and convention. The distinction made by Dicey is clear enough and worth maintaining. The evidence for the existence of law and convention is in standard cases characteristically different, whether the evidence is assessed by judges or by politicians.

Dicey's instinct was also right about the purpose of the conventions. Although conventions cover a wider area than that mentioned in *The law of the Constitution*, and although they do not always modify legal powers, the major purpose of the domestic conventions is to give effect to the principles of governmental accountability that constitute the structure of responsible government. The main external conventions have the comparable purpose of seeing that responsible government is shared equally by all the member states of the Commonwealth, and that accountability is allocated in accordance with political reality rather than legal form.

II
The Uses of the Queen

It is convention rather than law that fixes the practical role of the Crown — or what Walter Bagehot in *The English Constitution*, more precisely called 'the use of the Queen'.[1] By convention the Queen's prerogative powers are exercised on ministerial advice. The advice is either that of ministers collectively or of particular ministers. So, when Bagehot goes on to tell us that the Queen can do many things without consulting Parliament — that she can sell off the navy, declare war, dismiss civil servants, create peers and pardon offenders[2] — we are to understand that it is Ministers who authorize and carry out these actions.

But the conventional rule, like most of the major conventions, is framed in general terms and is subject to controversial limitations and exceptions. In Bagehot's description of the powers of the Crown there is an unexplained potential contradiction between two theories. One is implied by his assertion, often quoted, that the Sovereign has three rights only — the right to be consulted, the right to encourage, and the right to warn.[3] This, on the face of it, suggests that the Queen has no independent power of action or decision at all but only a power to decide and to act as Ministers — after consultation, warning, and possible discouragement — advise her to act. But compare this with Bagehot's remark that the Sovereign has a power 'for extreme use on a critical occasion but which he can in law use on any occasion'. In the exercise of this power 'He can dissolve; he can say to his ministers in fact if not in words, This Parliament sent you here, but I will see if I cannot get another Parliament to send someone else here.'[4] Bagehot's contrast between the legality of exercising such a power on any occasion and its

---

[1] *The English Constitution* (Oxford Pocket Classics edn.), p. 30. 'The use of the Queen, in a dignified capacity is incalculable. Without her in England the present English Government would fail and pass away.'

[2] Ibid., at p. 287.   [3] Ibid., at p. 111.

[4] Ibid., at p. 114.

availability on a critical occasion, suggests that in the latter
case he is asserting that the power may not merely legally
but politically and conventionally be used in accordance
with the Sovereign's independent judgment. This supposition
illustrates the possibility that the Queen is not in fact con-
strained on every occasion to act in accordance with ministerial advice, but is entitled on at least some occasions to
reject it and if necessary to find other Ministers who will
give better, or at least different, advice. Sir William Anson
was one constitutional authority who took this view. In 1913
his opinion was that 'If the King should decide in the interests
of the people to take a course which his ministers disapprove,
he must either convert his ministers to his point of view or,
before taking action, must find other ministers who agree
with him.'[5] 'Find other ministers', of course, slides over an
obvious question. Is the Sovereign permitted to dismiss his
Ministers? Is he to suggest that they should resign and make
way for alternative advisers? Or is he to do nothing other
than to decline ministerial advice and be willing to face a
threat of resignation and a possible political crisis? The first
course would obviously be more radical than the third.
Even so, a significant degree of independence of action
would be involved were the Crown simply to decline to act
on the Cabinet's or the Prime Minister's advice. Perhaps
Edward VIII, for example, might conceivably have declined
to follow the advice of his Cabinet that he could not as
King marry Mrs Simpson, calling the implied bluff that
Mr Baldwin would in such a situation have offered his government's resignation. Sir William Anson's view on its most
plausible interpretation would seem to be that before taking
such a stand the Crown would have to be assured that it
would be possible to find other Ministers who would be prepared to form a government. If this is so, a further question
arises. If the conventions of the Constitution permit such
a course, is it necessary to find alternative advisers who can
expect to be supported by a majority in the existing legislature? Or is it enough that someone should be willing to
take office and, if necessary, seek a majority by advising a
dissolution and fighting a General Election? Bagehot's and

---

[5] Sir W. Anson to *The Times* 10 Sept. 1913.

Anson's views seem to imply the second proposition. They amount to saying that the Queen, in what she judges to be a critical situation, is entitled to force a General Election on her Ministers for the time being and seek the support of the electorate against them.

Despite the authority of Bagehot and Anson some have rejected the constitutional propriety of such a course of action and propounded a so-called 'automatic theory'.[6] On this theory no rejection of the considered advice of Ministers currently in office is ever permissible. Between these two views there is a variety of possibilities. Some may reject the automatic theory but believe that only some extreme and possibly revolutionary crisis would entitle the Queen to act as a last bulwark of the Constitution. Others may believe that a wider field of potential independent action is possible but that the possibility cannot be stated in such open and general terms as those adopted in the Anson view.

It may be that some consensus can be reached by considering separately the various possible areas in which the Crown's agreement to governmental action is legally required. There are four main areas in which questions about the exercise of the prerogative arise. They are the giving of assent to legislation, the conferment of honours and creation of Peers, the appointment and dismissal of Ministers, and the dissolving of Parliament prior to a General Election. It may be that different conventions about the exercise of the Queen's powers have come to be recognized in relation to these different aspects of the prerogative.

Assent to Legislation

Perhaps an 'automatic' theory is most obviously justified in relation to the giving of assent to legislation that has received the assent of the Commons and the House of Lords. That the Royal Assent should not be refused in such circumstances is perhaps the least controvertible application

---

[6] The phrase seems to have originated with Lord Hugh Cecil: '... what may briefly be called the "automatic" theory is a serious misrepresentation of the constitution'. (*The Times*, 10 Sept. 1913. Reprinted in Sir Ivor Jennings, *Cabinet Government* (3rd edn.), App. III.)

of the general convention that prerogative powers are exercised on ministerial advice. This conclusion rests on a clear
negative precedent, that no such Bill has failed to receive
the Royal Assent since 1707 when Queen Anne refused
assent to a Militia Bill.[7] Normally, of course, ministerial
advice here coincides with, and is reinforced by, that of the
Queen's advisers in the assembled Houses. There could of
course be circumstances of an unusual kind in which the
two did not coincide. A Private Member's Bill perhaps might
be given the approval of both Houses and the government
not wish it to be enacted into law. Should the advice of
Ministers be complied with when it is clearly not supported
by a majority in Parliament?

Leaving aside such cases, however, can it be concluded
that the power to refuse assent to legislation is now a dead
letter? Under present constitutional arrangements it may
well be so. But there are conceivable constitutional changes
that might raise further questions about the Royal Assent.
Suppose, for example, that a Bill of Rights were to be introduced and protected against repeal by a special legislative
procedure requiring a specified majority in one or both
Houses. Alternatively, suppose that a similar constitutional
entrenchment were to require that some particular legal
change was to be submitted to a referendum before being
enacted into law. Though provisions of this kind have been
enacted in some Constitutions in the Commonwealth,[8] their
effectiveness in the United Kingdom is a matter of debate.[9] If
such provisions were introduced and subsequently disregarded
by a government that believed them to be ineffective and did
not wish to be bound by them, it might be that the Queen
would have to consider whether such a government's advice
to assent to legislation should be refused if the legislation had
not been submitted to the previously prescribed procedure. A
decision by the courts would be the most appropriate way of
deciding an issue of this kind but it might be that there

---

[7] The last occasion on which it was seriously contemplated was in relation to
the Irish Home Rule Bill of 1912.

[8] e.g. New South Wales and South Africa. See *A.-G. for New South Wales* v.
Trethowan. [1932] A.C. 526.

[9] See the *Report of the Select Committee of the House of Lords on a Bill of
Rights* HL 176 (1977-8), and J. Jaconelli, *Enacting a Bill of Rights: the Legal
Problems* (1980), chap. VI.

would be procedural difficulties inhibiting a judicial remedy to restrain an improper presentation of a Bill for assent.[10] A decision might therefore at some point have to be taken by the Queen and her advisers independently of Ministers.

Honours and Creation of Peers

The existence of the Political Honours Scrutiny Committee suggests that Prime Ministerial advice on the conferment of honours is not necessarily to be automatically accepted and that the Queen is entitled in appropriate cases to exercise an independent judgment on the basis of the Committee's advice. The Committee reports in the first place to the Prime Minister (since 1979 on all recommendations for honours). If the Prime Minister persists with the recommendation in the face of an adverse report, the Committee's view is made known to the Queen, presumably so that she can if necessary take her own view of the suitability of the Prime Minister's recommendations.

Some few appointments are made at the personal discretion of the Queen. The Royal Victorian Order is one such and membership of it was conferred by the Queen on the Governor of Rhodesia Sir Humphrey Gibbs after the rebellion of Southern Rhodesian Ministers in 1965.

Where honours are awarded on advice the advice appears to be that of the Prime Minister rather than of Ministers collectively. Honours are not normally the subject of Cabinet discussion and there appears in practice to be no ministerial responsibility for them, since Parliamentary questions on particular honours are inadmissible.[11]

It is the creation of peers, however, that has assumed a special constitutional significance in recent times, since it has figured and may yet again figure in arguments about the status of the second chamber and the delaying powers of the House of Lords. In some sections of the Labour Party the creation of a large number of Peers after a Labour government has achieved office has been seen as a desirable policy,

---

[10] See *Hughes and Vale Pty. Ltd. v. Gair* (1954), 90 C.L.R. 203; *Clayton v. Heffron* (1960), 105 C.L.R. 214.

[11] Erskine May, *Parliamentary Practice* (19th edn.), p. 328.

aimed at securing both an effective majority in both Houses and a facility for abolishing the House of Lords itself. Mr Wedgwood Benn, for example, has proposed that a Labour government should proceed to the creation of 1,000 Peers to vote the House out of existence. Such a course of action would plainly require the Queen's co-operation. Would she be bound to act on the advice of a Labour Prime Minister and agree to the creation of a thousand or as many Peers as might be necessary to secure a majority for abolition? Two considerations suggest that automatic acquiescence would not be required. It might be supposed in the first place that a step of such radical constitutional importance would entitle the Queen to insist that it be specifically put to the electorate either by referendum or at a further General Election. Suppose, however, that abolition of the Lords had been an item in the Labour Party's last election manifesto. It might be that the Queen would none the less be entitled to regard a mass creation of Peers as a constitutionally improper way of bringing about unicameral government, since it would be possible to achieve the abolition of the House of Lords by legislation and to do so even if the Lords were to exercise their veto, as the machinery established by the Parliament Acts of 1911 and 1949 would be available. It could be said that the undertaking to create Peers given by the Crown prior to the passing of the 1911 Parliament Act was a remedy necessary at that time to give effect to the convention that the will of the Commons should, when clearly supported by the people, be made to prevail. Before 1911 the two Houses had legally co-ordinate powers, and there was thus a possibility of deadlock with an emergency creation of Peers as the only available method for resolving it. But the passage of the Parliament Acts has provided a procedure through which a constitutional deadlock can be resolved. A Bill opposed by the Upper House — even a Bill to abolish the Upper House — may be passed again by the Commons and within the provisions of the Parliament Acts be assented to by the Crown with a delay of one year after the original second reading in the Commons. A refusal by the Crown on these grounds to act on governmental advice to create Peers might, of course, prevent the abolition of the House of Lords from being achieved in the last year of a Labour government's term of office. Defenders of the House of Lords would no doubt argue, however, that if a proposal for abolition were initiated at such a point for the first time it would be proper for it to be deferred until a further election had been fought on a manifesto that included abolition of the Lords.[12]

If these arguments for a non-automatic theory are valid they amount to saying that in relation to the creation of Peers the Queen is in some cases entitled to make her own judgment as to the constitutional propriety of the government's advice and to act on it by declining to exercise the prerogative.

Dismissal of Ministers

In some cases, however, allegedly unconstitutional behaviour by a government might not involve the use of prerogative powers or the offering of advice to the Crown. Could such behaviour be frustrated by a positive use of the royal prerogative to dismiss the allegedly culpable Ministers?

Dismissal of Ministers is certainly not supported by any modern United Kingdom precedent. The last occasion on which it was the subject of serious political discussion was in the pre-First World War Home Rule crisis. On 31 July 1913 Lansdowne and Bonar Law sent a memorandum to the King in which they argued that the Constitution was in a state of suspense, that a dissolution was the only method of averting civil war, and that if Asquith declined to recommend a dissolution, the King had a right to dismiss him and send for someone who would do so.[13] Both Sir William Anson and

---

[12] Before the Parliament Acts of 1911 and 1949 relations between the Lords and Commons raised a major question of convention. In recent years various practices have been followed restricting the kinds of issue on which rejection of measures supported by the Commons has been felt to be justified. But these policies are seriously in dispute between the political parties, and it cannot be said that any clear constitutional convention exists. Since the period for which the Lords can delay Commons legislation was fixed as the result of a political compromise in 1949, a putative convention would be that the Lords are constitutionally entitled to exercise the legal powers conferred upon them in the Parliament Acts of 1911 and 1949.

[13] See Lord Blake's life of Bonar Law, *The Unknown Prime Minister* (1955), at p. 152.

Professor A. V. Dicey concurred in this view, suggesting that the prerogative of dissolution might be exercised with constitutional propriety if it were done with the assurance that an alternative set of Ministers were prepared to assume responsibility for it. The justification for such an initiative was seen at that time by Lord Hugh Cecil as resting on 'the underlying principle of which the conventions of the Constitution are the expressions' that there should be no conflict between the King and his people or between the King and a House of Commons that correctly represented the people. It followed, he argued, that there was nothing unconstitutional about a disagreement between the King and his Ministers except in so far as it might imply disagreement with the Commons and the people. 'What is constitutional', he added, 'is not always judicious.'[14]

The injudiciousness of a dismissal of Ministers stems obviously from the danger that the Crown may become what Asquith called 'the football of contending factions'. Had George V dismissed his Ministers in 1913 he would undoubtedly have found himself in that undignified and impolitic situation. Sir Ivor Jennings did not think that a dismissal over the Home Rule proposals would have been justified.[15] In any political controversy in which the Queen was prepared to act on the assumption that the government of the day did not represent the settled view of the electorate, there are cogent reasons for thinking that the danger to the monarchy of proceeding on that assumption would be greater than that of allowing the electorate to form its own belated view of the matter. The conceivable exception would be if a government with a majority in the Commons were to take steps that in Sir Ivor Jennings's words 'subverted the democratic basis of the Constitution',[16] and prevented the electorate from exercising its electoral choice by interfering with the electoral process in some fundamental way. Extreme measures such as an Abolition of General Elections

---

[14] Lord Hugh Cecil to *The Times*, 10 Sept. 1913.
[15] *Cabinet Government* (2nd edn.), p. 412. Nor did Professor Arthur Berriedale Keith. See *The Constitution of England from Queen Victoria to George VI*, vol. i, p. 92. Nor for that matter did King George V. Asquith, however, considered that dismissal of Ministers would have been a less serious step than refusal of assent to the Home Rule Bill, which the King had seriously thought to be a possibility.   [16] *Cabinet Government*, p. 412.

Act or a partisan modification of the electoral system would however involve legislation, and a refusal of assent would be the more immediate and less radical remedy.

Dismissal would be appropriate if a government, by illegal or unconstitutional administrative action, were to violate some basic convention of constitutional behaviour. Even then it would be necessary for the breach to be a profound one for which no other remedy could be found, either political or legal.

In a great many cases in which it is alleged that Ministers have acted unconstitutionally (in the sense of violating constitutional convention or practice), the questions in issue are in any case debatable and usually a matter of controversy between the political parties or between government and opposition. The remedy for alleged convention-breaking is generally recognized to be, in the main, political. Either the government can be shamed by publicity and political debate into conceding error or changing its course of action, or its misdeeds can be made the subject of argument at the next General Election. There is perhaps only one breach of convention whose existence would, if it occurred, be sufficiently clear and undisputed to raise the question of a possible sanction by the Crown. That is a breach of the convention of collective responsibility which requires that a government defeated on a specific motion of confidence moved by it, or on a motion of no confidence moved by the opposition, should resign or advise a dissolution of Parliament and a General Election. Despite Dicey's view that obedience to conventions is supported by the requirements of the law, there does not seem any way in which a decision to stay in office after losing the support of the House of Commons could be discouraged by any immediate legal sanction. Ministers who clearly ignored a loss of confidence by the House of Commons and defied the conventional rule might properly be dismissed.

This proposition, if valid, rests on principle rather than precedent as far as the United Kingdom is concerned. There have, however, been occasions when Governors or Governors-General in Commonwealth countries have exercised the prerogative of dismissal.[17] The most recent was the dismissal

---

[17] A number of nineteenth-century cases are set out in Arthur Berriedale

of Mr Gough Whitlam's Government by the Governor-General of Australia in 1975. An earlier Australian dismissal was that of the Lang Ministry in New South Wales in 1932 by the Governor of New South Wales, Sir Philip Game. The Whitlam dismissal was undertaken by the Governor-General, Sir John Kerr, on the ground that the Government had been refused supply by the Senate, and that in the face of a financial crisis the Prime Minister had refused either to resign or to advise dissolution of the Lower House. The constitutionality of the dismissal has been debated with some vigour in Australia. On one view Sir John Kerr behaved injudiciously, concealing his intentions from his Ministers and removing a Government that maintained its majority in the Lower House at a point when dismissal was not the only conceivable political option. On the Governor-General's behalf it was argued that he acted properly to remove a Government that did not enjoy the confidence constitutionally required in Australia of both Houses, in order to appoint a Ministry willing to advise a dissolution of both Houses that would allow the electorate to resolve the issue.[18]

The 1932 dismissal of the Lang Government in New South Wales also stemmed from a financial crisis in which the Governor took the view that his Ministers were behaving illegally. Given the different constitutional structure of the Australian political system (where at the Federal level there is an unresolved dispute about the conditions under which the executive can be said to possess the confidence of the legislature), there is nothing that can be directly inferred about the prerogative of dismissal in the United Kingdom. The Commonwealth precedents, however, are consistent with the view that dismissal might properly be used as an act of last resort if a government were acting unlawfully in a way for which no conceivable legal remedy could be found, or if Ministers were to put themselves in breach of the convention that loss of Parliamentary confidence entails resignation or a General Election.[19]

Keith, *Responsible Government in the Dominions* (1912), vol. i, pp. 223–45.

    [18] The opposing viewpoints are set out in Sir John Kerr, *Matters for Judgment* (1978), and Gough Whitlam, *The Truth of the Matter* (1979). See also chaps. 7–9 of *Labour and the Constitution 1972–1975* (ed. Gareth Evans (1977)).

    [19] In *Adegbenro* v. *Akintola* [1963] A.C. 614, the Privy Council upheld

Appointment of Ministers

The appointment of a Prime Minister is an exercise of the prerogative that has been much affected by changes in the practice of politics and in the organization of political parties. The legal freedom of choice has always in modern times been encrusted with convention. An appointee must by convention be a member of one or other House of Parliament and in practice of the House of Commons. It is a nice question whether there is a convention that a Prime Minister cannot now be a member of the House of Lords. The last Prime Minister to hold office whilst a member of the Upper House was Lord Home (in the brief interval of four days between his appointment as Prime Minister and disclaiming his peerage), though Lord Halifax was considered as a possible leader of the wartime coalition government in 1940. It has sometimes been supposed that the choice of Baldwin in 1923 in preference to Lord Curzon set a firm precedent against Prime Ministers in the Lords. There were, however, other adequate reasons for Curzon's rejection, so it is not possible to affirm this with certainty. Since the passage of the Peerage Act of 1963 a potential appointee may disclaim his peerage within twelve months of succeeding or coming of age. Probably though, we shall never know whether or not there was any convention against Peers as Prime Ministers between 1923 and 1963. Today there almost certainly is such a convention, but it rests on principle rather than precedent.

Before 1965 the Crown's role in choosing a Prime Minister was greater than it has now become. If a Labour Prime Minister had died or retired whilst in office the Parliamentary Party election procedure would have produced a new leader. But the death or retirement of a Conservative Prime Minister made it necessary for a choice to be made by the Queen

the legal validity of a dismissal of a Prime Minister by the Governor-General on the ground that he no longer held the confidence of the majority of the members of the Western Nigerian legislature. The power to dismiss was in this case laid down in the Constitution but it was argued that British conventions should govern the exercise of the power. Cf. *Ningkan* v. *Government of Malaysia* [1970] A.C. 379.

in accordance with the convention that the office should be filled by an incumbent most likely to command the support of a Commons majority. That principle dictated the choice as the Prime Minister's successor of a leading figure in the party, but it did not indicate precisely who the appointee should be when the Conservative party was in office and there were competing claimants for the succession. Between 1945 and 1965 that situation arose on two occasions (in 1957 and in 1963), on the retirement of the Conservative Prime Ministers Eden and Macmillan. The practice was that the Queen with the aid of her Private Secretary[20] would take soundings from a variety of sources including Privy Councillors, senior politicians and party whips. It was agreed that the retiring Prime Minister did not have any right to nominate or give binding advice as to his successor, though he might be consulted along with others.

The choice by the Queen of Lord Home in 1963 was of some importance since the circumstances in which it took place illustrated the difficulties of the process and led fairly quickly to the adoption by the Conservative Party of a leadership election process that was designed (like the Labour Party's leadership election) to make the choice of a Prime Ministerial successor a constitutional formality.

The events surrounding the appointment of Lord Home (as he then was) have been the subject of rival accounts. A criticism made by those in both parties who were opposed to the appointment was that on Mr Harold Macmillan's prompting the Queen had allowed herself to be urged prematurely into a decision without having at her disposal all the available evidence about feeling in the Conservative Party. In effect the process of consultation and decision was cut off at a point where the situation was changing rapidly and when the leading contenders for office had in fact agreed to express their willingness to serve under Mr R. A. Butler. It was alleged that efforts to convey this information to the Queen's advisers on the morning when she saw Macmillan were unsuccessful. It is still unclear from the account given in Macmillan's memoirs what facts were made known to the Queen when the Prime Minister read to her

[20] The office of Private Secretary is described in Appendix B of Sir John Wheeler-Bennett's *George VI: His Life and Reign* (1958).

from his hospital bed a memorandum of advice containing the suggestion that she should invite Lord Home to attempt to form an administration. What is said is that mention was made of the 'so-called revolt of certain ministers'. When asked about this revolt the Prime Minister replied that he 'thought speed was important and hoped she would send for Lord Home immediately — as soon as she got back to the Palace'.[21] Randolph Churchill reported a similar sentiment as being expressed by Macmillan to Home: ' . . . We can't change our view now. All the troops are on the starting line. Everything is arranged.'[22]

This perhaps supports the criticism that the Queen's advisers should not have allowed her to be urged into an immediate invitation[23] to Lord Home and that she should have taken at least a little time fully to apprise herself of the changing political situation and of the views of the Conservative leadership, as it was then emerging. If she was aware of the situation as it was on the morning of 18 October 1963 she was possibly mistaken in her action. If she was not aware of it she was deceived. Mr Harold Macmillan was admittedly fortified by an informal poll of Conservative members and notables, but it may be argued that he should not have been the sole fountain-head of advice, if it is indeed a constitutional principle that a retiring Prime Minister has no special title or status to advise on the choice of his successor. In fact, at the time when Macmillan's advice was sought he had ceased to be Prime Minister[24] and it is the more odd that the Queen on this occasion should have, in Macmillan's words, said that 'she did not need and did not intend to seek any other advice but mine'.

Other criticisms were of less validity. Macmillan related that the Queen believed, or at least agreed, that 'Lord Home was really the best and strongest character'.[25] On the publication of Macmillan's memoirs Mr Humphrey Berkeley wrote

[21] *At the End of the Day* (1973), p. 515.
[22] *The Fight for the Tory Leadership: a Contemporary Chronicle* (1964), p. 137.
[23] Lord Home was not immediately appointed but invited to attempt the task of forming an administration.
[24] The announcement of his resignation was made from the Palace at 10.30 a.m. and the audience at the hospital took place at 11 a.m.
[25] Macmillan, at p. 515.

to *The Times* to complain about this as being a 'gross constitutional impropriety'.[26] The impropriety was not, it is to be
assumed, the expression of this arguably valid assessment
of the political talents of Messrs Maudling, Butler, and
Hogg, but the fact that it should have been revealed to the
general public. The complaint, if valid, would suggest the
existence of a constitutional practice or convention, which
has certainly not been observed with complete fidelity
in the past. Lord Attlee's memoirs, for example, as well
as Sir John Wheeler-Bennett's biography of George VI
described a number of views held by the King[27] without the
authors being accused of constitutional impropriety. In
1963 Queen Elizabeth, like her father, was exercising one
of Bagehot's three monarchical Prerogatives – the right
to encourage, the right to be consulted, and the right to
warn. No doubt she encouraged Mr Macmillan at a time
when he needed some encouragement; and there seemed
little danger to the Constitution in this fact being revealed
in 1973 to those readers of Sir Harold's memoirs who had
stayed the course through the *Winds of Change*, the *Blast
of War*, and the *Tides of Fortune* to the *End of the Day*.

Conservative dissatisfaction with the episode of 1963
led almost immediately to the adoption of a procedure
for election of the party leader by a ballot of members
taking the Conservative whip. Recent changes in the party
system, however, suggest that there may still be situations
in which it may be necessary for the Prerogative of appointment to be exercised in accordance with the independent
judgment of the Queen and her advisers.

For one thing it may be that future General Elections
will not produce a Parliament in which any one party has
an overall majority. That would not necessarily place the
Queen in any immediate difficulty since after a General
Election the existing Prime Minister, even if in a minority,
is entitled to remain in office[28] and to meet the House of

[26] *The Times*, 29 Sept. 1973.

[27] For example, his views on the merits of Lord Halifax as a successor to
Chamberlain in 1940 and his advice on ministerial appointments in 1945.

[28] After the election of February 1974 it was thought by some that the
Labour Party having the largest number of seats should have been invited to form
a government. But as Sir Harold Wilson acknowledged, 'This would have been

Commons. He may attempt, as Mr Edward Heath did in March 1974, to form a Government with the support of other party groups in the House. If he fails, he may still calculate that though lacking an overall majority he will not in fact be immediately defeated and decide to carry on as a minority government. If, however, he decides at that point to offer his resignation or if, having continued in office, his government is then defeated on the Address or on a subsequent vote of confidence, some problems appear.

If the Prime Minister resigns before the House has met, the Queen and her advisers would have to consider what course of action would be most likely to produce a government capable of surviving. It might be that discussions between parties, or some of them, made it relatively clear that a particular party leader would be acceptable to a majority of the House as a leader of a coalition. There might in such circumstances be a difficult choice to make between inviting that person to form a government and inviting the leader of the single largest party to form a minority government. Given the uncertainties of coalition governments, minority government has in the past been the preferred expedient. But if three-party politics were to become the normal setting of British government[29] (especially if proportional representation were to be adopted), coalition might become a strong competing alternative. One suggestion recently made is that in such circumstances the Queen's choice might be guided by a ballot of all members of Parliament under the superintendence of the Speaker.[30] It seems

contrary to precedent. A Prime Minister was there – at Downing Street.' (*The Governance of Britain* (1976), pp. 25-6.)

[29] The implications for the choice of Prime Ministers are discussed in Vernon Bogdanor, *Multi-Party Politics and the Constitution* (1983), chaps. 5-8, and David Butler, *Governing Without a Majority: Dilemmas for Hung Parliaments in Britain* (1983).

[30] Rodney Brazier, 'Choosing a Prime Minister', (1982) *Public Law* 395. Other problems have been envisaged as deriving from changes in the Labour Party constitution. The elected leader of the Labour Party might, it is suggested, not enjoy the confidence of the Parliamentary party or of a majority in the Commons and might be an inappropriate choice as Prime Minister after a General Election won by the Labour Party. See Brazier, loc. cit., pp. 411-16, and Dawn Oliver, 'Constitutional Implications of the Reforms of the Labour Party', (1982) *Public Law* 151.

safe to predict, however, that such a novel and adventurous constitutional expedient will not in fact be adopted.

If after a General Election that produces no clear majority the existing Prime Minister meets the House of Commons and is immediately defeated, the situation is significantly different, since there is an acknowledged leader of the Parliamentary opposition and precedent suggests that he — in the first instance at any rate — should be invited to form a government (or to attempt to form one). Sir Ivor Jennings suggested that this was a practice that had 'hardened into a rule comparatively recently'. He added that 'The rule is that on the defeat and resignation of the Government the Queen should first send for the leader of the Opposition.'[31] His view was that this rule followed from the need to demonstrate impartiality. The Queen's task, he wrote, was 'only to secure a government not to try to form a government which is likely to forward a policy of which she approves', and 'the only method by which this can be demonstrated clearly is to send at once for the leader of the Opposition'. It might, however, be argued that if in a three-party situation a coalition government seemed more likely to command the support of a majority of the House than a minority government led by the Leader of the Opposition, there would be no valid reason to suppose that an invitation to form such a coalition taken on that ground would suggest a preference on the Queen's part for any particular policies. The proposition that the Leader of the Opposition must always be sent for is clearly incompatible with the consideration of coalition as being on an equal footing with minority government. But if multi-party Parliaments were to become common it might well be necessary to reconsider the relative claims of coalition and minority government and to modify the existing practice.

Yet another question will fall for consideration by the Queen if a Prime Minister without an overall majority neither immediately resigns nor is immediately defeated, but carries on for a while, is then defeated and advises a dissolution of Parliament and the holding of a further election. May the Queen then reject his advice and insist upon one of the

---

[31] *Cabinet Government* (3rd edn.), p. 32.

other courses of action? Is the case any different if he advises the holding of a General Election without being defeated, or in anticipation of defeat? These questions lead directly to the contested issue of the right to refuse a dissolution.

Refusal of Advice

It is generally agreed that there are at least some occasions on which the Queen is entitled to refuse to act on ministerial advice to dissolve Parliament. Mr Harold Macmillan indeed preferred to speak of 'requesting a dissolution' rather than 'advising' one, on the ground that 'advice in the long run the Crown must today accept'.[32] It is not clear what he had in mind by 'the long run', but it seems unnecessary to treat ministerial 'advice' as if it meant 'binding advice' and better to suppose that there are degrees of freedom or discretion in complying with the advice offered by ministers.

A similar oddity about 'advice' is the notion that the Queen cannot act without advice and that for every act of the Crown some Minister is responsible. This presents difficulties both in relation to changes of government and to dissolution. When a Prime Minister resigns, his advice as to his successor is not treated as binding advice and indeed it is supposed that he is under no duty to volunteer it.[33] Some writers used to suggest that the responsibility for appointment of an incoming Prime Minister fell (by a curious piece of constitutional acrobatics) on the succeeding Minister himself. Professor Berriedale Keith, for example, held that when a Minister accepts office 'he assumes therewith the

[32] See *Riding the Storm 1956–1959* (1971), p. 750. His view was that a Prime Minister 'had no right to advise a dissolution'. With his recommendation the Queen could agree or not. 'This, the last great prerogative of the Crown, must be preserved. It might be of vital importance at a time of national crisis.'

[33] Sir· Harold Wilson writes, 'Contrary to widespread belief there is no duty on the prime minister, still less any inherent right, to recommend the man to be sent for. It is the sovereign who decides whom to send for and invite to form a government.' (*The Governance of Britain*, p. 22.) The same point was made to Bonar Law who was reluctant to advise on his successor. Lord Crewe mentioned to him that Victoria did not consult Gladstone in 1894 when appointing Rosebery, or Edward VII Campbell-Bannerman in 1908 when appointing Asquith. See Blake, *The Unknown Prime Minister*, pp. 514–15. There is however a distinction between a duty to volunteer advice and a duty to give it if asked to advise.

duty of defending the formation of the new ministry',[34] quoting Peel's remark after Melbourne's apparent dismissal in 1834 'I am by my acceptance of office responsible for the removal of the late government.' Sir Ivor Jennings disapproved of this notion as 'a pure fiction'.[35] A similar view may be taken of the supposition that a new appointee may be held to have retrospectively authorized or advised the refusal of a dissolution to his predecessor. That might be thought an even more rarefied fiction. The fiction or allegation is plainly inconsistent with the labelling of some prerogative acts, including appointment of Ministers and dissolution of Parliament, as personal prerogatives. If that means anything, it means that they are taken on the Queen's own responsibility and not on ministerial advice.

The term 'personal prerogative' is perhaps not entirely a happy label for appointment, dissolution, and assent to legislation (though Sir Ivor Jennings in *Cabinet Government* devotes a chapter to the personal prerogatives under that name). In fact all three prerogatives are in the great majority of cases not exercised in accordance with any personal discretion. They only become personally exercised prerogatives in the few exceptional cases in which an independent judgment must be exercised in appointing a Prime Minister or refusing ministerial advice. But in those cases it cannot be said that the Queen's powers are exercised indirectly or remotely on retrospective advice. The responsibility must be the Queen's own. No British monarch in modern times has in fact dismissed a government or refused to assent to legislation or to dissolve Parliament, but where the so-called personal prerogative has been exercised in a Commonwealth country, it clearly has not been possible to avoid direct popular judgment of the Governor-General's actions by any supposition that they were retrospectively underpinned by ministerial advice.

What then of the possible occasions in the United Kingdom for a personal exercise of the prerogative to refuse a dissolution of Parliament? Some have argued that the prerogative is obsolete or should be made so. In 1938 Professor Harold Laski in his *Parliamentary Government in England*

---

[34] *The British Cabinet System* (2nd edn. by N. H. Gibbs, 1952), p. 277.
[35] *Cabinet Government* (3rd edn.), p. 449.

argued that after disuse for over a hundred years the prerogative of refusal could not be revived,[36] and he expressed
a similar view in his *Reflections on the Constitution* in
1951.[37] In 1982 Mr Anthony Wedgwood Benn proposed that
Parliament should transfer the Crown's prerogative in relation
to appointment and dissolution to the Speaker of the House
of Commons.[38] In 1974 some Labour Members of Parliament
argued that the Prime Minister had 'an absolute right to
decide the date of the election and that the Queèn was
bound to grant a dissolution whenever the Prime Minister
after discussion with his Cabinet colleagues requested it'.
After the election of February 1974 no party had an absolute
majority in the House of Commons and Mr Wilson's supporters may well have felt some apprehension that refusal
of a request to dissolve Parliament might be the prelude to
the formation of a Conservative–Liberal coalition. A situation
in which a minority government is in office raises directly
the question whether such a government is entitled at a
time of its own choosing to appeal for a renewed electoral
mandate, though its political opponents might be willing to
assume office. Given the desirability of the Queen's remaining free from political involvement or partisan controversy,
and given the certainty that installation of a Conservative or
Liberal–SDP government by the Queen would attract violent
criticism by the Labour Party, the prudential arguments for
supposing that a General Election would present lesser evils
seem obvious.

On the other hand, to admit an automatic right of any
government to dissolve Parliament at any time would run
counter to the views expressed by most constitutional
authorities. That was conceded in 1974 by the Leader of the
House of Commons, Mr Edward Short, whose reply to his
back-benchers noted that 'Constitutional lawyers of the
highest authority are of the clear opinion that the sovereign
is not in all circumstances bound to grant a Prime Minister's

---

[36] Op. cit., p. 409. Marshall and Moodie in *Some Problems of the Constitution* (4th edn. 1967), pp. 46–8, seem inclined to the same conclusion.
[37] *Reflections on the Constitution*, p. 72.
[38] *The Times*, 28 Aug. 1982. In Australia Mr Gough Whitlam has argued
that prerogative powers of appointment should be transferred to 'a panel of
certain office-holders or the High Court' (see below p. 43).

request for a dissolution.'[39] That view was stated categorically by Asquith in 1923 in discussing the entitlement of Mac-Donald's minority Labour Government to dissolve Parliament. Dissolution, he said, was not a mere feudal survival but a useful part of the Constitution. He added:

> It does not mean that the Crown should act arbitrarily and without the advice of responsible ministers, but it does mean that the Crown is not bound to take the advice of a particular minister to put its subjects to the tumult and turmoil of a series of general elections so long as it can find other ministers who are prepared to give it a trial. The notion that a Minister — a Minister who cannot command a majority in the House of Commons — is invested with the right to demand a dissolution is as subversive of constitutional usage as it would, in my opinion, be pernicious to the general and paramount interests of the nation at large.[40]

Asquith was, of course, discussing the right of a minority government to appeal to the electorate. How far does his conclusion apply to a government that has a majority over all other parties? Can the existence of a prerogative power vary with the state of the parties? To that question the appropriate answer seems to be that whilst the existence of the legal prerogative is not affected, the conventional rules for its exercise are in fact different in situations of majority and minority government. There is perhaps one limitation that is generally perceived as applying even to a government with an overall majority; namely that a series of dissolutions aimed at securing successive increases in its majority would merit refusal. Repeated requests for dissolution would certainly be an improper putting of the country to the tumult and turmoil of General Elections. But it is so improbable a contingency that it has perhaps not been felt necessary to ask how the Queen could exercise the constitutional right to refuse advice even in the face of such an extreme course of action if the government could by its numerical support prevent the working of any alternative government.

[39] *The Times*, 11 May 1974. Chap. III and IV of Eugene A. Forsey's *The Royal Power of Dissolution of Parliament in the British Commonwealth* (1943), give a detailed account of the opinions of constitutional authorities including Dicey, Anson, Asquith, Keith, Jenks, Muir, Marriot, and Jennings. A more recent account (comparing United Kingdom and Greek practice) is Dr B. S. Markesinis's *The Theory and Practice of Dissolution of Parliament* (1972).
[40] *The Times*, 19 Dec. 1923. (Speech to Liberal MPs.)

The importance of that point became clear in 1950 when the Labour Government of Mr Clement Attlee took office. His 315 seats in the House of Commons gave him a majority over all other parties combined, though, being a majority of six, it was not one that was satisfactory to the Labour Party or one which in their opponents' view gave them a clear mandate to put their programme into effect. In his life of King George VI, Sir John Wheeler-Bennett noted that the majority was 'so narrow that it would not enable them to proceed nor justify them in trying to proceed'.[41] A question was thus faced by the King as to his proper course of action if Mr Attlee should request an immediate dissolution of Parliament. Mr Winston Churchill in a letter to the King's Private Secretary asserted the principle that 'a new House of Commons has a right to live if it can and should not be destroyed until some fresh issue or situation has arisen to place before the electors'.[42] This was perhaps reminiscent of earlier nineteenth-century views of dissolution that there should be some important political question at issue to justify an appeal to the electorate.[43] But Sir Alan Lascelles's advice to the King rested on the different and more expedient ground that there did not seem any possibility of forming an alternative government. When Sir Alan later wrote to *The Times* (under the pseudonym 'Senex'), he suggested that a dissolution might be refused if (1) the existing Parliament was still vital and capable of doing its job, (2) a General Election would be detrimental to the national economy, and (3) the King could rely on finding another Prime Minister who could carry on his government for a reasonable period with a working majority in the House of Commons.[44] Clearly the third consideration is the crucial one; and it was on that ground that the King was advised that though he would be 'perfectly entitled' to refuse a dissolution to Attlee if he were persuaded that the sitting Parliament had not exhausted its usefulness and that the

---

[41] *King George VI: His Life and Reign* (1958), p. 771.

[42] Wheeler-Bennett, op. cit., p. 772.

[43] See for example the views on dissolution expressed in Alpheus Todd *Parliamentary Government in England* (1894), vol. ii, pp. 504-10; and by Gladstone ('There should be an adequate cause of public policy; see C. S. Emden (ed.), *Selected Speeches on the Constitution*, vol. i, p. 89).

[44] *The Times*, 2 May 1950.

country's interests demanded the postponement of a General Election, it was 'doubtful whether the argument is valid in present circumstances'.[45] Perhaps a clearer way of summarizing the position would have been to say that in the absence of a viable alternative government the King was *not* constitutionally entitled to refuse a dissolution, whatever his views on the viability of Parliament or the need for a General Election. Sir Alan Lascelles's advice referred to the occasion in 1926 on which the then Prime Minister of Canada, Mr Mackenzie King, was refused a dissolution by the Governor-General. Lascelles remarked that it was questionable if this refusal did any good and that it left a considerable legacy of bitterness against the Crown.[46] The relevant point about the Canadian precedent, however, was that the Governor-General was not able, as it turned out, to meet the third condition as to an alternative government capable of carrying on for a reasonable period. A refusal of dissolution to the Hertzog government in South Africa in 1939, on the other hand, was followed by the establishment of an alternative government·under General Smuts. If that had happened in Canada, it might still have led to bitterness against the Crown and the Governor-General, but such criticism should presumably not in itself constitute a bar to the exercise of the prerogative in a proper case.

Clearly, situations in which there is no overall majority are those in which the possibility of finding alternative Ministers will occur. Asquith's declaration that a minority government does not have an automatic right to a dissolution does not distinguish between a government that has asked for a dissolution without having been defeated and a government that has been defeated either on a vote of confidence or on major legislative proposals. Nor is there anything in Lascelles's advice to George VI which turns on the question whether a government requesting dissolution has suffered defeat (since he was considering the likelihood of a request from Attlee's majority government). In summing up the

---

[45] Wheeler-Bennett, op. cit., p. 774.

[46] Wheeler-Bennett, ibid. Professor Berriedale Keith thought the 1926 refusal improper (see *Letters on Imperial Relations etc. 1916–1935* (1935), pp. 56–58). Dr Eugene Forsey however thought it to be justified (see *The Royal Power of Dissolution of Parliament in the British Commonwealth* (1943), chap. VI).

conclusions of his study of the dissolution power, Dr Markesinis makes no distinction, saying that 'The Crown may
under certain circumstances refuse a dissolution to a minority
government (whether defeated or undefeated), provided
an alternative government is possible and able to carry on
with the existing House.'[47] It is unclear whether in principle
being undefeated should increase or diminish a government's
entitlement to be allowed to dissolve. If a government were
undefeated because an immediate request to dissolve had
been made before the House had been allowed to meet, then
absence of defeat would not enhance the government's claim.
Moreover, a request that is made to avoid defeat or censure,
or a request made whilst a motion of censure is under debate
should equally not enhance a claim to dissolve.[48]

In the future situations that are likely to arise if electoral
reform or changes in the number and relationships of the
parties produce a House of Commons in which no single
party can take office with an overall majority, requests
for dissolution are likely to come from either single-party
minority governments or coalition governments that find
their programme obstructed, or who are defeated on issues
of confidence. Whether such a government should be allowed
to appeal to the country for support, or whether positive
efforts should be made by the Queen to enlist the support
of other party leaders in forming an alternative government
without an election, would present a difficult and delicate
question for decision. A Social Democratic/Liberal government would not easily be replaceable by any conceivable
combination of Conservative and Labour politicians. A
Labour minority government might more easily be replaced
by a formal or informal grouping of Conservatives and
Liberals or Alliance members. It might or might not be the
case that a different single party would be willing to take
office as a minority government. But should the issue be
raised by the Queen or, if raised by the parties, should
the Queen respond? A Labour government that was refused

---

[47] B. S. Markesinis, *The Theory and Practice of Dissolution of Parliament*,
p. 120.
[48] Cf. Eugene A. Forsey, *The Royal Power of Dissolution in the British Commonwealth* (1943), p. 269. 'If a government asks for dissolution whilst a motion
of censure is under debate it is clearly the Crown's *duty* to refuse.' (Italics added.)

a dissolution would almost certainly criticize the refusal as partisan, as the Liberals in Canada did in 1926, on the ground that the Crown would in due course be compelled to grant a dissolution to the alternative party or party grouping, having refused it to the government in office. That would not be a strong argument since the two refusals would be in different situations and on different grounds. Nevertheless the argument would certainly be used by critics of the Queen's action. It seems likely that if a government, whether minority or coalition, had been in office for a significant period and if some time had passed since the last General Election, the alternative of granting dissolution would present less difficulties and arouse less controversy than an attempt to send for an alternative Prime Minister or to issue invitations to opposition leaders to form a government (thus assuming the burden of judging whether any given combination of alternative office-holders could be assured of continuing support in the Commons). Nevertheless in other situations and if little time has passed since the last election, a difficult and controversial judgment by the Queen might still be required. There is also the possibility in an era of multi-party governmental groupings that requests for dissolution might be disputed or resisted within the governmental party or that the coalition leader might be held to be requesting dissolution to preserve his own position or for narrow party political reasons. (He might even have been removed from his leadership of the party by antagonistic party followers.) In these situations criticism of the Crown will be less if the conventions are clear. The last possibility suggests some consideration of the conventional rules governing the relationship of the Prime Minister and the Cabinet.[49]

A summary of the conventions that govern the exercise of the Crown's prerogative at the present time cannot usefully, as we have seen, be framed in terms of a general 'automatic' or 'non-automatic' theory, but calls for separate consideration of the four main so-called personal prerogatives. We have

---

[49] See chap. III below.

seen that in relation to withholding of assent to legislation and dismissal no practical problems arise, though improbable circumstances can be imagined in which such exercises might be a possibility. The Queen's judgment on the other hand may still sometimes be needed in bringing about changes of government if political power is divided, as it may be in the future, between more than two competing party groups.

It could be argued that powers of this kind, if necessary, need not be exercised by the Queen. In Australia Mr Gough Whitlam, and in Britain Mr Wedgwood Benn, have proposed that they should be vested elsewhere. Mr Whitlam writes:

We do not need a Head of State with any powers at all . . . . All that is needed is transitional machinery to hand over government from one party to another when the electorate so determines. A panel of certain office holders, or the High Court — not, obviously, the Chief Justice alone — would probably suffice. The idea that the orderly handing over of government can be guaranteed only by a head of state is a fallacy. In the United States . . . the transition from one administration to the next is made by the Electoral College. The great attraction and safeguard of a republican constitution are that a president, or whatever we might call the Head of State, would have no inherited or reserve powers at all.[50]

If comparison is to be made with the United States it must be remembered that the British and Australian cabinet systems are not based upon a system of fixed elections or a separation of powers with the executive placed in office for a definite period. Since in the Cabinet–Parliamentary system the appointment, continuation and cessation of governments in office is based upon the possession or loss of the confidence of the legislature, the transition from one government to the next is more complex. So also is the existence of prerogative powers alongside the law-making powers of British and Australian legislatures. It is not clear from Mr Whitlam's suggestion whether he envisages the *legal* prerogatives of the Crown being transferred to a committee or court, or simply the acceptance of a conventional rule that the committee's advice should be treated as binding. Since his chapter is headed 'Towards the Republic' it is probable that his proposal is to be seen as part of a new constitutional settlement

[50] *The Truth of the Matter* (1979), p. 184.

involving the abolition of the Crown and its prerogatives in Australia.

If it is conceded that the British cabinet system needs on occasion a reserve of independent judgment that stands apart from the party system, it seems unlikely that either Mr Benn's or Mr Whitlam's proposals would meet with widespread approval. In some political quarters in Britain High Court judges are not regarded as beyond criticism or best fitted to exercise delicate political choices. Nor would most judges regard themselves as qualified to assess the Parliamentary situation or the outcome of particular political courses of action. Nor is it easy to imagine any committee of persons, in or out of politics, whose standing would be such as to carry universal conviction and acceptance, especially on the part of those who might believe their judgment in particular cases to be misguided or disastrous. If the position of impartial arbitrator were to be filled by ballot it seems probable that the Queen (or whatever we choose to call the Head of State) would be a popular candidate.

III
The Practice of Dissolution

Some few constitutional responsibilities have been imputed specifically by convention to the Prime Minister rather than to Ministers generally. Of these the most important is the right to choose the date of a General Election and to advise the dissolution of Parliament. This is a discretionary power of some importance. Today it is normally asserted that responsibility for its exercise rests constitutionally with the Prime Minister and with him alone. This supposed convention, however, is one whose basis is unclear. Those who believe it to exist (including most recent Prime Ministers) are unsure about how it came to do so. It can be argued that it lacks the essential quality that should mark a constitutional convention, namely the combination of consistent historical precedents, and a convincing *raison d'être*. It is not, in fact, to be found mentioned in any discussion of the Prime Minister, the Cabinet or the conventions in Dicey, Bagehot or Sir William Anson.

Prime Ministerial Dissolution

The power to dissolve Parliament is in form an exercise of the Royal Prerogative, and the general rule about the prerogatives of the Crown is that they have come to be exercised in major matters on the advice of the Cabinet. In referring to dissolution Anson speaks of that prerogative being exercised on the advice of Ministers.[1] The powers to declare war, to make treaties or to assent to legislation are obviously so exercised. No one supposes that the Prime Minister has

---

[1] 'The prerogative of dissolution is one which the King exercises on the advice and at the request of *his ministers*.' Sir William Anson, *The Law and Custom of the Constitution* (5th edn.), vol. i, p. 327 (italics added). Cf. Morley, *Life of Walpole*, pp. 155-6: 'The cabinet is a unit — a unit as regards the Sovereign . . . . Its views are laid before the sovereign and before Parliament as if they were the views of one man.'

any peculiar constitutional primacy in these activities. Why should the prerogative power to dissolve Parliament be an exception? No compelling or even plausible reason seems ever to have been suggested. In practice the issue will only assume importance if there is cabinet and party dissension (as there was in the Labour administration of 1966–70), or possibly if there is disagreement between the leaders of a coalition government. If a Prime Minister at odds with his colleagues wished to dissolve and they did not, the Queen and her advisers might face conflicting advice from her Privy Councillors. This is an unusual but not an impossible event. At the time during the Labour Government of 1966–70 when a dissolution request from Mr Harold Wilson seemed a possibility, many seemed prepared to accept the contingency of alternative advice being offered. *The Times* suggested that 'If a Prime Minister defeated in Cabinet, unable to carry his policy in the party meeting were to ask for a dissolution for the apparent purpose of unnecessarily involving his party in his own downfall, the Queen would have ample grounds for refusing him and dismissing him, provided an alternative leader of the majority party was in sight.'

What then of the precedents? Between the second Reform Bill and 1914 there is no lack of instances of dissolutions debated in Cabinet. In 1880 'the Cabinet reconsidered the question of dissolution . . . the Commons ministers with the exception of Beach and Manners were in favour of an early election and were supported by the Whips and the Central Office. Northcote and Cross . . . were particularly enthusiastic. Disraeli backed them and the Cabinet decided to dissolve as soon as possible.'[2] Disraeli's letter to the Queen relates that every member of the Cabinet had been asked to give his opinion on the question of dissolution: 'The question, after exhausting arguments, really resolved itself to this: whether your Majesty should be advised to dissolve Parliament now or in the late autumn. The latter alternative was thought to involve too many risks; and perhaps was altogether impracticable, for the excitement of the existing House of Commons could hardly be restrained till that later period.'[3] The modern belief that dissolution

---

[2] Robert Blake, *Disraeli* (1966), pp. 703–4.
[3] Moneypenny and Buckle, *The Life of Benjamin Disraeli*, vol. vi, p. 514.

is a matter for decision by the Prime Minister appears to have sprung up after the First World War. In 1923, for example, Mr Baldwin's colleagues, whilst addressing to him a number of arguments about the date of dissolution, assured him (according to G. M. Young) that those views were submitted 'in great deference, recognising that fixing these matters is your special perquisite'.[4] In 1937 Professor Berriedale Keith wrote in critical terms of Baldwin's attitude to the Royal Prerogative and of his aggrandizement of the Prime Minister's office (anticipating the theories of Mr Richard Crossman by a quarter of a century). Baldwin, in Keith's view, had 'throughout his term of office . . . consistently increased the importance of the Prime Minister by transferring definitely to his office control of the discretionary power of the Crown'. In deciding upon his dissolution of 1935, he added, Baldwin had claimed for himself the full power to determine the issue. It was, he thought, 'remarkable that the claim to decide a dissolution should have been made and apparently enforced without effective or perhaps any protest'.[5]

Keith noted that in Canada the Prime Minister's primacy in recommending a dissolution had been affirmed by Order in Council in 1920 but that the recommendation was put forward with the assent of the Council. Subsequent Canadian practice is of some interest. For reasons that are unclear there appears to have been a change of procedure in the 1950s in the mechanism for signifying advice to the Governor-General on dissolution (as also on the summoning of Parliament and appointment of Ministers). Before 1957 the Governor-General was advised on these matters by a formal Minute of Council. In 1957 a different document termed an 'instrument of advice' was used. In reply to questions in the Canadian

---

[4] *Stanley Baldwin* (1952), p. 66. Baldwin himself seems to have regarded the question as one requiring persuasion rather than mere decision. Writing later to Tom Jones he said 'I came to the decision myself', but added ' . . . how I drove that Cabinet to take the plunge I shall never know'. (Keith Middlemas and John Barnes, *Baldwin: a biography* (1969), at p. 249.)

[5] Keith, *The King, the Constitution, the Empire and Foreign Affairs: Letters and Essays 1936-7*, pp. 41-2. Cf. Keith's view in *The King and the Imperial Crown* (1936), p. 176: ' . . . a dissolution is advised by the Cabinet, not the Prime Minister alone. There is no case on record where action has really occurred without the assent of a Cabinet majority'.

House of Commons in 1966 the Parliamentary Secretary to the Prime Minister said that 'The minute of Council was considered inappropriate as a means of addressing the Governor-General on those matters on which the tendering of advice is the responsibility of the Prime Minister alone and not of the Committee of the Privy Council.'[6]

Origin of the Theory

The manner in which the Prime Ministerial theory of dissolution came into existence in Britain deserves examination. In 1918 Mr Bonar Law made a remarkable statement in the House of Commons which is possibly the starting-point of the present received belief. At the end of 1918, suggestions of a dissolution were in the air, but in the House of Commons on 7 November Mr Bonar Law spoke of a General Election as being decided by the 'head of the Government'. 'In my belief,' he said, 'there is no custom more clearly defined than that what advice on this matter should be given to the Sovereign is a question not for the Cabinet but for the Prime Minister.'[7] Mr Lloyd George, he said, agreed with him on this. When challenged on the point,[8] he added that the doctrine as he had stated it had always been the regular practice; that he had himself known of recent cases where no intimation had been given to the Cabinet; and that members would recall the action of Mr Gladstone in 1874 when his colleagues received the intimation of the coming election from the public press.

A remark in a letter which he had received from Balfour several weeks before may conceivably have suggested this formulation.[9] In October 1918 Balfour, writing to Bonar Law about the timing of the election, had written that responsi-

---

[6] House of Commons Debates (Canada), 4 April 1966.

[7] 110 HC Deb. 5s., col. 2425.

[8] Mr Dillon (ibid.) replied 'That is not a recognised practice and I am amazed that the Right Hon. Gentleman should say that it is.'

[9] But Sir Ivor Jennings in *Cabinet Government* (3rd edn.), p. 417, quotes a much earlier letter to Balfour from George Wyndham in 1905 which contains the words 'It rests — as I understand the Constitution — with the Prime Minister *alone* to advise a dissolution.' Wyndham's suggestion is possibly the first mention of the Prime Ministerial theory of dissolution.

bility for it 'in fact' rested with the Prime Minister and that on some previous occasions the Prime Minister of the day 'had not even gone through the form of consulting his colleagues'. But wherever it originated, each part of Bonar Law's statement was open to question. Morley's account of the 1874 dissolution does not support it. Gladstone in January 1874 wrote to the Queen that he was about 'to recommend his colleagues humbly and dutifully to advise an immediate dissolution' and (two days later) that he 'laid before the Cabinet a pretty full outline of the case . . . and . . . the Cabinet unanimously concurred, upon a review of its grounds, in the wisdom of the proposed measure.'[10] What again were the recent cases of which Mr Bonar Law knew? The three previous dissolutions were in 1906 and 1910. If Mr Asquith's word is to be accepted each of those resulted from Cabinet decisions. Mr Asquith was particularly clear on the point: 'Such a question as the Dissolution of Parliament is always submitted to the Cabinet.'[11] In a survey of the eleven dissolutions between 1868 and 1910 in *Fifty Years of Parliament*, he could find no exception to this rule. Why then did Bonar Law and Balfour assert the contrary in 1918? The most plausible reason seems to be that they may have had in mind a quite different question about dissolution which had been raised in 1916. In December 1916, Bonar Law had had an interview with the King after the resignation of Mr Asquith. At this interview the question of dissolution of Parliament had been discussed. George V, being reluctant to contemplate a General Election in wartime, had consulted Lord Haldane upon the question whether Mr Bonar Law or any proposed successor to Asquith might properly make a dissolution of Parliament a condition upon which he would accept office. Lord Haldane had advised that the King could not entertain any such bargain with a *possible* Prime Minister not yet in a position to give advice as a responsible Minister of the Crown. Unfortunately the memorandum which Haldane sent to Lord Stamfordham summarized this position by the words 'The only minister who can properly give advice as to a dissolution of Parliament is the Prime Minister.' It rather looks as if Lord Haldane

[10] *Life of Gladstone* (1903), vol. ii, pp. 485-6.
[11] *Fifty Years of Parliament*, vol. ii, p. 194.

here unwittingly helped to originate the misunderstanding which Bonar Law in the heat of a Commons debate subsequently amplified and handed on to his post-war successors. Clearly Haldane, who had sat in Mr Asquith's Cabinet, did not mean to deal in his 1916 memorandum with the internal relationships of an administration in office. His mind was not directed to that issue. What he had been asked to advise upon, as the memorandum — printed in Sir Harold Nicolson's biography of George V — makes plain, was the right of a *potential* Prime Minister to advise or bargain for dissolution *before* assuming office. His categorical phrase 'The only minister who can properly give advice . . . ' was meant only to emphasize the right of the King to decline to guarantee in advance a particular use of the prerogative to a potential incumbent who, not yet being in office, would not be constitutionally entitled to proffer advice on anything. It was not intended to prejudge the quite different question, not then in issue, of a Cabinet's collective rights as against a Prime Minister.

Subsequent opinion seems, then, to have rested upon the plainly mistaken assertion about previous practice made in 1918 in a confused party situation, when Bonar Law, and possibly others, wished to leave the responsibility for dissolving Parliament to Lloyd George.[12] Balfour, as we have seen, concurred in the prime ministerial prerogative doctrine, but whether he got it from George Wyndham and gave it to Bonar Law, or whether Bonar Law was confused by the different issue raised in 1916 is less certain. Lloyd George, perhaps not surprisingly, agreed with Bonar Law's statement of Lloyd George's rights. In the debate on 7 November 1918 Bonar Law said that 'In the Prime Minister's view and in my view the question of deciding whether or not there should be an election is the duty of the Prime Minister.'[13] This certainly seems to be the point in time at which the Prime Ministerial heresy gained acceptance. Mr Bonar Law, however, could

---

[12] See Robert Blake, *The Unknown Prime Minister* (1955), p. 384. 'Balfour was inclined to the view that an early Election was desirable [and] that the responsibility should be left to Lloyd George.' Mr Bonar Law also was not so certain that there was any advantage to the Conservative Party in having a coalition election. 'On balance he was prepared to leave it to the Prime Minister.' (Jennings, *Cabinet Government* (3rd edn.), p. 419.)

[13] 110 HC Deb., col. 2227.

not be compared as a constitutional authority with Mr
Asquith, and why his opinion should have been adopted
as the popular view remains mysterious. It may be that the
better view should, if possible, be reinstated? Whatever
has been recently believed and acted upon, there seems
no adequate constitutional foundation for the view that
the discretionary power to dissolve and hold a General
Election is a peculiar personal perquisite of the office of
Prime Minister. It may perhaps be felt by some that the
Prime Ministerial view is the more realistic and that it is in
any event too firmly established to be overthrown. Neither
point is persuasive. Constitutional conventions are established through the medium of belief and conviction, both
of which can be changed. As to realism, it could be urged
that the more realistic and down-to-earth view lies with the
recognition that a decision to hold a General Election is
no less a piece of political decision-making than any other
issue of cabinet policy.

Recent Practice

In *Cabinet Government* Sir Ivor Jennings wrote that 'No
dissolution since 1918 has been brought before the Cabinet
and all Prime Ministers since Mr Lloyd George have assumed
a right to give the advice.'[14] But it may be that the first
part of that statement does not accurately reflect the practice
of Cabinets since 1945 and it may not be clear beyond doubt
that all Prime Ministers have assumed the right or that they
would have been correct to do so. If Cabinet Ministers have
discussed the question of dissolution and are in agreement,
it may not be possible to say with complete assurance that
the decision was that of the Prime Minister and not the
Cabinet. It may also be that the degree of formality with
which such discussions or consultations have been carried
on has differed between parties and Prime Ministers. Given
the different leadership philosophies of the Conservative and
Labour Parties, it would not be unusual if wider consultations have taken place before dissolutions advised by

[14]· *Cabinet Government* (3rd edn. 1959), p. 419.

Labour Prime Ministers. Patrick Gordon-Walker reports that in 1950 the Cabinet decided that if defeated on the Address they should advise immediate dissolution whereas Attlee had favoured resignation.[15] Sir Harold Wilson quotes John Mackintosh's statement[16] that Attlee 'consulted a few senior colleagues but clearly made up his mind about the dissolutions which terminated his two administrations'. Sir Harold adds: 'This is not my recollection in respect of 1950.'[17] He himself seems to have consulted more widely and more formally as time went on. In 1966 Brown and Callaghan as Deputy Leader and Chancellor were consulted[18] but the decision was, according to Richard Crossman's account, put before the Cabinet. Crossman's *Diary* for 28 February 1966, notes that 'In the morning Cabinet was summoned and we formally decided the election date.'[19] In 1970, Crossman reports a detailed discussion amongst Ministers held at Chequers on 8 March. 'The Prime Minister', he says, 'started by going round the table asking everyone for their views of the date of the election.' Various matters were discussed. 'Harold said one of the problems was the World Cup. If it wasn't for that he would favour the end of June and was now trying to find out what time of day the match was played because he felt this was a determining factor.'[20] In turn Ministers mentioned strikes, rising prices, likely Conservative tactics, and a number of other considerations. In *The Governance of Britain* Sir Harold stresses the propriety and usefulness of such consultations, though he adds that 'there is no obligation on the Prime Minister to consult'.[21]

Clearly the fact that Cabinet Ministers are consulted and discuss dissolution is not inconsistent with the belief that the Prime Minister has some special pre-eminence in the process that is different from that which he or she normally exercises

[15] Patrick Gordon-Walker, *The Cabinet* (2nd edn.), p. 135.
[16] *The British Cabinet* (1962), p. 24.
[17] Harold Wilson, *The Governance of Britain* (1976), p. 37.
[18] Harold Wilson, *The Labour Government 1964-70: a Personal Record* (1971), p. 201.
[19] Richard Crossman, *The Diaries of a Cabinet Minister*, vol. 1 (1975), p. 464.
[20] *Diaries*, vol. iii (1977), p. 847.
[21] *The Governance of Britain* (1976), p. 38. Before the General Election of 1983 it was reported that 'Mrs Thatcher has summoned her inner Cabinet to a special meeting at Chequers on Sunday 8 May to discuss whether to hold a General Election in June.' (*The Observer*, 24 April 1983).

in virtue of general leadership of the Cabinet and party. But the testing of that belief could only take place if a Cabinet unanimously or by majority persisted in a disagreement with the Prime Minister's judgment[22] or if a coalition Cabinet were to split on the question.[23] These might be considerations making against automatic acceptance of a dissolution request as might the rejection of a Prime Minister's leadership by his party.[24] If any such arguments are valid the Prime Ministerial theory of dissolution cannot be accepted in its present form.

Argument about this particular rule aptly illustrates the general proposition that conventions are not best thought of as being the beliefs that politicians actually hold at any one time about the conduct of government.[25] It may be that a view is widely held about the existence of a particular rule. But it may sometimes be possible to argue (as it is here) that the common or widespread conviction rests upon misconstruction of earlier precedents or on unconvincing assertions of principle. Even in politics convictions − and therefore conventions − are sometimes changed by argument.

[22] In *Cabinet Government* (3rd edn.), p. 86, Sir Ivor Jennings wrote that 'The Queen must not . . . support a Prime Minister against his colleagues. Accordingly it would be unconstitutional for the Queen to agree with the Prime Minister for the dissolution of the Government in order to allow the Prime Minister to override his colleagues.'

[23] See Rodney Brazier, 'Choosing a Prime Minister', (1982) *Public Law*, p. 400, on the implications of coalition splits for dissolution. Cf. Bogdanor, *Multi-party Politics and the Constitution* (1983), p. 184.

[24] See Gordon-Walker's view (in *The Cabinet* (2nd edn.), at p. 170) of a Prime Minister who is detached from his party support. ('A Prime Minister who has been overthrown either by a vote of his Cabinet or by the Parliamentary party or by both ceases to be a Prime Minister save in the most formal sense, and cannot therefore advise the Crown.')

[25] See chap. I above at pp. 10–12.

IV
The Doctrine of Ministerial Responsibility

A clear and succinct account of the principle or convention of ministerial responsibility is not easy to give. One reason may be that the convention is, like most British conventions, somewhat vague and slippery — resembling (to borrow a phrase) the procreation of eels.[1] Another reason is that collective and individual responsibility are two doctrines, not one, and each divides in turn into a series of disparate topics. The slipperiness shows itself when we see that propositions about both types of responsibility have to be formulated in some such form as: 'Ministers generally do or should do X in circumstances Y (but with various exceptions).' Thus:

1. The prerogatives of the Crown are exercised on the advice of Ministers (except in such cases as they are not).
2. The Government resigns when it loses the confidence of the House of Commons (except when it remains in office).
3. Ministers speak and vote together (except when they cannot agree to do so).
4. Ministers explain their policy and provide information to the House (except when they keep it to themselves).
5. Ministers offer their individual resignations if serious errors are made in their Departments (except when they retain their posts or are given peerages).
6. Every act of a civil servant is, legally speaking, the act of a Minister (except those that are, legally speaking, his own).

It is the filling in of the exception clauses that makes the drafting of a written Constitution for the United Kingdom such a hopeless, Utopian enterprise. Indeed, so far as individual responsibility goes, it has been urged that the exception clauses have blotted out the main principle and that no such convention now exists.[2] Ministers never (or very nearly

---

[1] Quoted by G. H. L. Le May (from Sir Claud Schuster) in *The Victorian Constitution* (1979), p. 97.

[2] S. E. Finer, 'The Individual Responsibility of Ministers', (1956) *Public Administration* 377.

never) offer their individual resignations as the result of condemnation by the House of Commons. We might perhaps even add that governments collectively never (or really hardly ever) resign as the result of condemnation by the House of Commons. So it may be that the convention of collective responsibility does not exist either. Despite this, politicians and textbook writers carry on as if these conventions do exist. From 1900 to about 1950 the textbooks, moreover, were more or less unanimous in what they had to say. But perhaps now some re-writing is needed.

Collective Responsibility

There are three traditional branches of the collective responsibility convention: the confidence rule, the unanimity rule, and the confidentiality rule. The first is to do with the conditions on which a government holds office; the others with the way in which its members behave whilst in office. If we look at each branch of the convention we seem to see some changes. It sometimes used to be said that a prime non-legal rule of the Constitution was that governments defeated by the House on central issues of policy were obliged to resign. But only one Prime Minister has resigned as the result of a defeat in the House in the twentieth century and that was immediately after being deprived of his majority by a General Election (Baldwin in January 1924). MacDonald was defeated on a confidence issue in 1924 and Callaghan in 1979, but neither resigned. Both fought the subsequent General Elections as leader of a government, having advised dissolution.

So the rule about a government that loses the confidence of the House seems to be that it must *either* resign *or* advise dissolution. Its right is only to advise, not to have, dissolution; since dissolution can, as we have seen, in some circumstances be refused. Resignation might therefore follow as the result of such a refusal (by the Queen), but that has not happened. As to what constitutes a loss of confidence there seems also to have been a development in doctrine. The books used to say that defeat on major legislative measures or policy proposals as well as on specifically worded confidence motions was fatal to the continuance of the government. But this no longer seems to be believed or acted on.[3] In 1977 *The Times* propounded the view that 'there is no constitutional principle that requires a government to regard any specific policy defeat as evidence that it no longer possesses the necessary confidence of the House of Commons'. Some were greatly shocked by this doctrine and Professor Max Beloff wrote to *The Times* to say that it was inconsistent with the principles of the Constitution as hitherto understood. Sir Ivor Jennings, he pointed out, had said in *Cabinet Government* that the government must go if the House failed to approve its policy.[4] What provoked the disagreement was that the Labour Government had just failed to carry a budget proposal about the rate of income tax and was proposing to remain in office in defiance of Sir Ivor Jennings's view of the established convention. Sir Ivor Jennings was of course dead, which is supposed to augment the authority of a textbook writer by allowing his views to be cited more freely in the course of litigation. Unfortunately there is a countervailing disadvantage in that his works may go out of print and are no longer constantly perused by Ministers, who are thereby enabled to fall into lax habits and disregard established constitutional conventions. In the 1960s and 1970s, in any event, governments seem to have been following a new rule, according to which only votes specifically stated by the Government to be matters of confidence, or votes of no confidence by the Opposition are allowed to count. Just conceivably one can imagine amongst recent Prime Ministers those who might have felt it their duty to soldier on in the general interest even in the face of such a vote.

If we turn to the second meaning or branch of the collective responsibility principle, namely the unanimity or solidarity of the Cabinet, we see further change and uncertainty.

---

[3] Compare earlier and later editions of, for example, Hood Phillips's *Constitutional and Administrative Law*. In 1962 the third edition said that a government was 'bound to resign or advise the Queen to dissolve Parliament if it is defeated in the House of Commons *on a major issue*'. In 1978 the sixth edition refers only to 'defeat *on a motion of confidence* or of no confidence' (italics added).

[4] In 1976, after a government defeat on the 1976 Expenditure White Paper, Mrs Thatcher said that 'When there is a defeat on a matter of major economic strategy, a matter central to the historic nature of the power of the House of Commons over the Executive, that is a resigning matter.' (907 HC Deb. 642-3.)

The doctrine of collective responsibility in this second sense was treated roughly in 1975 when Mr Harold Wilson suspended it before the EEC referendum in order to allow free play to the convictions of the Labour Cabinet's anti-Common Marketeers.[5] The reasons offered for the suspension were that it was necessary for a fair and free debate to take place and that the issue was one on which both political parties and 'many families and households' were divided. The 'divided parties and households' argument seemed unimpressive since neither parties nor families are Cabinets. Free and fair debate is certainly a good thing, but it is unclear why the debate would have been unfree and unfair if the opponents of cabinet policy had followed the normal practice and campaigned against it from outside the Cabinet. So the reasons given seemed suspect and the parallels drawn with the 1932 Coalition agreement to differ seemed not obviously applicable to a single-party government. It does not follow, however, that the Wilson Government were guilty of constitutional impropriety. Possibly Mr Wilson did not need to supply reasons for changing the Cabinet's customary practice. It may be that the custom of unanimity, like that of cabinet secrecy, is not a duty-imposing constitutional convention,[6] though undoubtedly a historically observed and politically convenient practice. It is acknowledged that the Prime Minister may decide to which members of a government the rule of unanimity extends and to what times and places; for example to party meetings such as the Labour Party's national executive committee. But perhaps the principle in its entirety is a matter for the Cabinet and the Prime Minister between them to apply or not as they wish.[7] The first sense of collective responsibility (resigning or dissolving after defeat on a confidence issue) is undoubtedly a duty-imposing convention since it entails an obligation

---

[5] The Cabinet dissenters were free to advocate their views in the EEC referendum campaign but not (unlike the National Government's 'agreement to differ' on the tariff issue in 1932) by speech or vote in Parliament. (Or at European Community meetings.)

[6] See the discussion of types of convention in chap. I at pp. 7–8.

[7] That seemed to be Mr James Callaghan's view when permitting dissent on the European Assembly Elections Bill in 1977. He believed that the doctrine of collective responsibility should apply 'except in cases where I announce that it does not'. (933 HC Deb., col. 552.)

or a duty to the House of Commons. Cabinet solidarity, on the other hand, is the subject matter of a right inhering in the Prime Minister correlative to a duty in his colleagues. It is not necessarily a right inhering in the House of Commons correlative to a duty in the Cabinet and Prime Minister. It has been said by some to be a duty to the Crown. But the traditional rationale for cabinet solidarity rather makes against that notion since it developed historically not as a right of the Crown but as a partial shield against the Crown to avoid the penalizing or attempted dismissal of particular Ministers for their opinions. So if a Cabinet and Prime Minister do not mind exposing their internal differences of opinion, is that course unconstitutional or a breach of convention, as distinct from being politically imprudent or tactically risky? In nineteenth-century Cabinets, subjects that excited keen disagreement, such as Catholic emancipation, women's suffrage, and tariff reform were treated as 'open questions'. Those who now esteem open government ought perhaps to encourage open disagreements, openly arrived at.

Similar considerations affect the third aspect of collective responsibility, namely confidentiality. Disclosure and briefing of the Press by Ministers has always taken place when they have felt it to be in their interest. The rules respecting exercises in communication by individual Ministers, however were significantly modified by Mr Richard Crossman whose *Diaries of a Cabinet Minister* were published after an unsuccessful attempt to prevent their appearance by the Attorney-General in 1976.[8] In the course of the proceedings a number of witnesses gave evidence about the nature of collective responsibility, including the Secretary of the Cabinet, Sir John Hunt. The Crossman manuscript had been submitted for security clearance to the Cabinet Secretary who had set out for Crossman's guidance a number of restrictive rules or 'parameters' (a term[9] new to constitutional theory).

---

[8] *Attorney-General v. Jonathan Cape*, [1976] Q.B. 752 (See App. A). See also Hugo Young, *The Crossman Affair* (1976).

[9] It means 'a constant occurring in the equation of a curve or surface, by the variation of which the equation is made to represent a family of such curves or surfaces'; or in conic sections 'the third proportional to any given diameter and its conjugate or, in the parabola, to any abscissa on a given diameter and the corresponding ordinate'.

The 'parameters' provided a basis for the Attorney-General's attempt to prevent publication of the *Diaries*. The injunction applied for against the literary executors and publishers sought to restrain the disclosure of communications or discussions falling into three classes: first, discussions in Cabinet or cabinet committees; secondly, any other communications between Ministers or between Ministers and civil servants about the formulation or execution of policy; and thirdly, discussions about the appointment, transfer or fitness for office of senior members of the public service (junior members being presumably expected to suffer in the higher interest of free discussion).

In arguing for the injunction, the Attorney-General suggested that publication of Mr Crossman's recollections would set off a process that would in due course put an end to the principle of collective ministerial responsibility. If the *Diaries* were published, he said, 'nothing could stop the snowball process of proliferation of information from rolling downhill and taking with it the shattered remains of the system of Cabinet collective responsibility'. Such a declension would, he implied, be cataclysmic. Affidavits were produced from Sir Peter Rawlinson and Lord Hailsham of St. Marylebone to the effect that they had attended cabinet meetings and had relied upon each other's discretion not to disclose what had passed between them in private on such occasions. If the courts could intervene, to shield from public curiosity, what had gone on between husband and wife,[10] how much more so should they be prepared to draw a veil in the public interest over the relations, one with another, of Privy Councillors?

Lord Widgery refused an injunction to restrain the publication of the first of Mr Crossman's volumes. He was, however, prepared to concede the substance of the Attorney-General's argument. Cabinet meetings were, he said, conducted in confidence and the publication of cabinet proceedings could be restrained by the courts whenever that was clearly necessary in the public interest. There was overwhelming evidence that the doctrine of collective responsibility was an established feature of the English form of government. Since

---

[10] See *Argyle* v. *Argyle*, [1967] Ch. 302.

confidentiality was imposed to enable the efficient conduct of the Queen's business, the confidence was owed to the Queen and was not something from which Cabinet Ministers could release themselves at will. For a Cabinet Minister to disclose his own views would enable experienced observers to identify the views of others, and to identify Ministers who voted one way or the other would undermine the whole doctrine of joint responsibility. In this case, however, the matters disclosed related to transactions that had taken place ten years earlier and there could, therefore, be no danger of free discussion being inhibited in the present Cabinet, even though some members might be the same people and the problems they were discussing distressingly similar to those of a decade earlier.

Given Lord Widgery's acceptance of the Attorney-General's interpretation of the doctrine of collective responsibility, there seems a confusion in the argument about past, present, and future. The argument appears to be that disclosure of what were confidential matters ten years ago will not inhibit free discussion now. But this argument seems to take no account of the importance of knowing now that because a breach of the rule of complete confidentiality has been accepted there may be further disclosure later on of what is at present confidential. If free and frank discussion really rests upon the confidence principle it may not survive in the same form if the participants are aware that present confidences are likely to share the same fate as past confidences. Moreover, if the maintenance of confidentiality really rests upon a duty to the Queen not to disclose the advice privily given to her, is not the obligation one to be dissolved by her, if at all? It is possible that Her Majesty may not mind readers of the *Sunday Times* knowing what advice was offered to her by Mr Macmillan or Sir Alec Douglas Home, whilst wishing to preserve more reticence about the inner working and thought processes of her current advisers. But ought not the point to be decided by her rather than by politicians with manuscripts to sell, or even by the Cabinet itself?

If cabinet confidentiality is considered as a politically useful practice Lord Widgery's concessions to the potential cabinet diarist seem too broad. On the other hand the Attorney-

General's description of the requirements of ministerial responsibility might also have been thought extreme. It may be that not every shred of the doctrine would crumble away even if it were to become known what arguments were used in Cabinet and by whom. This sometimes is known. Indeed the knowledge is frequently engineered by members of the Cabinet who seem on these occasions to find their oaths as Privy Councillors no encumbrance. The central strands of the doctrine of collective responsibility are that the government should stand or fall together, that the administration speaks formally to Parliament with one voice and that Ministers resign or dissolve if defeated on a Commons vote of confidence. None of these practices would be fatally impaired by greater public knowledge of the views of individual members of the administration.

The present practice is formally that set out in the *Report of the Radcliffe Committee of Privy Councillors on Ministerial Memoirs*.[11] Ministers should not disclose cabinet transactions for a period of fifteen years after their occurrence if they affect national security, or would be injurious to foreign relations or would publicize relationships between Ministers, or between Ministers and the Civil Service or outside advisers. Diarists who work to these guidelines do not seem likely to find a ready sale for their memoirs. It is intended that the guidelines should be accepted as a matter of honour by Cabinet Ministers, but they could presumably be enforced by a further application for an injunction sought by the Attorney-General or even perhaps by a disgruntled colleague.

Individual Responsibility

When we turn to individual responsibility to Parliament we find here also that the traditional rules are not wholly to be relied upon. Some things said by Sidney Low and Sir Ivor Jennings or Lord Morrison of Lambeth are not now said with conviction. 'Ministers are responsible for the misdeeds of civil servants.' 'The Minister is responsible for every stamp

[11] Cmnd. 6386 (1976).

stuck on an envelope.' 'When things go right ministers take the credit; when things go wrong they take the blame.' 'If necessary they offer their resignations.' These suppositions do not entirely square with either recent history or the present organization of central government.

If we look for instances of resignation by Ministers as the result of public or parliamentary criticism, there are since 1945 only about a dozen reasonably clear and one or two marginal cases. Of course resignations are not always what they seem. Some that seem to be without fault[12] may be in anticipation of future dismissal (as perhaps was the resignation of Attlee's Minister of Food, Sir Ben Smith, in 1947). Some others that are on the face of it stout-hearted withdrawals as the alleged result of policy differences may in reality be polite expulsions or prudent subterfuges. It has been alleged, for example, that one of the Ministers who resigned from the first Wilson administration was required to retire on a false pretext as the result of information from the security service that he had put himself in serious danger of being blackmailed by Soviet bloc intelligence agents.[13] Of the overt cases, moreover, none involved a blameless Minister resigning as the result of departmental faults. Nor did any case between Sir Thomas Dugdale's Crichel Down resignation in 1954 and that of Lord Carrington over the Falkland Islands' occupation in 1982 involve an issue of political or departmental policy, though perhaps Mr James Callaghan's 1967 post-devaluation departure from the Exchequer in a sideways direction towards the Home Office might possibly be treated as such a case (as might Mr Emanuel Shinwell's translation from Fuel and Power to the War Office in 1947). All the rest involved questions of personal behaviour or alleged moral scandal. Dalton resigned in 1947 having prematurely handed out budget information, and John Belcher in 1948 after the Lynskey Tribunal found him to have accepted small bribes for

---

[12] There are, of course, a great many instances of genuine 'no fault' resignations as the result of policy disagreements, such as Mr Harold Wilson's resignation from the Attlee Cabinet or Mr George Brown's withdrawal from Mr Wilson's. These resignations are relevant to the unanimity aspect of the collective responsibility rule rather than to the rules of individual responsibility for failure in office.

[13] Chapman Pincher, *Inside Story* (1978), p. 17.

ministerial favours at the Board of Trade. They were followed in 1962 by Galbraith, blamed for consorting with the spy Vassall, and in 1963 by Profumo, blamed for consorting with Christine Keeler. Then in 1973 there was Lord Jellicoe who entertained call girls under an assumed name and Lord Lambton who used his own. In 1975 a junior Minister in the Wilson government, Lord Brayley, resigned after financial inquiries had been made into the affairs of a company with which he had previously been associated. Adverse publicity related to their private behaviour also accounted for the resignations of Mr Ian Harvey in 1958 and Mr Nicholas Fairbairn in 1982.

An arguable case for inclusion in the list is Mr Reginald Maudling who, having had dealings with the architect John Poulson, whose affairs were under investigation, resigned from the Home Office under the misapprehension that he was in charge of the police force. Home Secretaries seem particularly prone to mistakes of this kind. According to Lord Denning's report on the Profumo case, Mr Henry Brooke in 1963 did not know that he was head of the Security Service. For cases where a Minister does not know the nature and quality of his office we perhaps need a special category. We might call it 'diminished ministerial responsibility'.

As to vicarious liability for departmental subordinates, Ministers have never been keen on it. Both Mr Herbert Morrison and Sir David Maxwell Fyfe (as they then were), who spoke at some length about ministerial responsibility in the Crichel Down debate in 1954, were in agreement that resignation must entail some degree of personal culpability. In 1977 Sir John Hunt giving evidence to the Expenditure Committee spoke thus, with clear intent if infirm syntax: 'The concept that because somebody whom the minister has never heard of has made a mistake means that the minister should resign, is out of date and rightly so.'[14] It is not certain what Sir John would have said about the concept of ministerial resignation when somebody whom the Minister *has* heard of has made a mistake. Possibly, that its parameters are indistinct.

[14] See *Eleventh Report from the Expenditure Committee (The Civil Service)*, HC 535-1 (1977), p. xlvii. Cf. the Committee's conclusions on 'accountable units' and the public accounting of civil servants for management decisions.

In considering what conclusions can be drawn about the convention of individual ministerial responsibility, it is useful to recall some of the well-known cases of non-resignations by Ministers when matters of one sort or another have gone wrong. The failure of the West African ground nuts scheme in Mr Attlee's post-war administration did not lead to the resignation of the nominally responsible Minister, Mr John Strachey. The Colonial Secretary Mr Lennox-Boyd did not resign when brutal treatment and killing of detainees at a prison camp at Hola in Kenya was debated in the House of Commons in 1959. In 1964 Mr Julian Amery did not resign when the Ministry of Aviation was found to have made large over-payments to Ferranti Ltd. for defence contract work. In 1971 the Vehicle and General Insurance Company collapsed and a Tribunal of Inquiry found that there had been negligence on the part of the Board of Trade in exercising its functions; but the President of the Board of Trade did not offer his resignation.

In the 1960s there were no ministerial resignations after the series of espionage scandals. Nor when large-scale mis-calculations were made about the cost of the Concorde aircraft development programme. Nor again when sanctions against Rhodesia were evaded by the major oil companies with covert governmental acquiescence. In 1982 Mr William Whitelaw, as Home Secretary and police authority for the Metropolitan area, did not offer to resign when the arrangements for protecting the Queen and the security of Buckingham Palace were seen to be defective.

These cases divide into two categories. One category is that in which responsibility, i.e. culpability, is shared by a number of Ministers, and particular Ministers are protected by the assumption of collective responsibility. In relation to security failures, for example, Mr Harold Macmillan was apt to say in response to calls for resignations that the government as a whole was responsible and that the electorate must judge it.

The other category is that in which the chain of command or accountability is extended either geographically or administratively, and mistakes have been made by someone of whom the Minister either has not heard or over whom he could not be expected to exert control or surveillance.

Mr Lennox-Boyd could not be expected to have personal familiarity with the day-to-day operations of prison guards in Kenya, or Mr Whitelaw with the precise arrangements for patrolling the grounds of Buckingham Palace.

From these cases of non-resignation the current rules of individual ministerial responsibility can be summarized. Sir Thomas Dugdale's resignation over the mishandling of his Department's policy towards the disposal of land revealed in the 1954 Crichel Down case, though it was accompanied by subordinate errors, was an assumption of personal responsibility by the Minister who had himself been involved in the particular misjudgment and who was held by his colleagues to have failed to organize his Department efficiently. He was not, as many alleged at the time, a Minister sacrificed in accordance with the hard doctrine that a ministerial head must roll for civil service error. No post-war case has involved such an assumption and it can be said with confidence that the convention of ministerial responsibility contains no requirement of any such vicarious accountability. Some Minister must of course answer in the House of Commons for civil service failings and must explain the reasons for their occurrence and the measures to be taken to prevent future failures. But the conclusions of Sir David Maxwell Fyfe in the Crichel Down debate in 1954 and the similar conclusions of the then Opposition spokesman Mr Herbert Morrison[15] may still be taken to state the present position. When action is taken of which a Minister disapproves and of which he has no prior knowledge, there is no obligation on his part to endorse it, to defend the errors of his officers, or to resign.

Lord Carrington's resignation in 1982, accepting personal responsibility for misjudgment of the danger from Argentina to the Falkland Islands (together with the resignations of the two junior Foreign Office Ministers Mr Richard Luce and Mr Humphrey Atkins) provides a further clear precedent for the existence of a rule requiring a Minister who is personally culpable of misjudgment or negligence to offer his resignation. In his survey of ministerial resignations some years

[15] See 530 HC Deb. 5s., col. 1278 et seq. Similar views are set out in chap. XIV (Ministers and Civil Servants) in Lord Morrison's *Government and Parliament: A Survey from the Inside* (1954).

ago,[16] Professor S. E. Finer rightly observed that the supposed rule about ministerial resignations at the instance of the House of Commons was not based upon any sequence of precedents and therefore might be thought to be of doubtful authenticity. Perhaps Sir Thomas Dugdale and Lord Carrington together do not constitute a sequence, or (since their downfall was not procured by the House of Commons) refute Professor Finer's thesis. None the less they are precedents and with a dash of principle may be treated as evidence of a convention whose existence is certainly not doubted in the House of Commons.

Civil Service Responsibility

One familiar corollary of the idea that Ministers were vicariously responsible for the acts of civil servants, taking both blame when due and credit when available, was that the civil servants themselves were anonymous and their personal failures not a matter of knowledge or debate. In the 1950s Mr Herbert Morrison suggested that civil servants, if blameworthy, might be named by a Minister in the course of explaining administrative failure to the House of Commons. No one contradicted him, but it was assumed that this would be a rare event, and so it was. Nor at this time was there any other common forum in or out of Parliament for inquiring into administrative or bureaucratic failure.

Since the middle 1950s however – and possibly beginning with the public inquiry into Crichel Down – there has been a number of changes in the machinery of government that have focussed inquiry or publicity on particular acts of administration and on the persons of particular administrators. Three such developments are the increasing use of formal inquiry procedures and tribunals of inquiry; the creation of the Parliamentary Commissioner (the Ombudsman); and the increased scrutiny of departmental administration through specialized Select Committees in Parliament. All of these have in some degree served to reveal and separate the internal division of responsibilities between Ministers and civil ser-

[16] (1956) *Public Administration* 377.

vants, though the logic of this has not been worked out, and there are some tensions between its implications and those of the familiar doctrine of ministerial responsibility.

In the post-war period, for example, numerous inquiries have been set up into political and administrative failures, many of them under the provisions of the 1921 Tribunals of Inquiry (Evidence) Act. The public evidence given before these inquiries and the final published reports often involve the activities of particular civil servants, who are named and if necessary blamed. The Crichel Down inquiry, though it was not set up as a tribunal under the 1921 Act, led to sanctions against a number of civil servants that were publicly announced.[17] Similarly the Tribunal of Inquiry into the Vehicle and General Insurance Company collapse reported that the Under-Secretary and two named assistant secretaries in the Insurance and Companies Division of the Board of Trade were responsible for the Department's failure to deal with the risk of the insurance company's insolvency and that their conduct had been negligent. How, in either of these two cases, would it have been possible for the Minister to adopt the fiction that he was responsible and that the blame should be laid at his door? When the facts are known and published, that appears an empty and groundless affirmation. A similar conclusion seems now to follow from the situation of civil servants when they are the subject of inquiry and report by the Ombudsman under the powers of the Parliamentary Commissioner for Administration Act of 1967. That was a thought that struck and puzzled Mr George Brown as Foreign Secretary when the conduct of his officials was criticized in one of the Commissioner's first and most important cases. The episode raised further questions about the implications for civil servants both of the Parliamentary Commissioner and of the activities of Parliamentary Select Committees (of which that on the Parliamentary Commissioner is one) since the work of the Commissioner and of the Committees involves the making of detailed inquiries into the administration of departmental policy.

[17] See *Report of a Committee appointed by the Prime Minister to consider whether certain Civil Servants should be transferred to other duties*, Cmd. 9220 (1954).

The Sachsenhausen Case

The Commissioner's report on the *Sachsenhausen* case, like the Crichel Down report, brought into question both the Minister's conduct and that of his civil servants. The complaint related to the treatment during the Second World War of twelve prisoners of war in a special camp and cell block at Sachsenhausen. An Anglo-German agreement in 1964 had made available £1 m. for United Kingdom nationals who were victims of Nazi persecution, but the Foreign Office had refused to pay compensation to the twelve applicants who alleged that they had suffered injustice by reason of the Foreign Office's maladministration. The issues were a mixture of fact and judgment. A lawyer might have said that they related solely to questions of fact, meaning that they involved matters of opinion about where to draw the line. The Foreign Office had laid down for itself certain criteria, which were roughly that a victim of persecution should, to qualify for compensation, have been interned in a concentration camp or in conditions which were equally severe. Amongst the questions in issue were the camp boundaries and whether the applicants had been interned inside them. In his report the Commissioner found in favour of the complainants' version of the facts about their internment. He held that there had been defects in the procedure by which the unfavourable decisions had been reached. 'The original decision was based,' Sir Edmund Compton stated, 'on partial and largely irrelevant information and the decision was maintained in disregard of additional information and evidence.'[18]

This characterization was disputed by the then Foreign Secretary, Mr George Brown. He himself had undoubtedly been involved. In February 1967 Mr Brown had seen three of the complainants at the Foreign Office. Mr Airey Neave's account of the meeting at which he had been present was as follows: 'After they had given an account of their sufferings, he told them "to forget it and get it out of their systems". He said that "all the money was gone."'[19] Indeed,

---

[18] HC 54 (1967-8), p. 18.
[19] Evidence to the Select Committee on the Parliamentary Commissioner for Administration, HC 258 (1967-8), p. 57.

Mr Brown's view of the decision was that it was entirely his. As he later said in the Commons, 'I read every piece of paper in the file. I came to my own conclusions by my own processes of judgement.' In the debate to take note of the Commissioner's report on 5 February 1968 he insisted that none of his officials had misled him. Nobody had blundered or bungled. The matter was one of judgment and he personally had judged it.

Having said this, the Foreign Secretary went on to suggest that a serious constitutional question had been placed in issue, namely the maintenance of the convention of ministerial responsibility. The House, he said, should not start holding officials responsible for things that had gone wrong. If things were wrongly done, they were wrongly done by Ministers. It was Ministers who must be attacked, not officials. If the office of Parliamentary Commissioner were to lead to changing this constitutional position, the whole function of ministerial accountability to Parliament would be undermined.

These reflections and the apparent conflict between the Minister's and the Parliamentary Commissioner's conclusions provoked an inquiry by the Select Committee on the Parliamentary Commissioner. The Committee, after examining the senior Foreign Office officials, reported to the House that there had been shortcomings on the part of both Ministers and officials. There were defects in the information and advice provided to Ministers and this was 'the collective responsibility of Foreign Office Officials'.[20] They were also dissatisfied by the evidence given to them by the Foreign Office. The Permanent Under-Secretary, Sir Paul Gore-Booth, they said, 'was unable to give your Committee any specific indication either of the defects of the system that the *Sachsenhausen* case had brought to light or of the action that was being taken to mend the system'.[21] This was not altogether surprising, since the Foreign Secretary had not conceded that any defects in the system had occurred. Sir Paul was placed in further difficulties by the Committee. They wished to know whether the Foreign Office now accepted the conclusions of the

---

[20] HC 258 (1971–8), pp. ix–xi.   [21] Ibid., p. xii.

Parliamentary Commissioner on the basis of which they were paying compensation. Sir Paul found it difficult to say, because his Minister had given no clear guidance. He had said that compensation should be paid, but he had completely rejected the Commissioner's conclusions, if not his facts. Did the Foreign Office (Mr Fletcher-Cooke wanted to know) now say, having reviewed the cases, that the complainants were or were not in the concentration camp? 'The answer', Sir Paul said, 'is that the Foreign Office takes its instructions from the Foreign Secretary.'[22] Sir Paul also declined to say which civil servants had dealt with the question: 'I am not authorised, certainly by the Foreign Secretary, to name individuals.'[23]

The Committee returned to the implications of this topic in their second report issued in July 1968. In the interim they had met with some opposition from Mr Brown's successor Mr Michael Stewart, who had sent the Attorney-General to tell the Committee that it must not take evidence from junior civil servants. Mr Airey Neave in his evidence to the Committee had named the official whom he thought had had the greatest responsibility for the day-to-day administration of the *Sachsenhausen* case (though the name does not appear in the minutes of evidence). Sir Elwyn Jones suggested that ministerial responsibility would be undermined if the Committee were to examine anyone other than the Permanent Under-Secretary.

To this the Committee replied that if the doctrine of ministerial responsibility had meant that all decisions were assumed to have been made by Ministers, the whole point of the Parliamentary Commissioner Act was to undermine it, since Parliament had authorized the Commissioner to find out exactly how decisions had been made and to interview civil servants. The legislature had decided 'to let this independent official go through the files behind the Minister's back and talk to Tom, Dick and Harry in his Department'.[24]

This, the Attorney-General suggested, would be dangerous to the morale of the Civil Service. They might, he thought, be terrified if the Commissioner's cases were to be reopened

---

[22] HC 258 p. 33.   [23] Ibid., p. 30.
[24] HC 350 (1967-8), p. 82.

by the Select Committee and they would lose the right of privacy guaranteed to them by the Act when questioned by the Commissioner. To this the Committee replied that they were not reopening investigations, but it was their duty to see how a Department had remedied defects discovered in its procedures and this they could only properly find out from those actually working the system. But, said the Attorney-General, a junior civil servant might, in defending himself, implicate others and even contradict his Minister. That, the Committee seemed to think, would not be fatal to the Constitution.

The report laid before the House clearly states the Committee's conclusion, that the complete anonymity of civil servants forms no part of the current doctrine of ministerial accountability. That anonymity can, with Parliament's authority in the 1967 Act, be infringed by the Commissioner's findings, since a complaint may be directed against specific individuals or branches of government. The Committee did not agree that they should confine themselves to taking evidence from the principal officer of a Department when they are considering what a Department should do to remedy administrative defects, since they might sometimes need the evidence of officials concerned at first hand with the working of the system, and they were satisfied that they would be able to take evidence from subordinate officials for this purpose without exposing them to unfair publicity or criticism.[25] Departments could be relied upon to indicate the appropriate witnesses. The Fulton Report, in commenting on the relations between the Civil Service and Parliament, had, they added, in any event envisaged a greater involvement of civil servants below the level of Permanent Secretary in explaining departmental policy.[26]

Select Committee Inquiries

The Wilson Government's refusal to allow junior civil servants to appear — a refusal contested by the Committee — is a special case of the wider unresolved issue, considered by

[25] HC 350 (1967–8), p. xii.   [26] See Cmnd. 3638 (1968), pp. 93–4.

the Select Committee on Procedure in 1978, namely the extent of the House's authority to compel the production of information by Ministers, or the giving of evidence by particular Ministers or officials through the use of power to send for persons, papers, and records. This is a contentious area in both Britain and the United States. The executive privilege that was acknowledged in general terms in *U.S.* v. *Nixon*[27] (though its extent as against Congress is undetermined), rests essentially on the separation of powers. Though the Crown in the United Kingdom is able in litigation to claim what used to be called Crown privilege (but is now depicted as an entitlement to claim a public interest immunity), there is no obvious parallel in the relations of the Crown's servants with the legislature. The theoretical autonomy and equality of the American executive contrast with a theoretical subordination and accountability of the executive in the United Kingdom. The question is admittedly complicated by the fact that the British executive is legally speaking the Crown, and between the Commons and the Crown there subsists a formal relationship of respect resting historically on feudal propriety. In that relationship it is hardly fitting for the Queen to be ordered about, and so in various ways ordering Ministers about tends to be a mixture of peremptory mandate and humble address. Where an address to the Crown is necessary, whether to secure papers or action of other kinds, there could in principle be a situation in which the Crown was faced with a clash between the advice tendered by Ministers and that offered by a resolution of the House.

A committee of the House with power to send for papers, persons, and records could, it seems, properly summon a named official but could not necessarily secure his evidence or order him to produce papers against the wishes of his Minister.[28] Securing the appearance of a particular Minister may on the same principle be a proper object of endeavour. In 1976, however, when the Expenditure Committee tried to secure the presence of Mr Harold Lever, he declined their invitation (on the instruction of the Prime Minister[29]), and

---

[27]   417 US 683 (1974).

[28]   See the memorandum of the Clerk of the House in *Report of the Select Committee on Procedure* (1977–8), HC 588-1.

[29]   The issue was government policy towards the car industry and Mr Lever

maintained that the doctrine of collective responsibility required him to decline it.

As to the supply of information to select committees, the Callaghan administration helpfully categorized the information that it would be unwilling to provide. The forbidden areas were briefly described under five heads in a letter sent in 1967 to the Chairman of Committees by Mr Richard Crossman (not always so single-minded a guardian of ministerial confidentiality). They were national security matters; information relating to private individuals; cases involving the exercise of appellate or quasi-judicial[30] powers; questions that were the subject of sensitive current negotiation; and legislative proposals not yet divulged to the House. Perhaps one might try to fit into these categories the lengthy list of topics barred to Parliamentary questioning by various Departments and periodically listed for the benefit of members. The list in fact contains a large number of miscellaneous items, not all of which fall within the Crossman categorization. For example, the Minister of Agriculture declares himself unwilling to respond to questions about agricultural workers' wages, and the Board of Trade wishes to keep to itself details of air-miss inquiries, neither topic being obviously matters of security, quasi-judiciality or sensitivity (except possibly to farm workers and air passengers). In 1976 also, the Government offered a memorandum of guidance to officials appearing before Select Committees from which some additional taboos may be inferred. In the main they relate to the internal structure of policy-making. Advice given to Ministers is not to be revealed; nor at the level at which decisions are taken;[31] nor the existence of particular cabinet committees. Cabinet committees have always had a curious status. They were known

was not the Minister principally responsible for Trade and Industry. Sir Harold Wilson later wrote: 'I felt it to be contrary to the principle of collective responsibility for a number of ministers to be called in an endeavour to establish the attitude each had taken up in Cabinet.' (*The Governance of Britain* (1976), p. 153.)

[30] Quasi-judicial is not a synonym for judicial or appellate, though nearly everybody seems to have forgotten this (see below p. 77).

[31] Gen. 76/78, 27 Sept. 1976 (see p. 38 of the 1977-8 Report of the Select Committee on Procedure).

to have existed when Ministers wrote their memoirs,[32] but never quite to be existing at any particular moment, lest Parliament or its select committees became too interested in their activities or membership. For a brief moment in early 1978 Mr James Callaghan contemplated the possibility of revealing all, but the consequences of such frankness were soon borne in upon him and he dispatched a personal minute to Ministers to the effect that neither select committees nor anybody else should be allowed to erode the convention that no details of cabinet committees are made available. Nothing was said about why nothing was to be said, but Mr Callaghan's thoughts were revealed in November 1978 by the editor of the *New Statesman*,[33] and they reduce to the relatively familiar points that disclosure of the main standing committees would 'give a partial picture only'; that select committees might seek to question committee chairmen; and that in any event a cabinet committee decision, unless referred to the cabinet, 'engages the collective responsibility of all ministers'.

Two other matters that witnesses before Parliamentary committees are instructed not to reveal are advice given to Ministers by the Law Officers (though the Law Officers themselves can presumably be questioned about their advice in the House); and information derived from the papers of previous administrations. The latter veto incidentally suggests that in relation to cabinet papers individual civil servants have a duty, beyond that to their immediate political masters, to protect certain papers of earlier administrations from scrutiny by their successors. The books do not reveal when this conventional duty was first acknowledged.[34] Indeed they

---

[32] They are discussed in some detail, for example, in Patrick Gordon-Walker's *The Cabinet* (1972).

[33] *New Statesman*, 19 Nov. 1978.

[34] In a letter to *The Times* (20 Dec. 1979), a former civil servant denied that any such rule or custom existed before 1945, adding that it must have been decided 'after the defeat of the Attlee government that incoming Ministers must not be allowed access to the Cabinet records or other policy papers of their predecessors'. Presumably a resolution of the House of Commons setting up a Parliamentary Committee of Inquiry to inquire into matters involving earlier cabinet decisions could authorize disclosure as would invocation of the Tribunals of Inquiry (Evidence) Act. The permission of previous Prime Ministers was obtained in 1982 for the Franks Falkland Islands Inquiry to see the cabinet papers of earlier administrations. It is fairly clear that the Bingham Inquiry of

hardly mention it at all. Sir Ivor Jennings noted briefly that 'the ministers of one government are not entitled to examine the Cabinet documents of their predecessors',[35] but he gave no reference or authority for the rule. It was mentioned in evidence to a Parliamentary select committee by the then Head of the Home Civil Service in 1972 as being a 'well-known rule and a self denying ordinance which each government had imposed on itself'. It was, he added, occasionally necessary for civil servants to draw the attention of Ministers to it. But 'if a request, notwithstanding that, is made, the civil servant has the right to refuse'.[36] The administration of the rule has been described by a former Cabinet Secretary, Lord Hunt.[37] It appears that Ministers may normally see the papers of former Ministers of the same political party if the need to do so arises in the course of their current ministerial duties. Officials, in addition, have a duty to provide Ministers with relevant information about departmental policy or past events, subject to not disclosing the views of previous Ministers or the advice tendered to them. It is recorded in the Franks report on Falkland Islands policy that in March 1982 the Foreign Office officials, after consulting the Permanent Under-Secretary of State, informed the Foreign Secretary Lord Carrington that in November 1977 the previous Government had covertly sent a small naval task force to the South Atlantic.

The need for officials to make such decisions points to the existence of a potential area in which civil servants have a direct personal responsibility as servants of the State

---

1977 into Rhodesian sanction-breaking did not see all the relevant cabinet documents. See the debate on the setting up of the Falklands Inquiry in the Commons on 8 July 1982.

[35] *Cabinet Government* (3rd edn.), p. 274.
[36] HC Deb. 393 (1972), p. 20 (Sir William Armstrong).
[37] 'Access to a Previous Government's Papers', (1982) *Public Law* 514. See also the statement by Mrs Margaret Thatcher on 17 Jan. 1983: 'Ministers of a current Administration may not see documents of a former Administration of a different political party, other than documents that can be regarded as being in the public domain, official communications to overseas governments and written opinions of the Law Officers. Ministers . . . may normally see documents of a former Administration of the same political party whether or not they saw those documents as members of that Administration, provided that the requirement to see them arises in the course of their Ministerial duties.' (35 HC Deb., cols. 29-30.)

or Crown, in addition to their role as servants of a particular political party in office. In relation to a Minister's activities in Parliament, however, the line between governmental and party political conduct is not easy to delimit. Indeed when objection was taken in 1971 to civil servants supplying parliamentary questions as part of an organized campaign to frustrate Opposition questions on particular topics by flooding the Order Paper, Sir William Armstrong, the Head of the Home Civil Service, said that he could see no distinction in Parliament between a Minister's political and his ministerial persona, and no general limit to the extent to which civil servants should carry out orders designed to assist Ministers in party stratagems against the Parliamentary Opposition.[38] The Select Committee, however, disagreed and their conclusion was that it was not the role of the Government machine to seek to redress the party balance of questions on the Order Paper, and civil servants should not be asked to prepare questions having this object.

It is recognized also that an Accounting Officer has in that capacity a personal responsibility to Parliament to place on record his disagreement with any decision of the Minister that he would have difficulty in defending as a matter of prudent administration. When the matter involves the safeguarding of public funds or the regularity or propriety of expenditure he 'should state in writing his objection and the reason for it and carry out the Minister's decision only on a written instruction from the Minister overruling his objection. He should then inform the Treasury of the circumstances and communicate the papers to the Comptroller and Auditor-General.'[39] This discharges his personal responsibility. The chief industrial adviser to Mr Anthony Wedgwood Benn felt obliged to act in this way, filing a written objection to his Minister's action when Mr Benn as Secretary of State for Industry in the Wilson Government made a State grant of £3-4m. to a workers' co-operative at Kirkby.

Another class of civil servants who now exercise a personal responsibility are inspectors holding public inquiries under

---

[38] *Report of the Select Committee on Parliamentary Questions*, HC 393 (1972), at pp. 19-20.

[39] *Government Accounting*, para. c-9 (cited by Sir William Armstrong), HC 393 (1972) at p. 20.

the provisions of various statutes. Here there may be some doubt about the degree of Parliamentary accountability where a Minister's functions have been delegated. Many final decisions on planning appeals, for example, are not now made by Ministers but by inspectors. The governing legislation provides that such decisions shall be treated for legal purposes as decisions of the Minister. This is ambiguous. Is it designed merely to deal with protecting decisions from legal challenges in the courts by giving them a status equivalent to that of a ministerial decision? Or does it mean that the decisions are ones for which the Minister is to be answerable in Parliament? Since the Minister may if he wishes reserve any decision for himself he could presumably be asked why in a particular case he had not reserved it. But would the Table Office accept a question about the substance of a decision made by an inspector? It is not one of the matters mentioned in the Department of the Environment's taboo list. One of the categories under which it was said that the government would be unwilling to give evidence to select committees, it will be remembered, was the exercise by Ministers of appellate or quasi-judicial functions. But if a Minister himself makes a decision it may not always be clear when he is acting in a purely judicial way as an appellate authority under statute, and when he is exercising the quasi-judicial function of reaching a final decision after a preliminary hearing process, possibly conducted on adversarial lines. For a purely judicial act of an appellate kind a Minister ought not to be accountable, but the final stage of a quasi-judicial decision is an 'administrative action, the character of which is determined by the Minister's free choice',[40] and for that he ought to be open to parliamentary questioning both in the House and in Committee.

Two Forms of Accountability

In some areas of administration there has developed in recent years a new form of accountability for which no term of art has emerged. It is characterized by a breaking of

[40] *Report of the Committee on Ministers' Powers* Cmd. 4060 (1932), pp. 73-4.

the normal connection between answerability and control. When, typically, a Minister is in direct executive charge of a Department, or when a decision is taken in his name, he answers for what he can forbid or enjoin. But decisions that have substantial political effects are sometimes taken by bodies or persons who are not hierarchically subordinate (in at least some aspects of their affairs) to a Minister of the Crown. There may nevertheless be both public and parliamentary interest in knowing what they are doing and why.

One obvious area is that of quasi-government or, as it may now be thought of, 'quango-government'. Quangos (or quangones?) have been variously and widely defined, but wherever we draw the lines there are a large number of corporate and non-corporate bodies, agencies, commissions, boards, panels, and authorities, mostly appointed by Ministers, some of which act on behalf of, or as agents of, Ministers and some of which do not. These bodies can be divided roughly into those exercising commercial, managerial and regulatory functions. The boards of the public commercial corporations are prominent examples of the first kind. From most of these bodies a Minister may receive, or have statutory authority to ask for, reports and information which he may retail in the House of Commons, thus satisfying curiosity, if he so wishes, on matters that are not within his personal control but within the independent authority or area of judgment of the body in question.

The other main area in which this style of accountability can be discerned is in the area of law enforcement where, in relation to the machinery of justice, public prosecution, and police, special and delicate problems arise from the need to balance public accountability and independence. The form of accountability appropriate to these areas of public activity may be termed 'explanatory accountability' in contrast to accountability having the direct or 'executive' form. Before turning to areas of government in which explanatory accountability is appropriate, we need however to take account of recent developments in the central departmental field for which Ministers are directly and executively accountable. Here there has been since 1967 a new instrument of accountability — the Parliamentary Commissoner for

Administration. His operations have imposed new obligations and a new form of restraint on the activities both of Ministers and Civil Servants.

V
The Principles of Ombudsmanship

Until 1967 a sharp distinction had in theory been maintained in British constitutional practice between law and policy. Ministers and their Departments must keep within the restraints imposed by law, but otherwise they were free to exercise discretions conferred by statute without any substantive check upon the merits or reasonableness of their policy decisions, except those imposed by the fear of political attacks in Parliament and the Press, and the proximity of the next General Election. Since governments have normally been strong, backed by a disciplined majority in the legislature and used to having their way, it was always clear that there would be some difficulty in defining the jurisdiction of any authority set up to provide redress for citizens against the discretionary decisions of government departments.

In 1957 the Committee on Administrative Tribunals and Enquiries under the chairmanship of Sir Oliver (now Lord) Franks surveyed those special areas of administration where machinery had already been provided for official decisions to be contested before independent administrative tribunals, or for objections to be registered at public inquiries (for example in town planning, compulsory purchase of land for urban development, major road developments, and road and air transport licensing). The Franks Committee's proposals improving and regularizing procedures in these fields were largely carried out in the Tribunals and Inquiries Act of 1958 which set up a Council on Tribunals to supervise the working of inquiry and tribunal procedures. The Franks Committee itself pointed out, however, that they had not been asked to examine the whole field of relationships between individuals and public authority, but only that part of it in which statutory opportunities for appealing against the merits of governmental action already existed. Outside this sphere were many offical activities whose merits could not be contested before any tribunal or public inquiry.

In 1961 Sir Oliver Franks stressed this point in writing the foreword to the report of Sir John Whyatt's unofficial committee of inquiry[1] which was set up to examine the possibility of adopting the Scandinavian Ombudsman scheme, a version of which was successfully grafted on to New Zealand's Parliamentary system in 1962. Prima facie the task which the putative British Ombudsman seemed required to carry out was that implied by Sir Oliver, namely the plugging of the gap in the citizen's array of weapons against officialdom so as to provide him with the means of appealing against, or objecting to, administrative decisions where Parliament had failed to provide any machinery. Lord Shawcross, chairman of the British branch of the International Commission of Jurists, and a former Attorney-General, echoed the belief that 'there *always* ought to be *some appeal* against administrative and executive decisions'.[2] The Whyatt Report itself, however, did not suggest this full-blooded role for the proposed Ombudsman. They recommended that 'A permanent body, to be known as the Parliamentary Commissioner . . . should be established . . . to receive and investigate *complaints of maladministration.*'

When the Parliamentary Commissioner Act was passed in 1967, the Commissioner was given the task of controlling 'maladministration',[3] but the Parliamentary draftsmen did not define the term and the Ministers who introduced the Bill confessed that they did not know what it meant and the Members who voted for it did not know either. 'Elements' of it have been discovered in a significant proportion of the cases investigated by the Commissioner, but it is admitted to be something different now from what it seemed to be in 1967.

Maladministration and Wrong Decisions

Though the New Zealand Ombudsman set up in 1962 was empowered to report on decisions that were 'unreasonable,

---

[1] *The Citizen and the Administration. A Report by Justice* (London, 1961).
[2] Preface to *The Citizen and the Administration*, p. xiii (italics added).
[3] S.5 (1) empowers the Commissioner to investigate complaints arising out of 'injustice in consequence of *maladministration* in connection with . . . action

unjust, oppressive' and 'wrong', the United Kingdom Act of 1967 clearly intended something different. The sphere of the British Ombudsman was intended (in the Whyatt Committee's phraseology) to be the control of 'maladministration', and not the provision of redress against 'wrong or unwelcome' decisions. 'Unwelcome' was probably not a very good word to choose since 'maladministration', whatever it is, is at least unwelcome. But a decision might be wrong, it was supposed, without violating proper standards of administration, or being a misuse of power. The Labour Government's White Paper of 1965 put it that the Parliamentary Commissioner was not intended to act as an appellate authority for discretionary decisions. All of this sounded as if maladministration was intended to encompass jurisdictional and procedural faults rather than substantive injustice. This was underlined by the declaration in the Parliamentary Commissioner Act itself that the Commissioner was not to question the merits of a decision taken without maladministration. Conceivably that might be understood to imply that he *may* question the merits of a decision that does embody maladministration, the maladministration being precisely its injustice or lack of merits. Clearly, however, in the light of the Whyatt Committee discussions and the White Paper, that was not the intention. Yet the original ministerial exegesis failed to draw a clear distinction between misuses or abuses of the decision procedure and the quality or lack of quality of the decision itself. In the Second Reading debate on the Bill in the House of Commons in 1966, Mr Richard Crossman conceded that the Government had not been able to define 'maladministration' or to list all its characteristics. Consequently they had decided to list some of them. They were such things as 'bias, neglect, inattention, delay, incompetence, ineptitude, perversity, turpitude, arbitrariness and so on'.[4]

This 'Crossman Catalogue', as it came to be known, seemed to be a mixture of procedural and substantive faults. Leaving aside 'and so on', two interesting categories are

taken by or on behalf of a government department of authority in the exercise of administrative functions'.

[4] 754 HC Deb., col. 51 (1966).

'perversity' and 'arbitrariness'. 'Unreasonableness' is not specifically mentioned,[5] but arbitrariness and perversity are undoubtedly forms of it. To be perverse is to be 'unreasonably or blindly or unaccountably wrong'. A decision that has those characteristics might be thought not to have any merits. This was the view that the Select Committee on the Parliamentary Commissioner formed in 1968 when they invited the Commissioner to consider it within his function to report on any decision which, judged by its effect upon an aggrieved person, appeared to be thoroughly bad in quality.

This course of action was impossible to square with the view implied in the Act, and initially adopted by the first Commissioner, Sir Edmund Compton, that merits and maladministration could be separated. Sir Edmund in 1968 had explained his task as follows:

My investigation is not directly concerned with the merits of the administrative action or decision complained of but rather with the way the Department acted or the way the Department reached its decision . . . . What I cannot do is to form a view about the merits of the decision, and whether the complainant suffered injustice from it if I have found no element of maladministration in the process by which the Department arrived at this decision.[6]

On this view there might well be decisions that had few or no merits and were thoroughly bad, but which were no concern of the Commissioner. He was not to enter into the question of the positive merit or lack of merit of a decision. But the view that the existence of maladministration may be inferred from, and can consist in, a complete lack of merits implies that the distinction between merits and maladministration drawn in the 1967 Act is incoherent, and that the merits must always be open to and indeed require inspection at least to the extent necessary to determine whether they constitute an instance of what the Select Committee and the Commissioner were prepared to classify as a 'bad decision'. If there is to be any doctrine of restraint in reviewing discretionary decisions by Departments it must obviously be by refining upon the category

---

[5] Nor is 'negligence', 'dishonesty', 'prejudice', 'capriciousness', 'obstinacy', 'tardiness', 'stubbornness', or 'absurdity'.

[6] (1968) *Journal of the Society of Public Teachers of Law* (NS) 101.

of 'bad decisions' and distinguishing between various types of fault in the decision-making process.

Types of Fault

One could in principle set out a number of ways in which such decision-making may go wrong. Five such categories might be:

(1) Gross improprieties of the bias, corruption, negligence kind that amount to dishonest abuse of the decision process.

(2) Less serious instances, ranging from the culpable to the excusable, of delay, inefficient collection and storage of information, loss of correspondence, deficiency in the communication process, honest or negligent misunderstandings, and understandable confusions (frequently involving messages passed via third parties or agencies).

(3) Failure to take into account, or to consider, or to appreciate the significance of all the relevant facts.

(4) Misweighing of facts, policies, or wrong balancing of relevant considerations.

(5) Faulty arguments. Insufficiency of alleged grounds, facts or reasons to justify the conclusions drawn.

So far the UK Parliamentary Commissioner has not uncovered any faults of the category (1) variety. Many of the cases in which 'elements of maladministration' are noted fall into category (2). Though some might class the first two categories as procedural and the last three as substantive faults, there seems no special reason to divide faults or errors in this way. There is an obvious sense in which they are all part of the decision process. Unless there are other ways of reaching wrong decisions, a decision which is wrong or without merits must be bad because of some deficiency in one or other of these processes. Mistakes in each of these categories may be present in a culpable or in a mild degree. Whether they are present at all, however, may be a matter of opinion and judgment.

It is at this point that the problem of reviewing the exercise of discretion calls for principles that have yet to be clearly set out. It resembles the difficulty of stating the principle upon which a judicial body should review the discretionary powers of a legislative body. In both cases the principle is easier to exemplify than to enunciate. It is not, unfortunately, made much clearer by the notion that he who reviews the exercise of discretion should not 'substitute his own decision' for that of the body on whom the discretion is conferred. In evidence to the Select Committee on the Parliamentary Commissioner in March 1971, Sir Edmund Compton remarked that 'the job of the Commissioner is to review the administration of Government and whilst I may question decisions taken with an element of maladministration it is not for me to *substitute my decision* for the Government decision'.[7] He could, he went on, say that the decision was faulty and ask for it to be taken again, but it was not for him to say what the decision should be. Many citizens did not, he added, understand this since what they wanted was an appellate authority or someone who would substitute his decision for a government decision that they did not like. There are perhaps three different senses of 'substitution' wrapped up here, namely (a) having power to give effect to a contrary decision, (b) stating what decision would be correct rather than stating that a wrong decision should be reconsidered, and (c) disregarding or contradicting administrative judgment in the course of reviewing it.

It is, of course, clear that the Parliamentary Commissioner has no executive power to substitute a different judgment in sense (a). But there must in some degree be a substitution of judgment in sense (c) whenever a decision falls into any of the categories of fault we have distinguished. To say that a decision has been wrongly or negligently reached or that it rests on irrelevant facts, wrongly-balanced considerations, faulty logic or insubstantial evidence is to substitute the judgment that such is the case for the administrator's judgment that such is not the case. Clearly the Parliamentary Commissioner does in the third sense substitute his judgment for that of civil servants.

In effect, since 1967 the character of British ombudsman-

---

[7] *Second Report from the Select Committee*, HC 513 (1970-1), at p. 10.

ship has changed. It was designed as a thin type of procedural appeal covering faults in the decision process not regarded as touching the merits. It has become a more substantial review of merits examined with restraint, or with what is in some jurisdictions called 'a margin of appreciation for administrative judgments'.

Interpretations of Maladministration

During the period of office of Sir Edmund Compton, the first Commissioner, some doubts as to the potency of the new machinery were dispelled when, with the approval of the Parliamentary Select Committee, he began to interpret his terms of reference more liberally. The Sachsenhausen prisoner of war compensation case in 1967 made it plain that the conduct of Ministers, as well as that of civil servants, might, if it were infected by departmental mishandling of evidence or information, be open to criticism. In the following year similar possibilities were revealed in the report on the Duccio affair, a complaint against the Board of Trade, alleging maladministration in its supervision of the law relating to auctions. In the course of his investigation, Sir Edmund Compton took evidence from Mr Anthony Crosland against whom complaint had been made on the ground that a speech by him in the House of Commons on 6 November 1968 had been damaging to the interests of two members of the Society of London Art Dealers. The Commissioner's special report was critical of the Board of Trade for not making its role in relation to auctions clearer at an earlier date, and vindicated the two complainants against criticisms of their actions made in Mr Crosland's Parliamentary statement. The Commissioner was careful to add that he did not think that he could properly investigate the Parliamentary statements themselves. An interesting constitutional question might have arisen had he done so, since Article 9 of the Bill of Rights of 1689 declares that debates or proceedings in Parliament are not to be impeached or questioned in any place out of Parliament. A breach of privilege by the Commissioner can, however, presumably be avoided if he confines his enquiries to the departmental briefing given to the Minister on which his parliamentary remarks are based.

In 1971 Sir Alan Marre took over as Parliamentary Commissioner. In his first annual report he remarked that there continued to be 'widespread misunderstanding about the scope of my office'. Complainants, he went on, 'not infrequently ask me to reverse decisions by Departments (including Ministers) simply because they disagree with the decisions and not with the way they have been taken'. The mystery of maladministration, in other words, had failed to make any impact on the public consciousness, and aggrieved citizens who believed that they had suffered hardship because of wrong or unjust decisions taken by the administration persisted in believing that they were the victims of administrative injustice. Luckily, some things that are objectionable can if necessary be called 'failure to give adequate consideration' to evidence germane to the decision. This is, we may suppose, a form of mishandling and in a wide sense a procedural fault. In many of his reports Sir Alan Marre did in fact characterize such faults not as 'maladministration' or even as 'elements of maladministration', but as 'shortcomings in the Department's actions' or 'muddles' or 'inadequacy of response'. Where some measure of maladministration occurred, it was, he noted, generally the result of a mistake or human error rather than of serious maladministration. The Departments most prone to human error have, not surprisingly, been the Departments of Inland Revenue, and Health and Social Security, the undisputed champions of the Commissioner's league tables, with the Department of the Environment in third place. The Inland Revenue has, however, claimed to be suffering hardship and a measure of administrative injustice as the result of its exposed position in these numerical tables. Given the very large number of individual cases handled, its large absolute total of registered complaints is no cause for surprise. Possibly an index of complaints per thousand citizen-contacts would exhibit the Revenue in a fairer light as against, say, the Public Trustee or the Scottish Office. The average percentage for all Departments of case reports in which there has been 'maladministration leading to some measure of injustice' was 37 per cent in 1971, 30 per cent in 1972, 37 per cent in 1973, 38 per cent in 1979, 48 per cent in 1980, 46 per cent in 1981, and 65 per cent in 1982. One striking feature of the Parliamentary Commissioner's jurisdiction is that it has not been much exploited by Members as a political weapon against Ministers. Several of Sir Alan Marre's cases did, however, relate to matters in which Ministers were involved and in which ministerial as well as departmental judgment was implicitly or explicitly criticized in his reports. One such case was the affair of the invalid tricycles. The motorized, three-wheel invalid carriage was the object of continual criticism by groups representing disabled drivers. The Commissioner's report on the Department of Health did not find that they had been guilty of indifference or a lack of concern for safety. But he did say that they were too slow to commission independent tests; that their initial refusal to publish the result of the tests was 'misconceived'; that their attitude of defensiveness was 'unwarranted and unwise'; and that replies given by Ministers to questions in the House had been 'less frank than they should have been'.[8] It seems clear that ministerial policy judgments must have been involved in the formulation of the Department's attitude.

Another such issue was the Television Licences case of 1975. There the essence of the complaints was that the Post Office and the Home Office had acted unlawfully and unreasonably in attempting to prevent licence-holders from holding overlapping licences, obtained before an announced increase in licence fees came into effect. The legality of the action taken was later disputed successfully in the courts,[9] but the Commissioner in his report criticized the Home Office for causing needless distress and confusion by their administrative arrangements. His conclusion was that they had acted with 'both inefficiency and lack of foresight'. In reaching that conclusion the Commissioner said he had directed his mind to the question 'whether, within the framework of their view of the law, the Home Office's actions have been administratively sound and reasonable'.[10] This sounds perilously close to a consideration of the merits

[8] HC 529 (1974-5).
[9] *Congreve* v. *Home Office*, [1976] QB 629.
[10] HC 680 (1974-5), at p. 14.

of the decision taken by the Department in the exercise of its discretion, the consideration specifically forbidden by s. 12 of the Parliamentary Commissioner Act.

Similar thoughts again might be suggested by the outcome of the *Court Line* case in August 1975. There the Commissioner blamed the Minister, Mr Benn, for giving misleading public assurances about the Court Line Company's holiday operations, though Mr Benn and his ministerial colleagues rejected the Commissioner's findings. Mr Benn's speech was the result of a Cabinet meeting in which a decision had been made striking a balance between the need to inform holiday-makers, and the possible danger of undermining public confidence. In the House, the Prime Minister, Mr Harold Wilson, said that he and the Government accepted full responsibility for the decision and that Mr Benn's speech in the House had been made in support of it. Yet the Commissioner was willing to say (in effect) that the Cabinet decision was misleading and the statement unjustified. This seems to be getting into the merits with a vengeance. But was the faulty decision one that arose out of maladministration? Some of the terms in Mr Richard Crossman's original parliamentary specification of the term might well have fitted it: 'delay', 'incompetence' or 'ineptitude' perhaps? Whatever it was, Opposition Members of Parliament may perhaps have drawn the encouraging conclusion that the Cabinet is capable of committing maladministration within the meaning of the 1967 Act.

In the *Court Line* case, the Commissioner was informed of the result of the Cabinet decision but he was not permitted to see Cabinet papers relating to it. Section 8 (4) of the Parliamentary Commissioner Act allows the Secretary to the Cabinet to certify that information or documents relate to the proceedings of the Cabinet or Cabinet Committees, and such papers or information are privileged from production. It is not clear, however, that this precludes Ministers from furnishing such documents. What the legislation says is that no person shall be required or authorized *'by virtue of this Act'* to furnish information in these categories. But it does not follow from that that it would be unlawful for Ministers voluntarily to provide the Commissioner with Cabinet papers; or that he is precluded from asking them to provide them in the exercise of their discretion.

Widening the Role

Ten years after the passage of the Parliamentary Commissioner legislation, Justice (the British section of the International Commission of Jurists) published a Report surveying its working, entitled, somewhat pointedly, *Our Fettered Ombudsman*. Their Report concluded that the system had proved disappointing in two respects. First, the Commissioner appeared to be known to and used by only a small section of the population. (Those who do know about him, it may be added, often complain about matters that they are not permitted to complain about, something like a half of the submitted complaints being rejected on jurisdictional grounds.) Secondly, the Commissioner's investigations were confined to inquiries into maladministration. One reason also for the relatively small number of complaints, the Justice committee thought, was the barrier imposed by the need to approach the Commissioner indirectly through a Member of Parliament. (In Sweden a citizen need only address his letter to the Justitie Ombudsman 'J. O. Stockholm'. In Quebec the Public Protector's Office will receive complaints by telephone.) As to the Commissioner's jurisdiction, the Report suggested that it was unnecessarily narrow when compared to that of the New Zealand Parliamentary Commissioner who is empowered to investigate complaints that action or inaction by a government department is unreasonable, unjust, oppressive or improperly discriminatory, while the French Médiateur may examine complaints that a public authority has 'failed in its mission of public service'. This latter expression sounds somewhat drastic and sententious (and therefore better in French than in English), so the Committee preferred something similar to the New Zealand formula.

These suggestions were considered by the Select Committee on the Parliamentary Commissioner when it undertook a comprehensive review of the Commissioner's powers in the 1977-8 Session. Neither of them found favour. In its

Report the Committee concluded that there was no need for a revision of s. 12 of the 1967 Act (ruling out consideration of the merits of discretionary departmental acts taken without maladministration), on the ground that they had persuaded the Commissioner to feel entitled to look at acts that were 'thoroughly bad'. But what about acts that are moderately bad or just plain bad? Sir Idwal Pugh claimed that he felt unconstrained by the term 'maladministration', and would have had no difficulty in looking for it in a decision that seemed clearly unreasonable. But it is hard to divorce a consideration of the reasonableness of a decision from a weighing of its merits and if the merits are to be weighed, it might be best simply to remove s. 12 (3) of the Act and leave the Commissioner to interpret 'injustice in consequence of maladministration' without any legislative restraint. Meanwhile it is to be hoped that successive Commissioners continue to treat the intention of the Queen in Parliament lightly and to ignore S.12(3)

On other issues the Commons Select Committee made a number of recommendations. They were:

(1) That the parliamentary convention that inhibits Members from taking up their colleagues' constituency cases should be interpreted flexibly. (It was recognized that complainants may for political or other reasons not wish to approach their own MPs.)

(2) That contacts between ordinary Members and the Commissioner should be strengthened, and that he should have an office in the Palace of Westminster to which Members could come to raise queries or to seek advice on complaints.

(3) That the Reports of the Commissioner and of the Select Committee should be debated in the House at least once a year.

(4) That the Commissioner should make more frequent occasional reports, and

(5) That the Commissioner should be able to investigate a number of matters excluded in the 1967 Act, namely complaints from British citizens resident abroad about consular offices and overseas posts; complaints about contractual or commercial relations with government

departments or agencies; complaints about public service personnel matters (except complaints from serving civil servants and members of the armed forces about discipline, establishment questions and terms of service); and complaints about Crown bodies not already scheduled to the Act. (Three interesting bodies mentioned in the report were the Law Officers' departments, the Privy Council Office, and the Cabinet Office.)

(6) That the Commissioner should be able to draw Parliament's attention to any unforeseen injustices arising from legislation. (The Committee envisage this facility being used 'sparingly' and no doubt it will be,[11] though there would be a broad vista of intervention opened up if it were in fact invoked whenever, in the Committee's words, 'Members were unaware of the consequences of the legislation they had enacted.')

(7) That the Commissioner should be able to carry out inspections of departments or bodies within his jurisdiction.

(8) That the Commissioner should have a right of access to Cabinet papers except where the Attorney-General certifies that such access would be prejudicial to the safety of the State or otherwise contrary to the public interest. (It is hard to imagine circumstances in which it could really be contrary to the interest of the State to allow the Commissioner to see a cabinet paper, but not so hard to imagine recent Attorneys-General who might think that it was.)

(9) That the Select Committee on the Parliamentary Commissioner should continue in existence.

The last recommendation conflicted with the conclusion of the Select Committee on Procedure that the function of considering reports from the Parliamentary Commissioner should be split up amongst the new specialized departmental scrutiny committees. Mercifully this proposal has not been put into operation and the Committee has survived. Being beyond question the most useful and effective of the existing select committees, it deserved to. A single 'grievance'

---

[11] The Government has taken the view that the Commissioner has power to do this under the existing legislation.

committee is needed because there are common strands in the technique of grievance supervision even between different departmental areas. (There is more in common between two maladministrators one of whom is a civil servant than between two civil servants one of whom is a maladministrator.)

Of the Select Committee's recommendations only one has been accepted. In 1981 the Parliamentary Commissioner (Consular Complaints) Act extended the Commissioner's jurisdiction to 'include complaints about the acts of British consuls overseas, made by persons with a right of abode in the United Kingdom. (The restriction in the last-mentioned phrase may have been incorporated because of a principled belief in the Burkean philosophy of 'a stake in the country', or it may bear some tangential relationship to the matter of immigration.) The proposals for bringing under the Act commercial, contractual, and personnel matters have not been accepted.[12]

In January 1979 Mr C. M. Clothier QC (the first Commissioner to be appointed from outside the Civil Service) took over from Sir Idwal Pugh. Sir Idwal before his retirement had already instituted a procedural reform of some importance. Complaints made direct to the Commissioner are now no longer returned to the complainant. Instead the Commissioner offers him the option of having his complaint referred to his Member of Parliament. If this offer is accepted the Commissioner asks the Member if he wishes formally to refer it for investigation and the Member may or may not do so. This short-circuiting of the formal requirements of indirect access may do something to meet the apprehension of Members (not apparently shared by Sir Idwal Pugh) that direct access would have the effect of changing the volume and character of the Commissioner's business, and remove the possibility of according the 'Rolls-Royce treatment' now alleged to be given to British complainants as compared with the production line service meted out to patrons of foreign ombudsmen. Whether this is so is not easy to say.

On balance, the restricted access to the Ombudsman seems

[12] See Cmnd. 7449 (1979); Cmnd. 8274 and Report of the Select Committee HC 243 (1980-1).

a defect in the system. There were originally two reasons for the MP 'filter': a fear of swamping the Commissioner, and a need to placate Members of Parliament who might otherwise have felt disinclined to support the 1967 legislation. Now that there are separate Ombudsmen for local government and for the Health Service the first fear seems exaggerated, whilst the continued disinclination of Members of Parliament to see any diminution in what they perceive to be their own role as popular ombudsmen, should perhaps be disregarded. Indeed, since Members of Parliament are more prone to feelings of self-importance than any other social group, any innovation that lessens the occasions for such feelings could be said to confer a valuable benefit on the community.

Meanwhile it remains a striking fact that citizens of the United Kingdom, in lacking direct access to their Ombudsman, are denied a facility that is freely available to the inhabitants of Sweden, Norway, Denmark, New Zealand, Alberta, Ontario, New Brunswick, Quebec, Manitoba, Saskatchewan, Nova Scotia, South Australia, Western Australia, Victoria, Queensland, New South Wales, Alaska, Nebraska, Iowa, and Hawaii, not to mention Uttar Pradesh, and Jackson County, Missouri.

VI
The Morality of Public Office

The responsibility of Ministers for their personal behaviour is a form of ministerial responsibility whose existence nobody doubts. But it raises a more general question about the morality of public life and the forms of behaviour that merit resignation or dismissal from public office. The most difficult cases are those concerning sexual activities, which in the case of ordinary citizens, or even Members of Parliament, might well be classified as questions of private morality. Though general moral standards may have changed or become more liberal since the time of Lloyd George and Asquith, the morality of public life is in some ways stiffer. Particularly since the 1950s, the role of Ministers and many other public office-holders as bearers of the nation's secrets has been thought to constrain their freedom as moral agents. But mere scandal in the absence of security dangers may conceivably be a hindrance to effective functioning in public life.

An implied code of morality can certainly be drawn from an examination of the major episodes since the Profumo case. There are however some odd quirks in it and, in the 1980s, a disposition to question some of its premisses.

The Profumo Case

The Profumo case of 1963 was probably the first post-war occasion in which the links between espionage and sexual indiscretion by politicans were drawn to public notice. The brief affair of Mr John Profumo with Miss Christine Keeler led to the appointment of Lord Denning[1] to inquire into the possible dangers to security as well as a wide range of rumours[2] about the behaviour of public figures. Profumo,

---

[1] See *Lord Denning's Report*, Cmnd. 2152 (1963).
[2] According to Mr Bernard Levin (*The Pendulum Years* (1970), p. 49), it was rumoured that nine High Court judges had indulged in sexual orgies, that a

whilst Secretary of State for War, had become acquainted with Miss Keeler at a swimming party to which she had been taken by her friend Stephen Ward, a London osteopath, an alleged procurer of women, with a wide circle of friends. One such friend was Captain Eugene Ivanov, a Russian working at the Soviet Embassy in London, nominally as a naval attaché, in fact as an intelligence officer. Ivanov does not seem to have been a very orthodox spy since he made no secret that he was on the look-out for information. The suggestion made later by Lord Denning was that he was a pioneer of a new form of social sabotage, aiming to weaken the confidence of the United States in Britain by manoeuvring Ministers or prominent people into compromising situations and making the Security Service appear incompetent. If these were his objectives, his tour of duty was, as Lord Denning concluded, a success.

It was the allegation that the Secretary of State for War had been sharing Miss Keeler with a Russian intelligence officer that provided the major justification for the setting up of Lord Denning's inquiry. The facts revealed in the Report seemed fairly dramatic. Keeler alleged that Ward had asked her to find out from Profumo on what date the United States would make nuclear weapons available to West Germany, though she had (she said) not asked him that question. The Security Service became aware of the Minister's connection with Ward and Keeler, and warned him about his association with Ward but after Ivanov's departure from the country they did not consider there to be a serious security risk and did not make the situation fully known to their political superiors. Thus in March 1963 Mr Henry Brooke, the Home Secretary and Head of the Security Service, had to send for the Director-General of Security Sir Roger Hollis and the Metropolitan Police Commissioner and ask to be 'put in the picture'. This was the first occasion on which any member of the Government

---

Cabinet Minister had served dinner at a private party clad only in a mask and a small apron and that another member of the Cabinet had been found by the police with a prostitute under a bush in Richmond Park. In 1980 in *The Due Process of Law* Lord Denning wrote that 'Some of the evidence I heard was so disgusting — even to my sophisticated mind. — that I sent the lady shorthand-writers out and had no note of it taken' (at p. 68).

was told about the request for information about nuclear weapons. The Prime Minister did not get to know of it until two months later on 29 May 1963. Mr Brooke did not immediately mention it to any other Minister since he did not know that they did not know.

The Directive issued to the Security Service in 1952 set out the convention that Ministers were not to concern themselves with the detailed information obtained by the Security Service in particular cases, but would be furnished only with such information as might be necessary for the determination of any issue on which guidance was sought. It added that no inquiry was to be carried out on behalf of any Government Department unless it was clear that an important public interest bearing on the defence of the realm was at stake.

Conservative Ministers felt, after the scandal had broken, that the Security Service had erred in neither taking the initiative to report on the Profumo-Keeler relationship nor asking for guidance on the question. Within the service it had been suggested to the Director-General in February 1963 that the information in their hands about Keeler's relationship with the Minister should be passed to the Prime Minister. A minute to the Head of Security suggested that 'If a scandal results from Mr Profumo's association with Christine Keeler there is likely to be a considerable political rumpus . . . If in any subsequent investigation we were found to have been in possession of this information about Profumo and to have taken no action on it, we would, I am sure, be subject to much criticism for failing to bring it to light.' The Director-General, however, after conferring with his senior officers rejected this advice. The Russians had moved Ivanov in January 1963. The serious risk of a security leakage, it was supposed, had been via Ward to Ivanov. But Profumo had been warned about Ward and was an honourable man. For that reason too they placed little weight on the allegation that Keeler had been asked by Ward to get information about West Germany and the atomic bomb. They did not believe that she had in fact asked Profumo about this or that he would ever have given her such information. It was not, in these circumstances, they concluded, within the proper scope of the Security Service to investigate the Minister's private life[3] and to find out whether Keeler was his mistress or not. All that was the concern of Profumo and his political colleagues, whom they knew to have suspicions on the matter. Profumo's colleagues, also honourable men, unfortified with telephone taps or informers' reports, equally trusted his assertion that the association, though foolish, was without impropriety.

Lord Denning's comments on the Security Service placed no blame upon them, on the ground that they had taken all reasonable steps to see that the interests of the country were defended and that there had not in fact been any security leakage. They were faced, he concluded, with an unprecedented situation for which the machinery of government did not cater. It was, for them, not a case of security at all, but of moral misbehaviour by a Minister. And he added, 'We have no machinery to deal with it.'

Lord Denning did not suggest that there should be any such machinery and his exoneration of the Security Service in the Profumo case suggests the conclusion that there should not be. Yet his arguments about the connections between immorality and security were not consistent with that view. They suggested, in fact, that machinery is needed to discern and expose at least some forms of immorality, namely those that lend themselves to the possibility of blackmail. In the circumstances of 1963 there was presumably at least a risk of damage to security. The Security Service did not believe that Profumo had supplied information, but some might have doubted their reasons for certainty on the point. Keeler said that she had neither obtained nor passed on information, but there was no independent evidence about it. There was in Profumo's situation a known exposure to a source of blackmail as distinct from a risk of exposure; and blackmail is the crux of the issue. The question is how seriously it is to be presumed that the possibility of blackmail (in London and Brighton, as well as in Moscow or in foreign bedrooms) is capable of erecting a permanent bridge between moral failings in senior poli-

---

[3] It has since been alleged that deliberate misuse was made of this principle by the Director-General and that he assisted the operations of Ivanov and withheld information from Ministers. See Chapman Pincher, *Their Trade is Treachery* (1981), chap. 9.

ticians and a danger to national security. A number of obvious questions arise. Since a man might conceivably be blackmailed for cheating at cards and for a great many things, how are we reliably to label blackmailable and non-blackmailable offences? Lord Denning seemed willing to attempt at least some generalizations. Because of the risk of blackmail or 'undue pressure', he regarded 'homosexual behaviour or perverted practices with a prostitute' as creating security risks 'at any rate if it was of recent date'. On the other hand 'adultery committed clandestinely with a person not likely to resort to blackmail' should not, he thought, ordinarily be regarded as a security risk, unless there were compromising photographs or letters.

These categorizations provide potential problems for a conscientious Security Service. How are they to divine whether a partner to a Minister's discreet adultery is likely to engage in blackmail, or for that matter whether transactions with a prostitute are perverted or non-perverted? They cannot know by simple instinct or clairvoyance. So whatever their use, these classifications do not provide criteria for investigating or not investigating Ministers; though they might, if confidently adhered to and roughly applied, provide some guide to subsequent action or non-action on the basis of security investigations. But the Denning Report admits almost in the next sentence that '*every* case of immorality and discreditable conduct' may come into the reckoning in some circumstance or other. An attempt to pervert the course of justice might, for example, it is suggested, set up extreme pressure to prevent exposure. Some persons also are inherently more exposed than others. Discreet clandestine adultery by the Lord Chancellor might be much more blackmailable than an Under-Secretary's unorthodox practices with prostitutes. And how are prostitutes to be set aside precisely from persons who resemble them in some respects?[4]

There is also the question of the kinds of evidence and the

---

[4] Two implicit criteria were suggested at p. 20 of the Denning Report, namely the wearing of certain kinds of bathing costumes and being photographed by the *News of the World*. On 3 February 1963 Miss Keeler appeared in a photograph in that paper 'with nothing on except the slightest of swimming garbs' and the Report notes that most people seeing the photograph would 'readily infer' her avocation.

burden of proof necessary for testing allegations that black-mailable activities have taken place. Here the Denning Report suggested that it would be unfair to any person to have to disprove allegations often based on hearsay and from informers who cannot be cross-examined. The test, it was suggested, was whether there was evidence of a kind that a judge would think fit to leave to a jury. Yet this approach seemed inconsistent with what was said in the Denning Report about the Conservative Ministers in 1963. They failed, the Report suggested, to deal properly with the situation because they asked themselves the wrong question. They asked themselves whether Mr Profumo had *in fact* committed adultery; whereas 'the proper question may have been: was his conduct, proved or admitted, such as to lead ordinary people *reasonably to believe* that he had committed adultery?' That sounds as if the facts of the matter are of less importance than the appearance.

At the outset of the Report, Lord Denning had said of his own inquiry that it was one in which no man should be condemned on suspicion, even presumably suspicion reasonably entertained by ordinary people. Whilst facts should be ascertained as completely as possible 'there is a yet higher public interest to be considered, namely the interest of justice to the individual which overrides all other'. And he added, 'speaking as a Judge, I put justice first'. Paradoxically it sounded as if Prime Ministers and politicians sitting in judgment on their colleagues were expected to have lower standards.

It would perhaps be instructive to reconstruct the sorts of judgments which might have been made about the Profumo affair if it had taken place with everything happening as it did but without the spy Ivanov's actual existence. On Lord Denning's theory it might be that if not Ivanov then some other foreign attaché with the same techniques must always be assumed by Ministers to be a permanent part of the social scene. If so, the risks of moving in that part of society which Mr Harold Macmillan found so alien and uncongenial,[5] must be calculated accordingly. Mr Profumo's

---

[5] ' . . . a raffish theatrical bohemian society, where no one really knows any-one and everyone is "darling."' (Harold Macmillan, *At the End of the Day* (1973), p. 439).

misfortune was to be a bad calculator. As a result he paid
a savage, permanent, and unjust penalty for a private moral
misdemeanour of a kind committed by many other public
figures before and since without disaster to their political
careers. If he had confessed all immediately, the outcome,
if not ideal, would have been more satisfactory than it turned
out to be. The House of Commons is not excessively censor-
ious about sexual misbehaviour, possibly out of an understandable reluctance to see uninhibited stone-throwing
in glass houses. What politicians care more about is their
image and supposed insults to it. So it was understandable
that when the Minister finally confessed his misdemeanour
after first denying it, he was told that what he had done
was not so much to deceive his wife as to deceive the House
of Commons. When the matter was debated in the House on
17 June 1963 some Members were incensed that the sudden
notoriety of Miss Keeler and her companion Miss Marilyn
Rice-Davies had earned them offers of £5,000 to appear
in a night club — a figure which as Mr Harold Wilson pointed
out, made them worth 250 times as much as Members of
Parliament.[6]

The Lambton and Jellicoe Cases

The questions with which Lord Denning struggled in 1963
were presented again ten years later in an affair with strik-
ingly similar features to its predecessor. Once again there was
a protagonist with socially distinguished connections, who
fled the country, whose life was threatened, who dabbled
in drugs, and whose activities led to rumours about the
involvement of ministerial figures. Once again one of her
clients was a Defence Minister.

Lord Lambton's involvement with Mrs Norma Levy was
distinguishable from the Profumo affair in a number of ways.
There was no evidence of any foreign agent taking any part in
it, but there was a serious attempt to exploit the situation by
criminal associates of Mrs Levy, and there were photographs

---

[6] One journalist suggested that this seemed reasonable enough since 'Nobody
sensible would go to a night club to see M.P.s coming down staircases dressed
in sequins and tail feathers unless there were at least 250 of them.'

and tape recordings which provided precisely the material for blackmail which Lord Denning had picked out as bringing moral failings into the security-risk area. Levy, like Keeler, became the prime agent in her client's downfall by talking to the police and by participating in the attempt to sell the photographs. At the same time gossip passed to the police brought about the resignation of a second Minister, Lord Jellicoe, Lord Privy Seal and Leader of the House of Lords, who stated in his letter of resignation that he had some casual assignations with call girls on five or six occasions between August 1972 and April 1973. The cases were not connected, but both were referred by the Prime Minister to the Security Commission who were asked to say whether there had been any danger to security and whether security procedures needed to be changed.

The Commission's report[7] appeared in July 1973, and the Commissioners' conclusions make an interesting comparison with those of Lord Denning. They point out that foreign intelligence services are known to make use of prostitutes in Western countries and that there is therefore a small risk that any call girl selected at random for an evening may turn out to have foreign contacts. A rough assessment might be made of the actual size of the risk (though the Commissioners did not make it) by dividing the number of such girls with intelligence connections[8] into an estimate of the total number of call girls available in the metropolitan area. Perhaps a risk of half of 1 per cent would be somewhere near the mark. This seems comparable with, or even less than, the risks involved in ordinary social intercourse or cocktail party conversations where indiscreet talk about official or confidential information is more likely than in prostitutes' beds. Even the security risk involved in blackmail should, as the Security Commission thought, be viewed in perspective, since it calls for a conjunction of fairly elaborate facilities for obtaining photographic or recorded evidence, and a victim who will yield to the temptation to betray his country.

The logic of these calculations is that intercourse with

---

[7] Cmnd. 5367 (1973). The Commissioners were Lord Diplock, Lord Sinclair, General Sir Dudley Ward, Lord Garner, and Sir Philip Allen.

[8] Subtracting, of course, those with *British* intelligence connections or retained by the Foreign Office.

prostitutes or call girls is in itself a negligible security risk and one that ought, therefore, to be ignored by those whose business it is to worry about the safety of the realm. This was the conclusion in fact reached by the Security Commission in considering Lord Jellicoe's case. He entertained girls supplied by an 'escort agency' in his own flat where there was no risk of compromising photographs, and behaved 'discreetly'. His discretion, on the Commission's view, consisted in assuming a false name and abstaining from 'abnormal sexual behaviour' (a point no doubt established by signed affidavits). The Commission added rather oddly, that it was inevitable that his true identity should leak out and become a subject of underworld gossip, a remark that leaves it uncertain whether the Commission thought the behaviour acceptable only because it was unrevealed or whether they thought it, though inevitably revealed, permissible conduct for a present-day politician or civil servant. There is the Commission's assurance that if it were disclosed in the course of positive vetting of a civil servant, it would not disqualify him from being employed on exceptionally secret work.

Lord Lambton's case was differently treated. The differences seem to be that he paid with cheques signed in his own name; that he used Mrs Levy's rather than his own flat (thus risking the photography that took place); and that he allowed himself to be photographed naked with Mrs Levy and another girl – a practice which 'deviated from the normal' (though it was unclear whether this last conclusion related to the absence of clothes or to the numbers present).[9] These transactions, however, were stated by the Commission to be less important than the fact that he had smoked cannabis and possibly taken other drugs in Mrs Levy's establishment. The conclusion was that 'the real risk lay in his use of drugs, even though this was confined, as we are prepared to assume that it was, to cannabis. Under the influence of this drug we consider that there would be a significant danger of his divulging, without any conscious intention of doing so, items of classified information.'

If this was indeed the major fault in Lord Lambton's

---

[9] If, as both Lord Denning and the Security Commission suggested, anything is to turn upon the nature of the proceedings, it may be necessary to draw a distinction between sexual excess and sexual perversion.

behaviour, the Commission's earlier comments about the relative incidence of indiscreet gossip in brothels and in other social venues might seem in point. If cannabis is a danger, it is a danger that is not confined to the sort of situation in question here. Where does cannabis-smoking in itself stand on the spectrum of blackmailable and non-blackmailable offences? How does it compare with, say, a moderate to high indulgence in alcohol?

Two further questions arise from the Lambton–Jellicoe inquiry. One is whether the same standards should apply to both Ministers and civil servants. The Security Commission thought that Ministers should not be subjected to the process of positive vetting by the Security Service, which is applied to officials before they are entrusted with exceptionally secret information. There are certainly some grounds for doubting whether positive vetting has shown itself to be efficacious in preventing serious leakages of security information. In the past such leakages have often stemmed from persons who would never have been rejected or found unreliable by any positive vetting. But if positive vetting is thought to be a necessary safeguard, it is hard to feel much confidence in the reasons given for not applying it to Ministers, at least those in sensitive positions. It was suggested implausibly that the Chief Whip's knowledge of Members of Parliament who become candidates for ministerial office was an acceptable substitute, and that the Prime Minister should 'bear in mind' the desirability of satisfying himself that potential Ministers without previous experience of the House of Commons, and therefore less well known to the whips, do not have character defects that might endanger security. Since the Prime Minister is unlikely to be able to engage in detailed personal investigations of this kind this was either a proposal that the Prime Minister should commission something analogous to the positive vetting which is declared to be impracticable or it was a pious evasion of the issue. Telling Ministers not to do something but to bear in mind the desirability of doing it could hardly be bettered as a recipe for inactivity.

A second question of some interest is why, given the conclusions of the Commission, Lord Jellicoe or even Lord Lambton should have been required to resign at all. To this there might perhaps be two replies. One might be that politicians who put themselves into the public arena should have, or at least appear to observe, a higher standard of behaviour than citizens at large; so that many activities might be tolerable in non-politicians that are not acceptable in those who represent them. This seems unrealistic both on grounds of democratic theory, which suggests that representative persons should resemble or share the characteristics of those they represent; and on the ground that all historical experience of the behaviour of Ministers and Members of Parliament suggests that their moral and intellectual standards are lower than those prevailing in many other walks of life. The other reply might be that Prime Ministers and their colleagues are entitled to have regard to other political factors than those connected with the existence of security risks and to enforce whatever rules of behaviour and apply whatever sanctions they feel are appropriate to the Government's or the party's electoral image. Nobody is entitled as of right to ministerial office. On the other hand Ministers ought possibly to be able to claim the same right to compensation for unfair dismissal as is accorded to all other persons in gainful employment.[10]

Neither the Denning Inquiry nor the Security Commission investigation could, when considered as forms of procedure, be regarded as very satisfactory. When the Prime Minister was questioned in the House of Commons about the basis for some of the Security Commision's conclusions he was compelled to confess ignorance and fall back upon the argument that the Security Commission was an independent body. No one, therefore, knows the basis for its conclusions or the persons from whom it took evidence or why it did not take evidence from some who might have been, but were said not to have been, questioned. A number of persons and two newspaper organizations were made the subjects of criticism but were not, it appeared, given any opportunity of commenting on or countering the allegations made against them.

Much the same was true of the Denning inquiry of 1963. Lord Denning, as he himself conceded in his report, had to combine the functions of detective, inquisitor, advocate,

---

[10] For example by the Employment Protection (Consolidation) Act, 1978, ss. 67–79, 138.

and judge. In his capacity as field investigator he visited the headquarters of the Security Service and watched the final stages of a security surveillance. He employed an accountant, a handwriting expert, and a physician. But no one gave evidence on oath or was cross-examined. Thus a large number of conclusions of fact rested on unpublished and unverifiable testimony and in many places it might well have been asked why anybody should be expected to believe a word of it. In 1966 the Royal Commission on Tribunals of Inquiry under the chairmanship of Lord Justice Salmon concluded that Lord Denning's inquiry should be regarded as 'a brilliant exception to what would normally occur when an investigation is carried out under such conditions'.[11] Alongside that description might be placed a contemporary impression by one of the leading participants Miss Mandy Rice-Davies.

I was asked to go and see Lord Denning. I was about an hour late because of a more pressing engagement with my hairdresser . . . We had quite a laugh together . . . . I kept wandering off the point and telling him all sorts of things that did not concern him . . . . He was not only interested in the security aspects of the affair, because he wanted to hear about anything I knew about any other member of the Government or the Opposition. I gave him a few names which are not in his report.

It was probably the feeling that justice was unlikely to be seen to be done under the forms of an investigation of this kind that led the Salmon Commission to recommend that 'no Government in the future should ever in any circumstances whatsoever set up a Tribunal of the type adopted in the Profumo case to investigate any matter causing nationwide public concern'.[12]

Where there is a matter 'of vital public importance, concerning which there is something in the nature of a nationwide crisis of confidence', the appropriate form of inquiry, the Commission thought, was a Tribunal of Inquiry under the 1921 Tribunals of Inquiry (Evidence) Act. There are some issues particularly in the security field where evidence cannot be given in public; and an affair of the Lambton-Levy kind may have security aspects intertwined with wider questions of public concern, as well as

---

[11] Cmnd. 3121 (1966), p. 19.   [12] Cmnd. 3121 (1966), p. 21.

some aspects which may not be proper subjects for anybody's concern. But the kind of evidence that needs to be confidential is often factual or technical evidence from government officials. The evidence from others is more likely to be of the kind that could either be given in public,[13] or should not be given at all. Where questions affecting the reputations or credibility of Ministers are concerned, it is a defect in the present arrangements that a decision as to the appropriate form of inquiry rests with Ministers themselves. One possible, though unexplored, use since 1967 of the Parliamentary Commissioner for Administration could be as a source of independent advice as to the most appropriate choice among the various possible forms of inquiry procedure.

The Thorpe and Trestrail Cases

At about the time that Lord Denning began his inquiries into the Profumo affair a situation of considerable political danger was in the making for Mr Jeremy Thorpe. In December 1962 Norman Josiffe, later known as Norman Scott, made a statement at Chelsea police station alleging the existence of a homosexual relationship between himself and Mr Thorpe, then a rising member of the Liberal Party. Nothing was publicly known about the statement at the time, but fourteen years later Scott's allegations were repeated in the course of minor court proceedings in which he was involved and were then widely reported in the national press. In December 1978 Thorpe and three others were committed for trial at the Old Bailey on charges of conspiracy, and in Thorpe's case, incitement, to murder Scott. The case was postponed until after the 1979 General Election. In his Devon constituency Thorpe was heavily defeated. At the trial in May 1979 all four defendants were acquitted. In his summing up Mr Justice Cantley called Scott 'a fraud, a whiner, a sponger

---

[13] At p. 20 the Commission pointed out that 'It is said that sometimes witnesses are willing to give evidence only if they are allowed to give it in private or in confidence . . . . But such evidence . . . is treated as suspect by the general public . . . . Secrecy increases the quantity of evidence but tends to debase its quality.'

and a parasite'. Inevitably, as it seemed, Thorpe was forced out of public life and the leadership of his party.

What general conclusions can be drawn? All the allegations against him were unproven. In the course of the trial it was conceded that he had had homosexual tendencies and that his relationship with Scott had once (as his letters showed) been affectionate. He maintained, however, that there had been no homosexual relationship between them and that Scott's account of their relationship was false.

It was argued by some at the outset of the affair that Thorpe and the Liberal Party would have been justified in saying that the private sexual behaviour even of a party leader, was not a matter of public interest or concern, whether heterosexual or homosexual. They should have conceded that there had been a past relationship of the kind claimed by Scott, if that indeed had been true. If there had been no other allegations of any kind against Thorpe such a stand on principle would certainly have its defenders at the present time. But past experience in both Britain and the United States suggests that such candour on the part of office-holders is unlikely to be rewarded by public support.

The question of homosexual conduct also brings out the potential conflict between the two principles mentioned in the Denning Report of 1963. One was that there is no machinery for dealing with moral misbehaviour by Ministers and that the probing of politicians' private lives is — in the absence of any security risk — not a matter with which the Security Services should concern themselves. The other was the assumption that homosexual behaviour, or 'perverted practices' of a heterosexual kind, in themselves create a risk to security. But the existence of the risk cannot be discovered with certainty unless detailed investigations into the recesses of politicians' private lives are in fact made by the Security Service. Discreet homosexual relationships, like discreet heterosexual liaisons, may sometimes be uncovered by routine positive vetting[14] but there is a significant chance that they will not be.[15]

---

[14] The Security Commission in May 1982 stated the purpose of positive vetting as being that of exposing security dangers or defects of character and circumstance which render uncertain the subject's trustworthiness or discretion and his ability to resist pecuniary temptation or exposure to blackmail.

[15] Positive vetting includes an investigation into the subject's character and

In relation to civil servants it seems that different principles are now being followed. The Security Commission has adopted the view that homosexuality should no longer be an absolute bar to security clearance (though clearance, it seems, is not given to practising homosexuals in the diplomatic or armed services since homosexual behaviour is still illegal in some foreign countries and is an offence against British military discipline).

The case of Commander Michael Trestrail in July 1982 drew attention to a number of these points. Commander Trestrail, who had served as police bodyguard to both the Duke of Edinburgh and the Queen, resigned after sixteen years' service when an informant telephoned a national newspaper claiming to be a homosexual prostitute with whom Commander Trestrail had had relations. The newspaper, though refusing payment for the story, printed it and informed the police.

Clearly there could have been a better outcome for Commander Trestrail if the newspaper and the Home Secretary had behaved differently. It would have been possible for him to have been allowed to resign without the Home Secretary revealing the reason in the House of Commons and for the newspaper not to have printed the story. If both had taken the view that Commander Trestrail's private sexual behaviour posed no risk to the country's security nor to his effectiveness as a police officer it would even have been possible for him not to have resigned at all, though of course conceivable that his immediate employers might not have wished him to continue in his existing post.

If the question is pressed why Trestrail should have resigned it would probably be suggested that despite the more tolerant attitude towards homosexuality in the Civil Service a security risk remains since the exposure of sexual irregularities of whatever sort remains a threat that blackmailers may use. Some will reply to that that it is only because sexual scandal leads to dismissal that blackmail is a credible threat. If this is so it might seem that the threat could be effectively neutralized if the Government were clearly to

circumstances by the Security Service, the completion of a standard security questionnaire, and letters to two referees named by the subject of the investigation (Security Procedures in the Public Service, Cmnd. 1681 (1961-2)).

state and follow a policy of not removing public servants (including Ministers) solely on account of their sexual relationships or behaviour.

An obvious objection to such a policy remains. Government is not in a position to control newspapers or public opinion and neither is invariably tolerant. Blackmailers are still able to rely upon the adverse effects of exposure and publicity, independently of the attitude of employers. There is, of course, a difference between junior civil servants and royal bodyguards or Ministers of the Crown. Junior civil servants and public employees working in Britain are less vulnerable to publicity than senior civil servants or public figures. If Commander Trestrail had been retained in his position on the supposition that no publicity had occurred, the Home Secretary would have been aware that fresh accusations or other informants might appear in the future. In that event he would certainly have had to face criticism from the Press and his political opponents urging that he had authorized a cover-up.

Those who are in the public eye are now more than ever subject to the threat of adverse publicity by informants actuated by cupidity, a sense of grievance, or political partisanship. Ministers and senior public servants cannot be insulated from the adverse impacts of public feeling, and the risk of publicity and ridicule. If the Russian security service were to retire from the scene, *Private Eye* and its successors would remain.

If in consequence a higher or at least more conventional standard of morality is required of politicians than is expected of private citizens that fact may not elicit much sympathy for them. It may be seen as one of the responsibilities and burdens entailed in thrusting oneself into public life, and a part of the heat that those who will not stay out of the political kitchen are often exhorted to endure. But the group of public servants about whom newspapers would buy or print salacious information is wider than the class of elected politicians. There are therefore many senior civil servants, police officers and soldiers to whom the two-tier doctrine of public morality is sadly unfair, and the heavens will sometimes fall on them without justice being done.

VII
The Politics of Justice and Security

In all the Commonwealth countries and in the United States questions have had to be asked about the desirable extent of political accountability for the actions of those who are in charge of the machinery of justice, and in particular of the mechanisms of prosecution and law enforcement. In the United States the Watergate experience pushed Congress into an attempt to establish a Special Prosecutor, separated from and not subject to the control of the political executive, the President having rapidly removed one earlier Special Prosecutor, one Attorney-General and one deputy Attorney-General. In Britain the independence of the Attorney-General, the principal public prosecutor, is legally insecure but conventionally safe. The Attorney-General is himself accountable as a member of the government to the House of Commons for all prosecution decisions conferred on him by statute, and in some sense or other he is answerable for the Director of Public Prosecutions.

But in what sense should those who start and stay the legal process be accountable at all? Should they be politicians, even politicians of a specially prim variety? Here, as elsewhere when debating questions of accountability, there is a need to make distinctions both between different senses or modes of accountability, and also between what is true in law and what is true or accepted in political or conventional practice.

The Independence of the Attorney-General

A good example of the latter difficulty is to be seen in the proposition that the Attorney-General cannot be directed in carrying out his duties by either his colleagues in the government or by Parliament. The United Kingdom Parliament has certainly not in recent times attempted to instruct the Attorney-General to prosecute. On the other hand its

112 The Politics of Justice and Security

entitlement to do so may not thereby have lapsed. Erskine
May remarks that 'where . . . the House has thought a proceeding at law necessary, either as a substitute for or in
addition to its own proceeding, the Attorney General has
been directed to prosecute the offender'.[1]

It would be equally difficult to find any clear *legal* ground
for asserting a right in the Attorney-General to act independently of his colleagues. He is one of the Queen's Ministers
and he shares the collective responsibility of the administration. He is a member of the House of Commons and
responsible to Parliament for the advice given to the Crown
and its servants.[2] In relation to prosecutions he exercises
a mixture of statutory and prerogative powers. Since the
prerogative of the Crown is exercised by convention on
the advice of Ministers, there seems nothing inherently
improper in the Ministry's forming a collective view about
the use of the prerogative in a particular case and directing
the Attorney-General to comply with it. There is no doubt
that they could enforce their view by the sanction of dismissal. Possibly a distinction should be made between cases
where the Attorney-General is acting under the prerogative
(for example to stop a prosecution by entering a *nolle
prosequi*), and cases in which he is empowered by statute
to assent or refuse assent to proceedings. But other Ministers
have statutory powers conferred upon them or upon their
Ministries by name without its being supposed that they
can in practice exercise them without regard to the collective
responsibility of the government. The power under discussion
is in theory an executive or administrative power. It is not
a judicial or even a quasi-judicial power (i.e. an administrative
or policy decision preceded by some form of judicialized
fact-finding procedure).[3]

Until the 1920s the Law Officers in the United Kingdom
seem to have acknowledged the entitlement of the Cabinet

[1] *The Law, Privileges, Proceedings and Usage of Parliament*, (19th edn. 1976),
p. 131. Reference is made to eleven such occasions, the last, however, being in
1866.
[2] Sir William Anson, *The Law and Custom of the Constitution* (4th edn.),
vol. ii, pt. 1, pp. 221-2.
[3] The definition adopted by the Committee on Ministers' Powers (Cmd.,
4060 (1932), pp. 73-4). Cf. H. W. R. Wade, 'Quasi-judicial and its Background',
(1949) 10 *Cambridge Law Journal* 216.

to exercise a right of ultimate decision where prosecutions raised important issues of political importance of public policy. It is generally supposed that the Campbell case in 1924 saw a change in this position, though it is not at all clear how it could in itself have changed the constitutional rule. Sir Patrick Hastings, MacDonald's Attorney-General, was alleged to have authorized withdrawal of a criminal prosecution after intervention by the Prime Minister. Though maintaining that he had taken his own decision in the case, he seemed to agree with his predecessors in office that the question whether prosecution was desirable in a matter such as sedition was a proper question for consideration by the Cabinet. The defeat of the Government hardly shows his view to have been mistaken. The Opposition parties defeated MacDonald because he had misled the House as to his own participation in the matter, because MacDonald refused to be rescued by the Liberals (who proposed the setting up of an inquiry) and because Baldwin wanted to bring the Labour Government to an end.[4]

Nevertheless it cannot be doubted that since 1924 the holders of the Attorney-General's office in both the major political parties have asserted that by convention in matters related to the institution and withdrawal of prosecutions the Attorney-General exercises his function independently of the Cabinet and could properly refuse to be instructed by them. All recent Law Officers have argued that it is proper and prudent for the Attorney-General to consult his political colleagues where prosecutions raise questions of public policy or issues of national or international importance, but that the final decision must be his. It must be taken on the merits of the case, which may include political considerations in a wide sense but no consideration of party advantage. Some matters about which questions may be raised are:

---

[4] A good deal of information is now available about MacDonald's and the Cabinet's part in the Campbell case. See Thomas Jones's *Whitehall Diary*, vol. i (1969), and David Marquand, *Ramsay MacDonald* (1977), pp. 366-377. Jones's note of the relevant discussion includes the words 'steps could be taken not to press the prosecution . . . if the Cabinet so desired' (*Diary*, at p. 1924). The Cabinet minute stated that (a) No public prosecution of a political character should be undertaken without the prior sanction of the Cabinet being obtained and (b) In the particular case under review the course indicated by the Attorney-General should be adopted.

First, is the Attorney-General *obliged* to consult his colleagues as well as entitled to consult them? Sir Hartley Shawcross, whose views are frequently quoted, suggested in 1951 that there was no obligation to consult, though he thought that it would in some cases be foolish not to do so.

Secondly should consultation be directly as to the desirability of the institution or withdrawal of proceedings? There is a difference between saying that Ministers may be asked if they think prosecution politically desirable, though the Attorney-General must make his own decision, and saying that the Attorney-General's decision must be made after hearing what Ministers have to say on matters of fact that he judges to be relevant. Sir Hartley Shawcross's view seemed (though not entirely unambiguously) to be the second. 'The assistance of his [the Attorney-General's] colleagues', he suggested, was to be 'confined to informing him of particular considerations which might affect his own decision. It does not and must not consist in telling him what that decision ought to be.'[5] When Mr Edward Heath's Attorney-General, Sir Peter Rawlinson, decided not to authorize proceedings against Miss Leila Khalid, an unsuccessful, aircraft hijacker, he did so after inquiring what danger a prosecution might entail for the lives of hostages in the hands of Palestinian guerillas. He explained that he had on three occasions asked the Foreign Secretary what he thought would be the effect of a prosecution on the lives of the hostages and was told on each occasion that it would increase the danger to them. The Secretary of State for Foreign Affairs was also consulted in 1970 before a prosecution under the Official Secrets Act was brought against a newspaper that had published a confidential memorandum about the Nigerian civil war,[6] but it is not known what questions were put.

Thirdly, given that a wide range of public policy considerations is permissible, but that partisan considerations are not, how is the distinction between the two to be drawn? Clearly 'partisan' would be too narrowly defined if it were

[5] 483 HC Deb., cols. 683-4.

[6] Jonathan Aitken (in *Officially Secret* (1971), pp. 136-7) states that the Secretary of the Cabinet, the Director of Public Prosecutions, and the Prime Minister 'pressed for the case to go forward'.

interpreted in terms of advantage of a purely party political kind. There are, for example, considerations of official or governmental convenience that have no direct connection with party advantage in a literal sense. Sir Hartley Shawcross's formulation was that what should be altogether ruled out was 'the repercussion of a particular decision upon my personal, or my party's or the Government's political fortunes'.[7] Even this, if taken literally, may be too narrow a conception of partial or partisan considerations, since there may be reasons or motives that do not in any evident sense bear upon the political fortunes of the government or party in office but may be thought to be ideological or clearly connected with doctrines that are part of the material of current political controversy. These indeed may be sincerely held convictions. Amongst legitimate grounds of public policy have been suggested such matters as the maintenance of harmonious international relations, the reduction of strife between ethnic groups, and the maintenance of industrial peace. But these are precisely the areas in which conservative and socialist politicians trust each other least. It might be, for example, that a politician holding the office of Attorney-General could believe that industrial peace would be endangered if legal proceedings were taken against strikers acting unlawfully in the alleged pursuance of a trade dispute. He might be right in this factual supposition, but those of a different political persuasion might not be willing to accept a decision based on this view as non-partisan.

This difference perhaps points in the direction of placing the Law Officers of the Crown as well as the Director of Public Prosecutions outside the political arena, in so far as this is possible, by appointing to the office from outside the ranks of elected politicians and by giving the office the same security of tenure as is enjoyed in the United Kingdom by the Director of Public Prosecutions, or the Comptroller and Auditor-General, or the Parliamentary Commissioner for Administration. The awkwardness of this course would be that of reconciling it with the answerability of the Law

[7] Loc. cit., at col. 682.

Officers to Parliament, since officials who were not members of Parliament could not be questioned in the House. The answer to this might be to leave the Attorney-General and Solicitor-General in the House of Commons as elected politicians but to vest all the existing prerogative and statutory powers in relation to prosecution in the Director of Public Prosecutions alone, removing also from the Prosecution of Offences regulations any rule requiring him to act under the direction of the Attorney-General. Questions might then be answered in Parliament by the Attorney-General, but his answerability would not be the full-scale kind now associated with the heads of ministries or departments but more closely analogous to the forms of Parliamentary explanation that occur in relation to independent public corporations and police matters. This application of explanatory accountability would be one way in which the dilemma of independence of decision and legislative accountability could be partly resolved.

Supporters of the present arrangements would, however, certainly object to the absence of full-scale direct answerability to Parliament entailed in the appointment of a non-political prosecutor exercising all the present powers of the Attorney-General. This objection was probably responsible for the withdrawal of the Consent to Prosecutions Bill considered by a Second Reading Committee of the House in March 1979.[8] Suppose (it may be said) that a non-political, independent prosecutor is appointed and he then makes a decision which is alleged to be 'a disgrace to our system of government and to our judicial system', a description applied by Mr Phillip Whitehead MP[9] in 1979 to the failure to bring prosecutions for admitted breaches of the Rhodesian sanctions orders. Suppose that he refrains from pressing prosecutions against offenders on the grounds that their offences have been condoned and encouraged by Ministers, or that their accounts are too complicated or that they cannot easily be found. Suppose that he prosecutes under outmoded statutes, offers immunities from prosecution to the wrong people or undermines the jury system. Shall we not want somebody acting on our behalf to tell him to stop

[8] See HC Deb., col. 657 (14 Mar. 1979).
[9] *The Times*, 20 Dec. 1979.

doing it or start doing something else? Is not the loss of such an opportunity (it may be asked) too high a price to pay for the possibility of securing his immunity from political influence?

To this the reformer may reply that the existence of an independent prosecutor is compatible with debate in the House of Commons. The decisions in both the Rhodesian sanctions case and the Thorpe prosecution were in fact taken by the Director of Public Prosecutions, under an arrangement with the Attorney-General. In the House of Commons Sir Michael Havers said of the Rhodesian sanctions decision that it was the DPP's, but that, since he agreed with it, he accepted equal responsibility with the DPP. He also accepted his own responsibility to answer in the House for the DPP's decision. It is clear, however, that there cannot be shared accountability in the direct executive sense for a decision which has been delegated to the DPP. All that the Attorney-General can in that case be accountable to the House for, is his decision to remit the question to the DPP. Where a decision is under present law given by statute to the DPP — as in many cases it is — the Attorney-General's existing responsibility for the Director's actions is in any event only explanatory and indirect. If all, or the majority of, prosecutorial decisions were transferred by statute that would be true more widely. But it would not prevent the Attorney-General being fixed with explanatory accountability. It is a nicely balanced point. The question is whether anything that the House of Commons in practice now has would be lost and whether the decisions of a non-political prosecutor would be less likely to be, or be felt to be less likely to be, influenced by the views, ideology and convenience of the government in power. Perhaps in relation to decisions in the field of industrial relations and public order they would be.

Parliamentary and Judicial Control

The Attorney-General's existing accountability to Parliament is suggested by some as a ground for the belief that judicial control of the Attorney-General's actions in authorizing prosecutions or giving leave for the institution of relator proceedings would be inappropriate. The House of Lords, at least, in *Gouriet* v. *Union of Post Office Workers*[10] declined to exercise any supervisory jurisdiction over the Attorney-General's use of his discretion. But a modicum of judicial control is not inconsistent with Parliamentary responsibility in this as in other areas. In *R.* v. *Metropolitan Police Commissioner, ex parte Blackburn*[11] it was held that even in matters of prosecutorial discretion there is a duty to the public which the courts might in an appropriate case enforce. In deciding whether a failure to enforce the law should be checked by mandamus it would be necessary for a court to canvass the reasons for non-prosecution (though the Metropolitan Police rather than the Attorney-General were the prosecutorial authority in question in Blackburn's case). If the argument is that a Minister could not accept a situation in which he was subject to judicial control for matters on which he had to answer to the House of Commons, an obvious rejoinder is that in recent times Ministers in the United Kingdom have on a number of occasions had to modify decisions which they felt to be matters of political judgment, and submit to judicial limitations on the exercise of powers for which they were politically responsible,[12] and it seems unlikely that any novel eruption of feeling would have occurred amongst Members of Parliament if the House of Lords had upheld Lord Denning's view in *Gouriet* that the Attorney-General's decisions were subject to judicial control. Parliamentary control is in any event no more substantial in practice in this than in any other area of administration. Though the House of Commons can in theory subject the Law Officers to an inquisition to ascertain the grounds for their actions, the instances in which this has been done have not been occasions for much Parliamentary satisfaction. What questioners have often been told is that the Attorney-General has considered the matter and reached a decision on the merits.[13]

---

[10] [1978] A.C. 435.   [11] [1968] 2 Q.B. 118.
[12] e.g. in *Laker Airways Ltd.* v. *Department of Trade*, [1977] Q.B. 643 and *Secretary of State for Education and Science* v. *Tameside Metropolitan Borough Council*, [1977] A.C. 1014.
[13] The following is an example. The Attorney-General in question had authorized prosecutions against a number of leading figures in the campaign for nuclear

Moreover, it is far too optimistic to suppose that elected members in a tightly disciplined legislature will consider the merits of the actions in question in a constitutional or objective manner, or eschew partisanship. The logical quid pro quo for such an approach would be for the government to refrain from whipping the House. Since no such restraint on either side is to be expected, it need not be a matter of great regret if the courts are in some degree able to exercise control of the Attorney-General's use of his prerogative and statutory powers. Such control, exercised with restraint, would not be out of line with other recent developments in the judicial review of discretionary powers.

The Home Secretary and Law Enforcement

Central or national ministerial responsibility for the machinery of justice and law enforcement is then a mixture of the two types of accountability already distinguished.[14]

In the traditional full-blooded executive form of accountability, a Minister answers to Parliament only for matters over which he exercises direct executive control and where he could by his own action, or the exercise of his authority, issue orders to put right what might be held to have gone wrong. In the more indirect diluted form a Minister may have power to make enquiries and to relay information to the House of Commons in answer to Parliamentary questions. In exercising this thinner type of 'explanatory accountability', a Minister gives information or explanations to the House without possessing any executive authority to issue instructions to those from whom the information is obtained.

disarmament for holding a demonstration on an airfield (*Chandler* v. *D.P.P.*, [1964] A.C. 763). On 5 April 1962 Mr Driberg asked the Attorney-General if he would state the principles which guided him in deciding whether or not to authorize prosecutions under the Official Secrets Act. Sir Reginald Manningham-Buller's reply was 'I authorise prosecutions under the Official Secrets Acts in those cases where, having regard to the relevant facts I consider it to be in the public interest to institute proceedings'. It is fair to say that subsequent Attorneys-General have on a number of occasions given fuller explanations to the House of the reasons for prosecution or non-prosecution.

[14] See chap. IV above at pp. 7–8.

This type of accountability we have seen could be retained, if the present powers of the Attorney-General were exercised by an independent non-political appointee.

'Informative' or 'explanatory' ministerial responsibility is also of some significance in relation to other parts of the machinery of justice. Under the Police Act of 1964, for example, the Home Secretary is given a power to require the Chief Constable of any police area to submit a report to him on any matter connected with the policing of the area. Parliamentary questions may accordingly take the form of asking the Minister to use his power to require such a report and inform the House of its contents. As to many administrative and logistical matters, on the other hand, the Home Secretary has full authority and executive accountability. He maintains a force of Inspectors of Constabulary. He pays out of central funds half of the expenditure of each local force. He can make regulations relating to their administration and conditions of service. He approves their establishment figures. He can require a local police committee to effect the retirement of a chief police officer. He exercises an appellate authority in disciplinary matters. He can set up a formal inquiry into any local policing matter. He is required to exercise his powers in such manner as appears to him to be best calculated to promote the efficiency of the police. But he claims no power to give operational directions. The investigation of crime, the arrest and charging of offenders, and the enforcement of the law are the responsibility of the forty-three county and regional forces in England and Wales. In the metropolitan area the Home Secretary as police authority stands in place of the local police committee and his powers of control may, in theory at any rate, be somewhat larger than elsewhere. In the nineteenth century the Home Office accepted and exercised a considerable responsibility for police operations in the metropolis involving public order. Sir William Harcourt's words are often quoted. The Home Secretary, he said, was responsible for the policy of the police and although it was unwise to interfere with the Police Commissioner's exercise of his powers it was 'a matter entirely at the discretion of the Secretary of State how far the principle of responsible authority should interfere with executive action'.[15] In the past thirty or forty years, however, the Home Office seems to have changed its attitude and in practice treats the Metropolitan Police Commissioner as having more or less the same independent authority in matters of law enforcement as it concedes to local Chief Constables[16] (though detailed questions on enforcement matters in London are sometimes put in Parliament to the Home Secretary[17]). Some central elements of control and co-ordination of local policing also reside in the inspectorate, Home Office advisory circulars, the sharing of some statutory powers in the public order field with local authorities and Chief Constables, and in the control over prosecutions of certain kinds exercised by the Attorney-General and Director of Public Prosecutions. But otherwise the Chief Constables exercise a large degree of independence both of the Secretary of State and of their own local police authority committees; and their degree of independence has probably increased since the amalgamation of small into larger county and regional forces.[18]

Police operations in relation to security matters are an exception in that this does involve some element of central control. The tapping of telephones, for example, for the purpose of detecting serious crime or offences against security or the Official Secrets Acts is an aspect of law enforcement but one in which Ministers take an interest.[19] Indeed the Home Office maintains a system of authorization by

[15] 330 Parl. Deb. 3 s. col. 1163 (1888). See chap. VIII below on this point.

[16] See for example the *Home Office Memorandum of Evidence to the Royal Commission on the Police* (Cmnd. 1728 (1962)).

[17] In 1961 the then Home Secretary said (somewhat ambiguously) that he was 'responsible to the House for answering for what the Commissioner does, even though under Statute it is the Commissioner who has to decide how to do it' (646 HC Deb. 5 s., col. 162).

[18] This is the expressed view of Sir Robert Mark, who retired from the Commissionership of the Metropolitan Police Force in 1976. See the final chapter of his autobiography *In the Office of Constable* (London, 1978) and see chap. VIII below.

[19] Sir Harold Wilson claimed that he had personally put an end to the tapping of MPs' telephones. Speaking of November 1966 when he was questioned on the matter, he said 'My answers made clear, first that there had been tapping of M.P.s' telephones up to the time Labour came into office; second that this had covered members of more than one party; third that I had peremptorily stopped it when I became Prime Minister. From that moment no member had his telephone tapped so long as Labour remained in office.' (*The Labour Government 1964–1970: a Personal Record* (1971), at p. 303.)

warrant for each interception. But it is not entirely clear what authority the Home Secretary would have to prevent a Chief Constable from ordering an interception if he believed it necessary for the detection of serious crime, and could get the co-operation of British Telecom or the Post Office.[20]

Responsibility for National Security

The Security Service in the United Kingdom is a civil agency separate from the police and directly under the control of government, the Director-General of the Security Service being departmentally accountable to the Home Secretary (though the service he controls is not a department of the Home Office). However, what is commonly called the Security Service accounts for only a portion of the intelligence activity carried out inside the United Kingdom. A significant part of the country's internal security work is carried out by police officers in the Special Branch which has no direct hierarchical relationship with the Home Office though it maintains liaison with and supplies information to the Home Office on public order and internal security matters. As police officers the Special Branch are under the authority of the Metropolitan Police Commissioner.

The Directive, published for the first time in 1963[21] and issued to the Director-General of the Security Service by the Home Secretary in 1952, relates therefore not to the totality of domestic security activity but only to that carried out by the relatively small agency that has been variously known as M.I.5 or D.I.5 that is concerned with counter-intelligence

---

[20] Both services are now controlled by independent corporations and not by a government department. The absence of a warrant from the Secretary of State might remove one defence to a prosecution of a post office employee for improperly divulging the contents of a communication. See Post Office Act, 1969, sched. 5, para. 1 (1). Interception powers were considered in *Malone* v. *Metropolitan Police Commissioner*, [1979] Ch. 344. See also *The Interception of Communications in Great Britain*, Cmnd. 7873 (1980).

[21] Cmnd. 2152 (1963) at p. 80. The Directive states that the Security Service 'is part of the Defence Forces of the country' having as its task 'the Defence of the Realm as a whole from external and internal dangers arising from attempts at espionage and sabotage or from actions of persons and organisations, whether directed from within or without the country and which may be judged to be subversive of the State'.

and anti-subversion work. Its agents are employees of the Crown but they have no powers not possessed by private citizens and they rely upon the police and Special Branch to carry out any arrests or prepare prosecutions that may result from their investigations. The documents made available in 1963 make it clear that eleven years earlier at the suggestion of Sir Norman Brook the Security Service was placed under the Home Office, though without being made a part of it and without depriving the Head of the Service of his right of access to the Prime Minister. Before 1952 it had been assumed that the Prime Minister exercised such ministerial accountability as existed for these activities. The transfer was not, however, a perfectly clear-cut one. Indeed, Ministers themselves did not seem to be aware that it had happened and nothing was done to make Parliament aware of it. In the 1950s questions in the House on security matters were put down to the Prime Minister, and both Sir Anthony Eden and Sir Winston Churchill answered them without making any reference to the Home Secretary's answerability. In the Report of the Privy Councillors on Security in 1956 there was no mention of it, and in the 1960s (for example in the debate on the Vassall spy case) the Prime Minister was referred to as being 'the Head of our Security Services'.[22] In 1961 the position was obscured by Mr Harold Macmillan who asserted that 'The actual responsibility rests on the Home Secretary, who is responsible for the Security Services, their discipline, pay and organisation.' 'But', he added, 'I retain a general responsibility for seeing that security is maintained.'[23] The Head of the Security Service's right of direct access to the Prime Minister is not presumably to be seen as displaying any lack of confidence in the Home Secretary or as being designed for use in the event of disagreement between the Home Secretary and the Director-General of the Service. It is more probably an acknowledgement of the Prime Minister's traditional defence responsibilities and of the relevance

---

[22] 676 HC Deb., cols. 264, 331.
[23] 642 HC Deb. 213 of col. 215, where Mr Macmillan also said that each individual Minister was responsible for security matters in his own Department. 'Ministers are responsible, I am responsible, the First Lord is responsible and the Government as a whole is responsible.'

of security to the Cabinet's collective responsibility. It would be going too far to make anything of the fact that the Security Service is not a department of the Home Office. There is no question of the service acting independently of direction by the Home Office or of Ministers collectively. It has no independent area for judgment analogous to that established by statute in relation to the management of quasi-governmental bodies. Nor can the Director-General or the members of the service lay claim to any independence in the law enforcement sphere that might have inhered in them had they been organized as part of a police force. It is true that the 1952 Directive to the Security Service spoke of 'the well-established convention whereby Ministers do not concern themselves with the detailed information which may be obtained by the Security Service in particular cases but are furnished with such information only as may be necessary for the determination of any issue on which guidance is sought'. But this is not intended to confer any entitlement to withhold detailed information if it should be required, or to set up any constitutional limitation to the particularity with which Ministers may concern themselves with security matters if they so wish or in any case they may think appropriate.

There is nevertheless a potential limitation on the ambit of ministerial responsibility for security matters depending upon whether the activities involved are carried out by Security Service personnel or by Special Branch or other police officers as part of their duty of investigating and preventing unlawful acts of sabotage, subversion or espionage. As to the activity of the former, Ministers are entirely in control of and executively answerable for them both in general and in detail. That is to say that questions in the House to the Home Secretary or Prime Minister are in order. (It does not of course follow that they will or should in all circumstances be answered, and it has been the practice of Ministers not to answer questions about the operations of the Security Service.[24] As to the Special Branch and

---

[24] In 1956 the Leader of the Opposition said that Parliament's acceptance of a limitation of answerability in security matters was conditional upon effective control of security and intelligence operations by Ministers. See 552 HC Deb., cols. 1220 and 1760-4.

the police, neither the Home Secretary nor any other Minister has any direct control (except for the Attorney-General's rights in relation to prosecutions), and ministerial responsibility in so far as it exists would rest upon the exercise of the Secretary of State's Police Act powers to require reports on matters of policing, and on his status as police authority for the metropolitan force.

The Prime Minister and Home Secretary together, therefore, are executively accountable for the detailed operations carried out by the Security Service. It might, however, be questioned whether in relation to routine day-to-day operations, their accountability is affected by the convention that Ministers are not normally furnished with details of individual cases.[25] The implications of such 'distancing' of Ministers from security operations has in recent times been extensively debated in Canada. In 1975 the Prime Minister Mr Pierre Trudeau said 'We in this government . . . have removed ourselves from the day to day operations of the Security Services and from the operations of the police on the criminal side.'[26] Ministers, it was implied, were not culpable for improper activities of the Security Services, since Ministers not only were unaware of them but were properly unaware of them. The ministerial situation was complicated in Canada, however, by the fact that the domestic security and intelligence services were organized as a part of the Royal Canadian Mounted Police, the federal police force, and its operations were directly under the command of the RCMP Commissioner. The Commissioner, giving evidence to a standing committee of the Canadian House of Commons in November 1977 stated his position shortly: 'I would buck like a steer', he said, 'if anyone tried to tell me who I could investigate and how I must go about it.'

Whether the British Metropolitan Police Commissioner could adopt the same attitude towards the Home Secretary is a matter that is not entirely settled, but in relation to the Director of the Security Service, no such difficulty arises. Any 'distancing' is not dictated by constitutional, but only by conventional and administrative, considerations. That

---

[25] See the 1952 Directive to the Security Services (above at p. 124).
[26] HC Deb. (Canada) vol. 121, p. 568 (2 November 1977).

being so, the accountability of the Home Secretary rests on the ordinary principles of individual ministerial responsibility. He cannot be expected to resign if mistakes or mischief of a detailed or technical kind occur that he could not be aware of. On the other hand, he must make sure that his Department is organised in such a way that he is made aware of matters that require policy direction. The security field in this respect raises peculiar difficulties. The Canadian Royal Commission that reported in 1981 suggested that proper areas of ministerial responsibility might be neglected under the misapprehension that they fell into the category of 'operations'. 'Policy' and 'operations' in the security field, they considered, were not clearly severable.[27] Methods of surveillance, the legitimacy of particular targets, and the propriety of different methods of collecting intelligence all raised questions about what might be called 'policies of operations', and required direction from the ministerial level. The Minister could not direct such day-to-day operations but he should not simply react to the proposals of the security agency. He should take the initiative in clarifying policies and guidelines, particularly in relation to investigation techniques and reporting arrangements. In the United Kingdom also, the Home Secretary is responsible for the efficient running of the security aspects of his Department, but given the seriousness of errors or failure at the operational level, it may be that more rigorous and detailed arrangements for reporting and control are necessary than in other Departments. No doubt some amendments were made to the Security Services directives after 1963, but they have not been given wide, or indeed any, publicity.

The reorganization of security arrangements in Canada suggests two general questions about accountability. First,

---

[27] *Commission of Inquiry Concerning Certain Activities of the Royal Canadian Mounted Police* (1981), Second Report, vol. ii, pp. 868-9. New Canadian security legislation, nevertheless, will in effect attempt to separate general policy from particular investigations. A new Security Intelligence Service is to be set up outside the RCMP. Its Director may be given general directions in writing but the Minister (the Solicitor-General) is not empowered to override the Director's decisions on the question of whether the Service should collect or disclose information or intelligence with respect to a particular person or group of persons, or as to the specific information, intelligence, or advice that should be given by the Service to the Government of Canada.

should the security service, like the police, be insulated in relation to particular investigative operations from detailed political direction? Secondly, can any effective method of legislative supervision be devised? Canada is to have an external review body (the Security Intelligence Review Committee). The Committee will consist of three Privy Councillors who are not members of Parliament, but they will review Security Service policy and submit to Parliament an annual report for consideration by the appropriate Parliamentary Committee.[28]

At Westminster it has been claimed that the work of the security services falls within the ambit of the departmental select committee system. That view was taken in the first report in 1982-3 from the House of Commons Liaison Committee. Mrs Thatcher's Government has set its face against any select committee involvement in the supervision of security activities[29] but the issue is, like some others, one in which the select committees could, if they had the will, have their way.

[28] See now the Canadian Security Intelligence Services Act 1984.
[29] See 42 H.C. Deb. col. 444 (1983).

VIII
The Status of the Police

Lord Haldane, when he became Secretary of State for War in Mr Asquith's Government, once said (being a philosopher as well as a politician) that he intended to have a Hegelian army. If, theorizing about our institutions in the same vein, we were to ask what sort of police force we have had in England, one thing we might say is that it has certainly been an un-Hegelian police force, meaning roughly that it has not been an organ of the State and that the whole of it has somehow or other been less than the sum of its parts.

Perhaps not everyone would agree that the British police are not organs or agents of the State. There are many radical theorists who say fiercely that the police are not only agents of the State but repressive agents of the State whose role is to ensure the stability and reproduction of the capitalist system. But theorists of this kind are not very particular about their use of the term 'State', and treat a great many things as being parts or tools or emanations of the capitalist State, including such institutions as the Stock Exchange, the Boys' Brigade and the Oxford University Press.

If we speak with reasonable care, however, it is clear that one characteristic feature of the history of policing in England has been its separation from the State in the sense of the central government. That is one thing that has moulded the attitude of the public towards the police. Policing has been by tradition, and is even now, a matter of localities or regions policing themselves. The psychological linkage between this system of local, and to some extent independent, forces, and the liberties of Englishmen has been a strong one. That local police forces could ever be an effective bulwark against real political extremism at the centre is of course one of those happy fragments of our political mythology that goes along with similar and equally unreliable convictions about habeas corpus and the House of Lords.

Two other connected features of British political history

are also relevant. One is the libertarian tradition (as compared to the nations of Europe or some of them); and another is the common law that has treated public officials as if they were nothing more than citizens.

We can see all these features in the development of policing in the nineteenth century. In London in the 1820s the prospect of organized policing, bringing about a reduction in crime and a restraint on popular unrest, was not sufficient entirely to quiet Parliamentary suspicion of police powers as a threat to liberty. The House of Commons Select Committee of 1822 said that it would be 'difficult to reconcile an effective system of police with that perfect freedom of action and exemption from interference which are the great privileges and blessings of society in this country'.[1]

By the end of the nineteenth century, nevertheless, the new police of London had been set up and spread to the provincial towns and counties under national legislation that involved a uniform system of police administration, in part financed from national funds, nationally inspected, and subject to a degree of national supervision by the Secretary of State for Home Affairs. Yet, despite the recommendation of the 1839 Royal Commission in favour of a national force and the urging of Benthamites from Chadwick onwards, local operational control remained one of the firm tenets of British policing.

As to the libertarian and common law tradition, it seems plausible to assume that the standards of behaviour required by the London Commissioners and instilled into the police from 1829 onwards were not totally unconnected with the vulnerable status of the constable, the availability of legal remedies against him if he exceeded his statutory or common law powers, and his personal liability to suit in respect of those powers. Certainly the standards set for the police of Victorian England were high, even unrealistically so. The first metropolitan regulations required perfect command of the constable's temper at all times and no indulgence in conversation except on matters of duty (and in particular not with servant girls), a level of behaviour which it has

---

[1] Cited by T. A. Critchley, *A History of Police in England and Wales 1900–1966* (1967), p. 47.

been noted was too demanding for 'bodies of barely literate and often drunken ex-labourers with a rapidly changing membership'.[2] (It has been estimated that in the first thirty years of the Metropolitan Police nearly a third were dismissed and the proportion in the boroughs down to 1874 was about the same.[3])

Police and Police Authorities

The English constable as a private person is a theme that bears examination. The constable, it has been said, was only a citizen whose business it was to keep order.[4] He was merely being paid, it used to be said, to perform as a matter of duty acts which, if he were so minded, he might have done voluntarily. That was hardly ever quite the case. Even in the eighteenth and nineteenth centuries citizens could hardly, for example, go around executing warrants or entering the premises of pawnbrokers or inspecting unfenced steam threshing machines. And in the twentieth century the differences between the accumulated powers of the professional law enforcement officer and those of the ordinary citizen have widened still further. Nevertheless there is still a point in stressing the English national prejudice against the policeman as bureaucrat. There is a connection here with our theory of prosecution, a matter in which, as Maitland noted in 1885, 'Englishmen began to see that they had against them the practice of almost all other countries' in believing that 'to put the control of the criminal law into the hands of state officials is not the way to make that law respected'.[5] Since Maitland's time, we have at the national level state directors and officers with statutory powers in matters of prosecution, but the subjection of powers to prosecute to the discretion or leave of such officers is still regarded as an exception to the general principle that any citizen should be able to invoke the processes of the criminal law.

---

[2] Jenifer Hart, in *Government and Society in Nineteenth Century Britain: Commentaries on British Parliamentary Papers*, 179 at 209.
[3] Ibid., p. 200.
[4] Lord Devlin, *The Criminal Prosecution in England* (1960), p. 14.
[5] F. W. Maitland, *Justice and Police* (1885), p. 148.

The role of the police in the local prosecution process in England has, it may be surmised, had some influence on the relations of the police with other public persons and administrators, particularly those in local government and on police committees. That relationship in theory is mysterious though it has changed in some ways over the past half century. If the police were merely bureaucrats their role would be a different one. In a sense they once were much nearer to a position of bureaucratic servitude than they now are. The old parish constables were directed in many ways in the conduct of their offices by the justices of the peace who themselves played a considerable part in law enforcement. With the emergence of organized police forces this role of the justices withered away, though they might be involved with the police in relation to their administrative jurisdiction. The 1856 County and Borough Police Act in fact provided that the constables should perform all such duties connected with the police as the justices in General and Quarter Sessions or the Watch Committees in their respective boroughs and counties should demand and require. The case of *Andrews* v. *Nott-Bower*[6] in 1895, for example, shows the borough magistrates instructing the Head Constable through the Watch Committee to carry out certain duties in relation to licensed premises. When the Head Constable issued a libellous notice to a landlord alleging that his barmaids had been observed in a partitioned-off snug, serving male customers in an unprofessional manner (unprofessional for barmaids that is), the Head Constable was held to be acting under a lawful order. In the boroughs, Watch Committees in the mid nineteenth century often took an interest in the fortunes of the liquor trade, a number of their members being brewers, and the Chief Constable of Norwich was dismissed for prosecuting publicans without the approval of his Watch Committee.[7]

The Watch Committees' powers under the Municipal Corporations Act of appointing and dismissing Chief Constables were sometimes used to enforce their right to interfere in prosecution policy. In Birmingham in 1880, for example,

[6] [1895] 1 Q.B. 888.
[7] Henry Parris, 'The Home Office and the Provincial Police in England and Wales', (1961) *Public Law* 251.

the Watch Committee intervened to prevent the Chief Constable from revising the amiable practice of not proceeding
against persons who were drunk without being disorderly[8] (a
form of municipal tolerance not altogether unknown in the
university cities of Oxford and Cambridge).

In both counties and boroughs, Watch and police Committees in the course of the last half-century have given
up the practice of exercising control over the law enforcement duties of the police. So has the Home Secretary in
relation to the Metropolitan Police. But since the events
that led to the appointment of the last Royal Commission
on the Police in 1962, there have been protracted but incon-
clusive arguments about the accountability of the police to
the public and the public's elected representatives.

The Controversy of 1959–64

Surprisingly enough, very little debate on police accountability seems to have taken place before the late 1950s although, in the latter years of the nineteenth century, control
over police operations in London had raised the issue of the
Metropolitan Commissioner's responsibility to the Home
Secretary (as police authority for the metropolitan force).
Outside London disagreements between county and borough
police authorities and their chief officers had been rare.
In 1959, however, a brief contest of wills in Nottingham
brought to the surface two contrasting views about the
independence of chief police officers *vis-à-vis* the county
and borough police authorities. The issue in Nottingham
turned upon a refusal by the Chief Constable to report to
the Watch Committee on inquiries being made into the
activities of council members and officers. The Town Clerk
and Watch Committee considered the inquiries to have
manifested a lack of impartiality on the Chief Constable's
part and, in view of his refusal to comply with their instructions, suspended him from duty in the exercise of their
powers under the Municipal Corporations Act of 1882,
legislation which authorized Watch Committees to suspend

---

[8] See T. H. Critchley, op. cit. at p. 131.

or dismiss any constable whom they considered negligent or otherwise unfit for his duty. At this point the Home Secretary intervened and informed the Watch Committee that he did not consider the suspension justified and that in enforcing the criminal law a chief officer of police should not be subject to control or interference by the police authority. This was an explicit assertion by the Home Office of the view that a Chief Constable, like any constable, held an independent position as an officer of the Crown. The point had been succinctly put by an earlier Home Secretary, Sir John Anderson. 'The policeman', he wrote, 'is nobody's servant . . . he executes a public office under the Law and it is the Law . . . which is the policeman's master.'[9] Legal support for this view was drawn from the absence of any master and servant relationship between police officers and police authorities. In 1930 in *Fisher v. Oldham Corporation*[10] it had been held that the Watch Committee could not be made liable for the wrongful actions of constables in carrying out their law enforcement duties as (to use the words of Mr Justice McCardie) 'servants of the state' and 'officers of the Crown or central power'.

The implications of this thesis did not commend themselves to the local authority associations, and when the Willink Commission began taking evidence in 1961 the Municipal Corporations Association and a number of other witnesses argued strongly that the supervisory powers of Watch Committees were not as narrow as had been implied; that the Oldham and Nottingham cases were in many ways special cases; and that they could not be used as foundations for a general theory of police independence in all matters of law enforcement.[11]

One sceptic who gave evidence to the Commission was Professor E. C. S. Wade, editor of Dicey's *Law of the Constitution* and Downing Professor of the Laws of England at Cambridge University. Professor Wade suggested that the prosecuting discretion of a Chief Constable was not peculiar to him 'since anyone can normally start a prosecution on his

---

[9] 'The Police', (1929) 7 *Public Administration*, p. 192.
[10] [1930] 2 K.B. 364.
[11] See the *Minutes of Evidence to the Royal Commission on the Police* (Cmnd. 1728 (1962)). Days 11–12, pp. 630–1 and 668–72.

own initiative and therefore there is nothing exceptional
in a local police authority requiring the police to carry
out this duty since each has an equal responsibility for
it'.[12] The police authority, he added, could not be absolved
from responsibility for enforcement of the law. The maintenance of public order was an executive function not
requiring the freedom from interference attaching to judicial
functions. In relation to some questions of law enforcement
policy (such, conceivably, as the excessive use of force in
maintaining order) it would not, he suggested, be *ultra
vires* for the Watch Committee to issue instructions to the
Chief Constable.

These views were not accepted by the police or by the
government in so far as they thought about the issue. The
Royal Commission certainly thought about it, but what
exactly their thoughts were never became clear. Two different questions arose and neither was clearly resolved by
the Commission. First, what did statute and common law
have to say, if anything, about the legal relationships of
police and police authorities? Did it establish the independence of chief officers in all matters of law enforcement
and the impropriety of all instructions even on matters of
general policy? Secondly, what, irrespective of the legal
position, ought sound administrative practice or constitutional morality to suggest as a proper relationship between
police and an elected supervisory authority? Twenty years
later two further questions need to be put. One is whether the
1964 police legislation that followed the Royal Commission,

[12] Cmnd. 1728, *Minutes of Evidence*, App. 11, pp. 33-4. The right of private
prosecution is, of course, a right exercised in England and Wales. Scotland, like
the United States, gives a practical monopoly to what are in effect public or
state prosecutors. How far this fact modifies the conclusions drawn in England
and Wales about the position of the police perhaps requires more discussion than
it has had. The rights of private prosecutors, including the police, are now circum-
scribed in England and Wales by a considerable number of statutes requiring
leave to be given by the Attorney-General or the Director of Public Prosecutions.
For a list of statutes containing such restrictions see *Hansard*, 14 March 1977.
The Director of Public Prosecutions is also empowered by statute to take over
and discontinue any prosecution (under the Prosecution of Offences Act, 1979).
See Royal Commission on Criminal Procedure (Cmnd. 8092-1, 1981) *The Investigation and Prosecution of Criminal Offences in England and Wales: The Law and
Procedure*. The Royal Commission recommended the setting up of an independent public prosecution service in England and Wales. Legislation is projected
in 1983 to give effect to this. So state prosecutors seem on the way.

or any subsequent development has changed the law? The other is whether anything has happened since 1964 that might affect views about sound or prudent administrative practice and convention. In assessing the conventional accountability and independence of the police some consideration of the legal status of constables is a necessary preliminary.

The Independence of the Constable

It may still be argued that too much importance has been placed on *Fisher* v. *Oldham* in assessing the degree of independence enjoyed by chief officers in the exercise of their constabulary functions. The thesis of the constable's operational independence rests essentially on the basis of civil liability cases in England and in Commonwealth jurisdictions.[13] In England the doctrine of constabulary independence in all law enforcement matters is not a long-established constitutional principle, but, on the contrary, one of which it is difficult to find any trace at all in the nineteenth and early twentieth centuries, either in the metropolis or in the provinces. The metropolitan relationship is particularly significant since it has figured prominently in several recent cases about the exercise of police discretion.[14] Though the exact chronology is unclear there has obviously been a change in the Home Office view of the Secretary of State's powers in relation to operational matters in the metropolitan area. In the nineteenth century Home Secretaries did not doubt their right to issue instructions in matters of law enforcement. Sir William Harcourt and Henry Matthews insisted upon and gave effect to the doctrine that it was for the Secretary of State to decide how far he should go in

---

[13] Cases such as *A.-G. for N. S. Wales* v. *Perpetual Trustee Co.* (1952), 85 C.L.R. 237; [1955] A.C. 457 also indicate that constables are not servants in that their employers cannot recover against third parties for loss of their 'services'. But 'servant', 'serve', and 'service' are many-coloured terms and it is hazardous to draw any direct implications about subjection to lawful superior orders from the use of these terms in different contexts. Compare for example the situations of civil servants, judges, and soldiers all of whom 'serve' the Crown in some sense, though not the same sense.

[14] See below p. 140.

exercising his responsibility for what Matthews called 'the
general policy of the police in the discharge of their duty'.[15]
Many examples of intervention in police operations could
be given. In 1880 the Home Secretary directed that no action
should be taken to suppress advertisements for Irish lotteries.
In 1881 Harcourt said that he had instructed that *agents
provocateurs* were not to be used without his authority,
and in 1888 he insisted that whether public meetings were
to be allowed or prohibited in the metropolis was 'a question
of policy' for the Home Secretary to decide. In 1913 the
Home Office told the Commissioner that proceedings were
not to be instituted against whist drives except where there
was evidence of serious gambling or profiteering.[16] In fact
it could reasonably be concluded that 'the authority of the
Home Secretary over the Metropolitan Police was regarded
as unlimited, subject of course to the normal principle
that public officers cannot be ordered to act unlawfully'.[17]
Also it was not supposed that any conflict arose between
lawful instructions relating to law enforcement or prosecution policy and the original independent common law
status of constables in the metropolis. One fact is perhaps
worth noting about the examples of intervention here cited,
namely that they involved for the most part either public
order, or cases where the law was unclear, or the morality
of its enforcement a matter of dispute. Such cases are of
course precisely those where advocates of greater accountability might want to argue that the exercise of discretion
should be subject to challenge through some mechanism
of accountability. By the 1930s, however, the Home Office
seems to have begun to disclaim responsibility. Conceivably
they had by then breathed in the spirit of *Fisher* v. *Oldham*.
Possibly also they were motivated by a desire to ward off
Parliamentary questions directed to the Home Secretary.
When the Home Office came to give evidence to the Willink
Commission in 1960 they went as far as to say that the

---

[15] 330 Parl. Deb. 3s., col. 1174. See G. Marshall, *Police and Government*
(1965), chap. 2, pp. 29–32 and 53–4; and Sir Frank Newsam, *The Home Office*
(1925), p. 104.
[16] See R. Plehwe, 'Police and Government: The Commissioner of Police for
the Metropolis', (1974) *Public Law* 316.
[17] Plehwe at p. 332.

Home Secretary 'could not be questioned . . . about the discharge by individual police officers of the duties of law enforcement'. Any glance at the index to *Hansard* would reveal that there is something amiss with this statement. In fact the 1929 and 1963 Royal Commissions on Police were both set up as the result of persistent Parliamentary questioning of Home Secretaries about the discharge by individual police officers of their duties of law enforcement,[18] as also were the special inquiries into actions undertaken by the Thurso Police in 1959,[19] the Sheffield Police in 1963,[20] and the Challenor case in the Metropolitan force in 1965.[21]

Outside the metropolitan area a parallel development took place. In the nineteenth century, borough Watch Committees frequently treated themselves as being competent to issue general instructions on matters of policing. A good example is the action of the Liverpool Watch Committee in 1890 which issued orders to the Head Constable, Sir William Nott-Bower 'to proceed against all brothels at present known to the police without any undue delay and such proceedings shall be by way of prosecution'. Sir William saw nothing improper in this. In a public speech he remarked that the police 'were not responsible for Policy or for Results. Policy was made for them not by them.' The police, he added, 'should be judged by the simple test of whether they carried out their duties in a fair and honest manner in accordance with the policy laid down for them by superior authority, which authority alone must take the responsibility both for it and for its results.'[22] Can it have been *Fisher's* case alone that brought about a change of heart on the part of the police and the Home Office (though not on the part

---

[18] For the episodes leading to the 1929 Commission see Cmd. 3147 (1928). (*Inquiry in regard to the interrogation by the Police of Miss Savidge.*)

[19] *Report of the Tribunal appointed to inquire into the allegation of assault on John Waters* (Cmnd. 718 (1959)).

[20] *Sheffield Police Appeal Inquiry* (Cmnd. 2176 (1963)).

[21] *Report of Inquiry by Mr A. E. James Q.C.* (Cmnd. 2735 (1965)).

[22] Sir William Nott-Bower, *Fifty Two Years a Policeman* (1926), p. 145. The Watch Committee had complained that Liverpool had 443 brothels whilst Manchester had only 5. Sir William's response was that 'such figures only profess to show the number of such houses "known to the Police" and all that they can prove is the very superior knowledge of the Police of Liverpool to that of the other towns quoted'.

of the local authority associations)? All that *Fisher's* case essentially decided was that no action in tort for a constable's wrongful acts would lie against anybody but him. Since no vicarious liability could be fixed upon those who appointed him he could not be in a master-servant relationship for civil liability purposes. Since there was almost a complete absence of any decided cases directly bearing on the constitutional status of the police, it may have been natural enough for the decision in *Fisher's* case to the effect that the police were not 'servants' for purposes of civil liability, to be picked out by textbook writers and others, and given a wider constitutional significance. Since 1964 the police have for civil liability purposes in effect become 'servants', since responsibility for their wrongful acts is now borne by the Chief Constable. Section 48 of the 1964 Police Act provided that the chief officer of police in any police area should be liable in respect of torts committed by constables under his direction and control in the performance or purported performance of their functions in like manner as a master is liable in respect of torts committed by his servants in the course of their employment. The imposition of this 'servitude' upon constables as an incident of a new master-servant relationship for purposes of the law of tort is however as much or as little relevant to the constitutional status of constables as was its absence in *Fisher's* case. If *Fisher's* case had really been the foundation of the constable's autonomy then the Act of 1964 must have enslaved him again. But in fact neither the one nor the other helps to delimit the scope of the lawful orders of the degree of constitutional subordination to which constables are subject.

It is clear, of course, that constables cannot be given orders to do what it would be unlawful for anyone to do, or what would amount to an obstruction of the course of justice if done by them, or involve a neglect of any common law or statutory duty. A police constable is a person who, although not a Crown servant, holds an office under Her Majesty.[23] The oath that he takes on assuming the office is to serve our sovereign lady the Queen in the office of constable without favour or affection; to cause the peace to be kept

---

[23] *Lewis* v. *Cattle*, [1938] 2 K.B. 454, 457.

and preserved; to prevent all offences against the person and property of Her Majesty's subjects; and to discharge all his duties according to law. So clearly no constable or Chief Constable can be told to act in a partisan way, to show favour or affection or not to keep the peace or protect property. Neither his superior officers 'nor the Crown itself can lawfully require him to abstain from performing the duties which the law imposes upon him with respect to the preservation of the peace and the apprehension of offenders'.[24] The acts he may lawfully be required to do, however, depend upon the statutes and regulations that govern police organization and upon the powers conferred on police authorities and Chief Constables.

The Position Since 1964

Could it be argued that any change in the constitutional position was effected by the 1964 Police Act? The answer would seem to be that it left the law in this respect unchanged. The legislation was based, with some exceptions, on the recommendations of the Willink Commission. The Commission's Report, though not a model of clarity, certainly suggests that they did not accept all the implications drawn by the Home Office and the police from the *Fisher* case. Indeed one section of the Report is even given the title 'Subordination of Chief Constables to Democratic Supervision'. The supervision the Commission had in mind was related to what they called 'police policies in matters affecting the public interest': the regulation for example of traffic, political demonstrations, strikes, processions, and public order generally. The Commission argued that such policies, though involving the enforcement of the law, 'do not require the immunity from external influences that is generally thought necessary in regard to the enforcement of the law in particular cases'.[25] Various provisions were made in the Act to increase accountability to local police authorities and to

---

[24] *Attorney-General for New South Wales* v. *Perpetual Trustee Co.* (1952), 85 C.L.R. 237 at 303.
[25] *Report of the Royal Commission on Police* (Cmnd. 1728 (1962), para. 91).

the Home Secretary, by way of formal powers to request reports from Chief Constables, but they did not involve any obvious alteration in the police authorities' direct powers in the field of law enforcement as they existed before the Act. The Act provided that police forces should be under the direction and control of the chief officer, but since Chief Constables had always exercised the immediate operational direction and control of their forces, these words do not seem intended to alter the pre-existing situation. It is noticeable that nothing was enacted directly about the *exclusive* control of the Chief Constable or the nature of his powers *vis-à-vis* the police authority. What really happened was that the government avoided this direct issue, in view of the inherent difficulty of framing any precise prescription, and relied upon the Home Secretary's powers to act as a potential buffer and arbitrator between police authorities and Chief Constables.

Perhaps the most significant legal decision related to the exercise of police powers since 1964, has been the decision of the Court of Appeal in *Ex parte Blackburn*.[26] The question in issue here was whether the courts could control the exercise of police discretion in prosecuting, on the supposition that the police owed a duty to the public to enforce the law. Surprisingly, an affirmative answer was given to this question. A policy instruction by the Metropolitan Police Commissioner not to enforce the provisions of the Betting and Gaming legislation could, had it not been withdrawn, have been controlled by the issue of mandamus. It was not asserted that a breach of the duty to enforce the law could be inferred from the mere existence of a policy of non-prosecution (as, for example, when prosecutions were not brought in relation to attempted suicide or juvenile

---

[26] *R.* v. *Metropolitan Police Commissioner, ex parte Blackburn,* [1968] 2 Q.B. 118. On the issues raised by Blackburn's case see D. G. T. Williams, 'The Police and Law Enforcement', (1968) *Criminal Law Review* 351 and 'Prosecution, Discretion and the Accountability of the Police' in *Crime, Criminology and Public Policy* (ed. Roger Hood (1974)). Compare the discretion conceded in *R.* v. *Metropolitan Police Commissioner, ex parte Blackburn (No. 3),* [1973] Q.B. 241 (enforcement of obscenity legislation) and *R.* v. *Chief Constable of Devon and Cornwall, ex parte Central Electricity Generating Board,* [1982] 1 Q.B. 458.

sexual offences[27]). But some policies would be improper (for example an instruction not to prosecute any person for stealing goods worth less than £100). In the course of the decision, however, both Lord Denning and Lord Justice Salmon made remarks about the status of the Police Commissioner *vis-à-vis* the Metropolitan Police authority, suggesting amongst other things that he was not subject to the orders of the Home Secretary. 'No minister of the Crown', Lord Denning remarked, 'can tell him that he must or must not keep observation on this place or that; or that he must or must not prosecute this man or that one, nor can any police authority tell him so.' Like every Chief Constable 'he is not the servant of anyone save of the law itself. The responsibility for law enforcement lies on him. He is answerable to the law and to the law alone.'[28]

What weight should be placed on these remarks? Both Salmon LJ and Lord Denning said clearly that it would be impermissible for the Secretary of State to issue any order to the police in respect of law enforcement.[29] But it was by no means clear on what this view was based except the insistence on the responsibility of the Commissioner to the law. No distinction was drawn between individual instances of law enforcement and policies of law enforcement of the kind referred to by the Royal Commission, and there was no detailed consideration of the historical relationship of the Secretary of State with the Metropolitan Police. It is fairly plain that these categorical remarks were merely unargued repetitions of the orthodox and questionable inferences from *Fisher's* case. In any event the points were not in issue. It was unnecessary to decide what the relations of the Home Secretary and the Commissioner were, or what the relations of Chief Constables to police authorities were. The question for decision was not the amenability of the police to political control, but how far the admitted legal duty to enforce the law was subject to judicial control and enforcement. The *ratio decidendi* of the decision was that

---

[27] For a number of similar examples and of the uses of prosecutionary discretion generally see *The Decision to Prosecute* (1972) by A. E. Wilcox (a former Chief Constable of Hertfordshire).

[28] [1968] 2 Q.B. 118 at 135-6.

[29] For Salmon LJ's view see [1968] 2 Q.B. at 138.

in a proper case judicial enforcement of the duty would be appropriate, and it seems justifiable to treat the tangential views of Lord Denning and Lord Justice Salmon on the powers of police authorities and the Secretary of State as being *obiter*.

One other episode since 1964 deserves mention since it suggests another possible basis for independence in the institution of individual prosecutions, by illustrating the traditional thesis that the initiation of prosecutions in England is, generally speaking, a right of the private citizen. In 1974 a police constable (PC Joy) successfully pursued a private prosecution of a Member of Parliament which his superior officers were unwilling to authorize and in consequence of which it was reported that he might be made subject to disciplinary action (though no action was in fact taken). Joy's case perhaps illustrates the virtue of the English (as against the American and Scottish) system in not permitting the State to monopolize the prosecution function, but it adds nothing to the argument about the relative powers of constables and police authorities in law enforcement matters other than prosecution.

It seems fair to conclude that neither the 1964 Act nor any subsequent development has changed the law on this subject or given the police any legal immunity which they did not enjoy before 1964. If that is so the legal basis for constabulary autonomy remains uncertain.

Given, however, the possibility that control of policing in some of its aspects might not be unlawful, the question that must be faced is whether and how that control should be exercised, not as a matter of law but as a matter of constitutional and administrative morality. What convention should govern the issue?

Independence by Convention

We have seen that in the British system convention often modifies law. The law may say one thing, but the political and moral rules followed in practice may differ. So even if it is the case that the issuing of instructions by police committees in some matters affecting law enforcement would not be unlawful, we still need to ask whether it would be a defensible or desirable administrative practice. And in asking that question in the 1980s, it may be necessary to take heed of some considerations that were not present twenty years earlier. In 1959 anyone who believed in the value of local control of administration and in democratic accountability could well believe in the need for greater political control of police discretion. Situations could even be conceived where, in the interests of more effective or uniform or equitable law enforcement, even positive instructions might in theory be justified. Few would have believed that such instructions could ever properly issue in relation to the institution or withdrawal of particular prosecutions. But the argument of the Willink Royal Commission about democratic supervision implied that police operations and the disposal of police resources, and even general prosecution policies in some areas of public interest, were matters over which police authorities might properly exercise influence and in the last resort exert control.

All such feelings are, however, contingent upon a number of assumptions about the processes of politics and administration at a particular time. An unspoken premiss is that the executive officers and elected persons through whom democratic control is exerted can be assumed to exercise it honestly and in the public interest. But our experience in the last two decades raises a question as to whether that pristine assumption can still be made. Nothing in British government is quite what it was in 1959 or ever will be. We are not now as sure as we were that elected politicians will respect the rule of law, or reject bribes, or refrain from exploiting their positions for self-interested or party political, or even corrupt and unlawful ends. Nobody's faith in councillors or Congressmen or Members of Parliament can now be as firmly held as it was twenty years ago.

What is the moral? Perhaps that democratic theory no longer gives a simple or straightforward guide to action here any more than it does in some other fields. In many areas such as financial and economic regulation (including such issues as control of the money supply, and health and safety requirements), there may be a tension between technical judgment and political ideology or party preference.

The long-run interests and rights of citizens may well be furthered by the construction of buttresses against some kinds of overt political pressures, even when exerted honestly and in the name of democratic majorities. The occasional frustration of such majority pressures may be required by the need to protect civil liberties and secure the impartial treatment of individuals. Bills of Rights are a standing acknowledgement of this. If, therefore, in the field of law enforcement we have to give a calculated and unprejudiced answer in the 1980s to the question whether civil liberties and impartial justice are more to be expected from party politicians (whether on police committees or in the House of Commons or in charge of ministerial departments) than from a body of rules or conventions that restricts their scope for intervention in police operations, many liberal democrats would feel justified in placing more trust in the latter than in the former. If that is so, then the thesis of police independence may, despite its uncertain legal foundations, be something that it is now necessary to defend as a constitutional and administrative convention.

Such a convention would suggest that orders or directives, whether related to prosecution or other law enforcement measures, and whether related to individual cases or general policies should as a matter of sound administrative practice be regarded as improper. That conclusion, it must be admitted, runs counter to a number of proposals that have been made to amend the existing legislation so as to confer wider powers on local police authorities. In November 1979, for example, Mr Jack Straw MP introduced into the House of Commons a Police Authorities (Powers) Bill[30] whose purpose was to extend the powers and duties of police authorities in respect of police operations and organization. Its principal sections proposed to amend the 1964 Police Act to add to the definition of a police authority's function that of determining the general policing policies of the area. It provided that the Chief Constable should report annually on his general policing policies but that the police authority should have power to amend or reject his recommendations. The Chief Constable would be thereafter required by the Act

---

[30] Bill 78, 14 Nov. 1978.

to exercise his powers in accordance with the general policing policies determined by the police authority committee's resolutions, subject to a right of appeal to the Home Secretary, against the authority's proposals.

If the Straw Bill, or something like it, were to be enacted it is not easy to predict what kinds of policies would be embodied in the police committees' resolutions. If local options and democratic control are taken seriously there would presumably be very different patterns of law enforcement from area to area, depending upon the policy preferences of the various police authority members. In some areas they might prefer to have certain laws enforced more strictly; in others they might wish to have them enforced less strictly, or not enforced at all. Area A might aim to have more prosecutions for racial incitement and fewer for speeding; Area B might have the opposite priorities. Some radical critics of police independence see democratic control as a means of securing greater respect for policies of social equality or more respect for minority rights. But the democratically elected majority in some areas might conceivably be in favour of less social equality and set out to have a more élitist set of enforcement policies, with more police time spent on protecting property and more stringent enforcement of drug and public order legislation. In the industrial relations field there may be very different views, all strongly held, about the way in which offences committed in the course of picketing are dealt with, or about the handling of secondary picketing or mass demonstrations. Many of these issues are presumably those the Royal Commission of 1962 had in mind in speaking of 'police policies in matters which vitally concern the public interest'. They also spoke of the need to provide opportunities for 'effective challenges' to police policies in these areas. But the subjection of such decisions to direct reversal by committees of elected politicians and the substitution by such committees of their own policies would not be a happy solution. Nevertheless if there is to be no direct executive accountability, some of the deficiencies of the present machinery need to be repaired. The principal requirements are better explanatory accountability and a satisfactory solution to the problem of the complaints machinery procedure.

Explanatory Accountability

The corollary of a conventional constabulary immunity from mandatory instructions in operational matters ought to be that explanatory accountability is not then confined within any particular bounds. It should extend to police operations and to prosecution matters, even sometimes to particular cases of prosecution or non-prosecution, as well as to general policies. Its effectiveness also depends on opportunities for debate and questioning on police matters at the local level. The central and local machinery that was set up in 1964 and subsequently modified by police reorganization has not, in fact, been very effectively used in the interests of explanatory accountability. In some degree this is perhaps more the fault of elected members than of the legislative machinery. The Police Act provisions for requesting and debating reports from Chief Constables on the policing of their areas have not been extensively used either in the House of Commons or in local councils.[31] In the new District Councils, to which many of the former cities and boroughs have been reduced by local government reorganization, these powers cannot be used at all. Nor does there appear to have been much significant debate in local council chambers of either annual police estimates or of the decisions or activities of police authority committees.

Lord Scarman's Report on the Brixton disorders of April 1981 took as one of its themes the relation between consultation and accountability. In his Report,[32] Lord Scarman recommended that a statutory duty should be imposed on police authorities and on chief officers of police to co-operate in the establishment of local consultative committees. That recommendation was embodied in the 1983 Police and Criminal Evidence Bill.

---

[31] There is no easily available information on the use made by local police authorities and councils of their police powers. In Oxford City Council for example, between 1964 and 1974 only one request was made for a report from the Chief Constable under s. 12 of the 1964 Police Act. This may not be untypical. Two useful articles on police committees are Barry Loveday, 'The Role of the Police Committee', (1983) *Local Government Studies*, p. 39; and D. E. Regan, 'Enhancing the Role of Police Committees', (1983) *Public Administration* 97.

[32] Cmnd. 8427 (1981), pp. 130-1.

The Home Office meanwhile has published a document of guidance for Chief Constables and local authorities in an attempt to set out in detail what community consultation might involve, and to say with whom — besides each other — police authorities and chief officers might be expected to co-operate. The Home Office guidelines suggest that the consultative bodies should be 'flexible in their membership, wide-ranging in the views they can reflect, but none the less of manageable size'. Existing bodies may be consulted about the consultation process. (Such bodies, for example, as the Rural Community Council, or the Council for Voluntary Services, or the Community Relations Council.) They could be used to nominate suitably flexible representatives of the community. Other local organizations — such as local churches, chambers of commerce, and Trades Councils — may themselves, it is suggested, be included in a consultative group, together with residents' and tenants' associations, youth organizations, and ethnic minority associations. At this point one begins to see the force in the Secretary of State's admonition that 'groups should not be so large that they become mere talking shops' (or perhaps, more to the point, have to be found accommodation in some suitable open-air arena).

Some topics for discussion are listed in the guidelines. They include: issues of local concern which it is desired to bring to the attention of the police; ways in which police procedures in relation to law enforcement operate; ways in which young people can contribute to crime prevention; the promotion of better community understanding of problems facing the police; discussion of police responses to crime; and the implications of any general complaints about police response to the public. The guidelines add that 'there are some operational aspects of policing such as criminal investigations or security matters which it would be wrong to make the subject of local consultation'. On this point Lord Scarman was cited on the necessity for non-intervention in police operations, but in his Report Lord Scarman did not rule out all discussion of police operations or even perhaps all aspects of criminal investigation. He remarked that 'the boundary between what may and what may not be discussed has not been subjected to a close enough scrutiny'.

Until recently, he said, operational decisions were held by senior police officers to be inopportune topics for community consultation. However, some police officers had recognized 'the propriety of consultation and discussion which could cover not only policy but the planning stage of some operational decisions' so that the community could be heard 'not only in the development of policing policy, but in the planning of many, though not all, operations against crime'. It is not clear from the Home Office guidelines whether the Home Secretary agrees with Lord Scarman on this point and it is probable that many senior police officers would not.

It seems improbable, however, that better police accountability can be effectively established on the basis recommended in the Home Office Guidelines. What is proposed is a hotchpotch reminiscent of participatory and consultative devices in other walks of life. It would be better to base consultation and debate about police matters on the existing local government structure. When police reorganization took place and larger police authorities were created, many areas lost their local police committee. To restore District Council police committees would create a useful adjunct to the county or regional police authorities in whose hands the statutory powers of the old Watch and police committees were placed by the 1964 Police Act. That seems the right level and the right degree of formality for a public forum devoted to police–public relations.

Consultation, debate, and questioning are of course different activities. Prior consultation as to law enforcement operations may involve matters of operational judgment. Questioning however can cover a wider area, and debate perhaps an unlimited area.

Complaints Machinery

The problem of creating an independent mechanism to consider complaints about the activities of the police is, of course, not on all fours with that of creating either an ordinary administrative appeals tribunal or an ombudsman-type review. Since the 1976 Police Act, some of the difficulties that arise have been experienced by the Police Complaints Board which is neither one thing nor the other. The Board was not intended to provide, as was the Parliamentary Commissioner, a general *ex post facto* review of decisions already made. In 1980 in its triennial review report, the Board noted that decisions on disciplinary proceedings, once taken, could not easily be overturned by the Board without creating an'element of double jeopardy for accused officers. So a finding disagreeing with a Chief Constable's disciplinary decision would be ineffective and unsatisfying to a complainant. They see their function as being supervisory in the sense that they inject an independent judgment at the point at which disciplinary charges are brought; and they determine also the procedure and the degree of formality with which the charge is heard.

As to double jeopardy the Home Office advised the Board that avoidance of it required not only that a police officer tried and acquitted by a court ought not to be subject to disciplinary proceedings for the same offence, but that there should normally be no disciplinary charge when the Director of Public Prosecutions has decided that criminal proceedings should *not* be taken (if the evidence necessary to substantiate the disciplinary charge was the same as that necessary to found the criminal proceedings). In December 1982, however, that view was successfully challenged in the High Court,[33] and the Board concluded that notwithstanding the Director's view they were free to recommend or direct a disciplinary charge on their own evaluation of the evidence.

A more important question is raised by the scale and ambit of the Board's operations. Are the Board's operations confined to the question of whether an offence has been committed under the Police Disciplinary Code by an individual officer? That appears to be the intention of the 1976 Act and the Home Office has advised the police that 'the requirement to record a complaint under section 49 of the Police Act 1964 does not extend to complaints about the general administration, efficiency or procedures of the force, which do not amount to a complaint about the conduct

---

[33] *R. v. Police Complaints Board, ex parte Madden* [1983] I.W.L.R. 447.

of an individual officer.'[34] But s. 49 of the 1964 Police Act, though it does not define a 'complaint', says nothing about a complaint from a member of the public being confined to a complaint about a police officer's having committed an offence against the disciplinary code. A complaint about what an individual officer does may be about conduct that is authorized by his force's standing orders and which does not raise any question of disciplinary proceedings, though it may be alleged to be objectionable or unfair or oppressive or unreasonable or a cause of hardship or injustice. As such it might in effect be a complaint about force policy and by implication involve senior officers or the Chief Constable. The supposition may be that complaints against the Chief Constable are a matter for police authorities. But it has never been entirely clear what is supposed to happen to a complaint about a decision of a senior police officer or of the Chief Constable that is not about the commission of a disciplinary offence. Police committees neither have the competence nor the willingness to deal with them, though they retain the statutory obligation under s. 49 of the 1964 Act to keep themselves informed as to the manner in which the Chief Constable deals with complaints (which is not the same thing as a duty to see that they are dealt with properly). There is perhaps a possibility that a dissatisfied complainant might pursue his complaint through one of the Commissioners for Local Administration on the ground that a police authority had failed to deal with his complaint. Though the local government complaints commissioner's jurisdiction does not extend to the police it does include the actions of police authorities.

In October 1982 the Government published proposals for a new set of complaints procedures.[35] They reflect the view that the police should continue to be responsible for the investigation of complaints, but that the investigation should be carried out under the supervision of the Chairman

---

[34] Home Office Circular 63/1977. Also paras. 21-2 of the *Police Complaints Board Triennial Review 1980* (Cmnd. 7966). S. 8 of the 1976 Police Act does, however, authorize the Board to make a report on matters coming to their notice to which attention should be drawn.

[35] *Police Complaints Procedure*, Cmnd. 8681 (1982). Legislative effect will be given to the revised procedure in the Police and Criminal Evidence Bill, 1983.

of the Police Complaints Board (or one of his deputies) acting as an independent assessor.

The new system specifies three different categories of complaints, each to be handled differently. On receipt of a complaint a chief police officer will cause it to be recorded and decide whether it can best be resolved by informal conciliation or by formal investigation. If conciliation is attempted an officer of a rank not less than inspector will interview the complainant who will be given the opportunity to choose a formal investigation. The supervising officer can arrange a meeting with the complainant accompanied if he wishes by some other person (not a lawyer), though any police officer involved is not obliged to attend. The interview is recorded in a register open to inspection by the police authority or the Inspector of Constabulary and the complainant may ask for a copy of the recorded entry. Conciliation cannot be used for alleged criminal or disciplinary offences. This latter exclusion seems a severe limitation on the potential area for conciliation.

Where a complaint cannot be resolved informally it will be investigated by a senior police officer of the rank of chief inspector as above, unless a dispensation for any investigation is given by the Police Complaints Board. Investigation reports will no longer be submitted automatically to the Director of Public Prosecutions in every case involving allegations of criminal conduct. The Chief Constable will be able to bring either criminal or disciplinary charges himself without consulting the DPP, though the Police Complaints Board's supervisory role will remain and they will be able to direct in any particular case that a reference of the papers be made to the DPP. After such reference the Police Complaints Board will consider the necessity for disciplinary charges as at present.

A third category of complaints relates to those in which allegations are made that police action has been responsible for death or serious injury (more than 'bruising or superficial laceration'). In these cases, where the Chief Constable considers that the injury could have been caused in the way alleged, there is mandatory reference to the independent assessor. Any other case, however, may be referred to the assessor if the Chief Constable wishes to refer it as being of an exceptional or serious character. The assessor himself has also a reserve power to require the Chief Constable to submit for his consideration any case not already referred to him. Cases thus referred to the assessor may be returned by him for investigation by the chief officer (as in the second category of complaints) or they may be handled under the assessor's supervision by an officer from a different division of the force or from another force. Thus the assessor will not himself investigate any cases; but where they are investigated under his direct supervision he may, with the consent of the DPP, give reasonable directions as to the collection of evidence and require interim reports from the investigating officer. The investigating officer's report to the assessor will be submitted to the DPP (if necessary) only when the assessor has signified his satisfaction with the investigation. Assistant assessors may be appointed as members of the Police Complaints Board, such appointments possibly being on a regional basis.

The revised complaints machinery, if developed like the commissioners for administration in local government on a regional basis (or even on a county or single-force basis), could provide the nucleus of a police ombudsman system. In several ways, however, it falls short of filling that role. In the first place the investigation of complaints is not carried out by an agency independent of the body investigated. Over a certain range of complaints that may be acceptable, since the problems of policing and criminal investigation are different from those of administration in general. The necessity for investigation by police officers may be less obvious, however, in complaints that are not directly about particular criminal action or individual acts of indiscipline. There seems room in the scheme for complaints about police activity falling outside these areas to be referred to the assessor at his own instance or at the instance of the Chief Constable. What needs to be added is provision for direct access to the assessor by complainants or the public for the purpose of submitting complaints of a more general character such as those falling into the Willink Commission's category of 'police policies in matters affecting the public interest'. In relation to these questions, however, it is not obviously appropriate that investigation of disputed facts or allegations should be undertaken only by police officers, rather than by staff employed by the assessor. The undertaking of such a function would involve regorganization of the Police Complaints Board, but it would be possible to deploy assistant assessors and staff in regional or local offices of the Board, and to transmute its function into something nearer to the existing ombudsman systems for local government, central government and health service administration.

In his autobiography *In the Office of Constable*, Sir Robert Mark concluded that 'the greatest challenge for the police of tomorrow is the threat of change in their constitutional position . . . As political and industrial tensions rise the police will inevitably become the focus of political controversy centred upon their constitutional accountability.'[36] That seemed at the time too dramatic a judgment. But questions that were once academic now figure in party manifestos.

Effective machinery for complaint investigation[37] and for extended local debate of police matters will not satisfy radical critics of the police but it will provide an institutional basis for the convention that operational policing should not be subject to direct executive accountability, but be exposed to virtually unlimited explanatory accountability procedures.

[36] *In the Office of Constable* (1979), p. 284.

[37] The arrangements described here have been introduced in modified form in the Police and Criminal Evidence Act 1984, which has set up a new Police Complaints Authority. Its function, like that of the Complaints Board, is essentially to supervise the propriety of the investigation of complaints by the police.

IX
The Duties of the Army

The rules and conventions that govern the use of the armed forces for purposes internal to the govenment of a community are an important segment of its constitutional framework. As such their character and content need to be clearly established. In Britain there is little help to be had in the matter from the traditional sources of constitutional doctrine. The common law cases involving the army or military action have arisen mainly from forgotten episodes in South Africa and Ireland, and they provide a few fragmentary rules governing the provision of military aid to the civil power. Perhaps all of them need to be reviewed in the light of twentieth-century developments.

In recent times the occasions of military aid to the civil authorities have been almost entirely in the context of industrial disturbances threatening the maintenance of essential services (or at least important public facilities). These episodes have raised a number of questions that are easier to ask than to answer. There is frequently a contrast between constitutional propriety and political practicality in the United Kingdom, and the impact of informal practice on formal rules of law is nowhere more obvious than in the regulation of industrial affairs. What is politically practicable is itself not always easy to predict with confidence. What is possible for some governments at some times may be less possible or impossible for others. And what is feasible in the case of a particular industrial conflict may be inconceivable in the event of a more generalized confrontation between government and organized labour. Since 1974, when Mr Edward Heath's government retired from office after a General Election precipitated by coal and power workers' strikes, these questions have been pondered by politicians on both sides of the House of Commons. Some thought has also been given to them by senior civil servants, who, as permanent employees of the Crown, differ from their political masters in having the duty not merely to learn lessons from the past but to foresee and make provision for the future.

The Pre-1914 Period

A conspectus of the use of the armed forces in the course of industrial disputes in the twentieth century may conveniently begin in 1908. In that year a select committee of the House of Commons reported on *The Employment of Military in Cases of Disturbance*.[1] The Report noted that troops had been called upon to aid the police twenty-four times in the past thirty-nine years, and on two occasions had been ordered to open fire. The committee's recommendations did not favour the use of troops in riot situations but suggested that the Home Secretary should have power to draft a proportion of the police force from any county to assist any other area threatened by disorder. This advice may well have played its part in the Welsh mining disturbances of 1910-11. In the early part of 1910 a strike at the Newport Docks led to looting, and the Home Secretary, Mr Winston Churchill, was asked to provide for police and military assistance. Extra police from neighbouring forces plus the offer of Metropolitan Police proved sufficient, but troops were made ready, since in the Home Office's view they must be available should the local magistrates requisition them. Churchill expressed the view that if military assistance were needed mounted troops should be sent as being more effective than infantry in dealing with rioters. In November 1910 a coal strike broke out in the Rhondda valley and the Chief Constable of Glamorgan, faced with disorder and damage to property, called for troops from the local army command. The troops were sent, but — after consultation between the Home Office and the War Office — were stopped on Churchill's instructions, and Metropolitan Police sent instead. Some doubts were expressed at the time about the propriety of the Home Secretary's intervention, but it reflected his view that troops and especially infantry were inferior as instruments of riot control to constables trained

[1] Parliamentary Papers, HC 236 (1908).

in handling crowds and not equipped with lethal weapons. 'Infantry soldiers', Churchill wrote to the King, 'can if attacked or stoned only reply by fire from long range rifles which often kills foolish sightseers unconnected with the riot or innocent people at some distance from it.'[2] Troops were, on this occasions, sent into the mining areas to protect the police and on at least one occasion offered 'a little gentle persuasion with the bayonet'.[3] But Churchill insisted that the troops must not be used as strike-breakers. There could, he said in the House of Commons in August 1911, be 'no question of the military forces of the Crown intervening in a labour dispute'.

The dock strikes of 1911, however, supported by transport and other workers appeared to Churchill to be 'the manifestation of a new force in trade unionism'. 'Shipping, coal, railways, dockers etc. are all breaking out at once', he noted. 'The general strike policy is a factor that must be dealt with.'[4] In such a situation the use of military or naval forces to maintain essential services as well as to maintain order appeared to Churchill in a different light, the intervention being not on behalf of a particular employer. Accordingly in Liverpool troops and police were used to move goods; the municipal authorities asked for a warship to be sent to Merseyside with instructions for naval personnel to work the river ferries, and HMS *Antrim* was in fact sent.

In the summer of 1911, Churchill asked for 25,000 troops to be made ready to move into the Port of London, but Asquith and Lloyd George dissuaded him from taking this step after warnings from the strikers' leaders that it would cause armed conflict and bloodshed. In August 1911, however, when the railwaymen joined the strike, troops were sent to over thirty places. Violent demonstrations broke out in many of them. In Liverpool, London, and Llanelly troops opened fire and a number of deaths resulted. On 19 August 1911 officers commanding the various military areas were told to use their discretion as to the sending of troops to any particular point, and the Army regulation requiring a

---

[2] Letter from Churchill to the King, 10 Nov. 1910. See Randolph Churchill, *Winston Churchill* (1967) vol. ii, p. 372.
[3] General Sir Nevil Macready, *Annals of an Active Life* (1924), vol. i, p. 136.
[4] Randolph Churchill, op. cit., p. 379.

requisition for troops from a civil authority was suspended. (The legal significance of this step was perhaps debatable as is the force of the regulation. At common law it would not, if the situation made it necessary, be unlawful in any event for the military to assist in keeping order. Indeed it could be argued that in such a situation they would have a duty to do so whether requested or not.)

The Inter-War Period

In the course of the twentieth century Churchill's principle that troops, and for that matter police, should not be used as strike-breakers has been stretched to breaking-point in three sets of circumstances: first, where a combination of strikes occurs or there is sympathetic strike action over a wide area; secondly, where a strike or strikes affects a service essential or important to the general economic welfare; thirdly, where a strike has avowed or patent political objectives unconnected with the traditional trade dispute about wages or working conditions. Any application of general principles here is admittedly complicated for a number of reasons. For one thing there are degrees of economic importance. Some facilities are more essential than others. In addition the distinction between industrial and political disputes has become less clear than it once may have been. Governments now interevene more radically in the wage and price arena and provoke strikes as a result of their policies. Governments also themselves employ large numbers of people in the public sector, and not every strike against the government as employer is a political strike. Moreover, disputes that in some degree fit the definition of trade disputes as being about remuneration or conditions of work may be connected with trade union campaigns of a political or international kind. In situations also where law and order is threatened, the practical application of theoretical maxims of constitutional propriety becomes more difficult. The years immediately after the First World War did in fact usher in a period of turbulence and industrial conflict in which the peace could only be kept by military reinforcement of the police, or on occasion by way of substitution for the police. Such was the case, for example, in 1918 and 1919 when there were widespread police strikes.[5] In Liverpool in 1919 rioting and looting in the dock areas had to be suppressed by both military and naval intervention. In 1920 Parliament passed Emergency Powers legislation authorizing the proclamation of a state of emergency and wide powers to act by regulation where it appeared 'that any action has been taken or is immediately threatened by any person or body of persons of such a nature and on so extensive a scale as to be calculated by interfering with the supply and distribution of food, water, fuel or light or with the means of locomotion, to deprive the community or any substantial part of the community of the essentials of life'.[6] States of emergency were declared in 1921, 1924, and 1926, all in response to strike action. In 1926 the outbreak first of the miners' strike and then of the General Strike appeared to threaten all the communal dangers envisaged in the Emergency Powers Act. Even here, however — at least at the outset — the instinct for separating the industrial issue from questions of public order could be seen. On one occasion, for example, it was proposed that medical supplies should be conveyed to London hospitals by police vans, but the proposal was dropped when Sir John Anderson, Permanent Under-Secretary to the Home Office, objected that it 'would involve the contravention of a very big principle — the principle that in a dispute the police do not help either side'.[7] Anderson's concern was that strike-breaking action by the police would compromise existing respect for the constabulary in their role of preserving the peace. There may well be in the English context a psychological difference between civil and military forces conceived as strike-breakers. Given the common law doctrine that police officers are not servants of either local or central government,

---

[5] For accounts of these see T. A. Critchley, *A History of Police in England and Wales* (1967), chap. 6, and G. W. Reynolds and A. Judge, *The Night the Police Went on Strike* (1968). This was the last occasion on which a police strike has occurred in the United Kingdom. All the strikers were dismissed from the force and none of them ever secured reinstatement.

[6] Emergency Powers Act, 1920 s. 1 (i).

[7] J. W. Wheeler-Bennett, *John Anderson, Viscount Waverley* (1962), p. 106. This principle, however, did not prevent the involvement of the police during the ambulance drivers' and social workers' strikes in 1979.

it may be plausible to suppose that the belief in the impartiality of the police and their perceived independence of political instructions is an asset worth preserving. The armed forces, by contrast, are undoubtedly employees of the Crown and, in general, subject to the orders of Ministers. They have, therefore, no such impartial and independent reputation to dissipate; and their use to take the place of strikers is to that extent less objectionable. In 1926 the armed forces were utilized to break the strikers' blockade of the London Docks. Police and special constables failed to clear a way for lorries to remove food supplies, but on the orders of the Home Secretary volunteer stevedores were taken down the Thames by the Navy under cover of darkness, and the dock entrances were cleared by two battalions of the Brigade of Guards with armoured cars. When a local authority sympathetic to the strikers cut off electrical power to the docks, Sir William Joynson-Hicks and the Admiralty produced a counterstroke. 'At the appointed time the supply was cut off but to the astonishment of the Council and the general body of strikers the lights of the docks did not go out and work continued without interruption. The explanation was that Joynson-Hicks had authorised a submarine to be brought up to the docks. From this vessel a cable was transferred to the shore and connected with the electrical plant at the docks. The submarine generated the necessary electricity with her own engines and the lights of the docks continued without a flicker.'[8] It is noticeable that in more recent times Sir William's successors in office have either lacked the inventiveness or lost the appetite for such tactical innovations in the industrial relations field.

The Post-1945 Period

Since 1945 even more states of emergency have been proclaimed than in the inter-war period in response to strike action by dockers, miners, power workers, merchant seamen, and other workers in public service industries; and on many

---

[8] H. A. Taylor, *Jix, Viscount Brentford* (1933), p. 199.

of these occasions military personnel have been used to replace strikers in carrying out work deemed to be essential. In 1948 and 1949 there were dock strikes, and troops were called in to unload ships and move perishable cargoes. In 1950 servicemen were employed in gas works. In 1953, during a petrol-tanker drivers' strike, they delivered petrol, and in 1955 they helped the Post Office to deliver mail. In the 1960s naval vessels carried supplies to the Western Isles of Scotland during strikes by the Seamen's Union. During the 1966 strike the Union stated that they did not regard this action as intervention in the strike, but would take steps to boycott and 'black' merchant ships if they were manned by naval personnel. On that occasion the Government made it clear that the armed forces would not be used, although tugs manned by the Navy might be used to tow away ships if the ports became congested. All these examples illustrate the reluctance both of Labour and Conservative governments to use servicemen except in marginal ways or as a last resort. In the 1970 dock strike, when emergency powers were again invoked, dockers agreed to move perishable cargoes in order to prevent the use of troops. Ministers acknowledged that they had a duty at least to maintain the supply of essential services: an action that produced a parliamentary revolt from a number of left-wing members (whose implicit major premiss must have been either that food was not an essential service or that, if it was, its supply should not be maintained).

The maintenance of public health certainly seems to qualify as an essential service. Troops were placed on standby in 1970 to pump sewage stations when a strike of local government workers occurred. In the same year the Grenadier Guards were sent to the London Borough of Tower Hamlets to remove refuse; and in the Glasgow dustmen's strike of 1975 about a thousand troops (working a seventy-five-hour week for no extra pay) mounted a major and successful refuse removal operation. During the national strike of water workers in 1983 it was stated that troops would be used if the emergency required it. But in the event they were not needed.

In the case of two other equally essential services, the use of troops has been more contentious. One is the maintenance of power supplies. Power is perhaps the single most vital commodity of life as now organized. But it seems doubtful whether, whatever may once have been the case, the Army could now without assistance run power stations. Quite apart from the numbers of trained engineers needed, the maintenance of stations in continuous operation requires the ready availability of a number of materials whose supply and delivery may be difficult to guarantee in a situation where transport and other workers may be on strike and where there may be simultaneous non-co-operation from both manual and technical workers in the power industry. In the House of Commons during the electricity dispute of December 1970, the Secretary for Trade and Industry said, 'My Right Hon. Friend the Chancellor of the Exchequer certainly never said that troops could take over and run the generating stations. It is not practical; my Right Hon. Friend and I know that.'[9]

A second controversial case that again underlines governmental inhibitions in strike situations was the affair of the firemen in the autumn of 1977, an episode of Gilbertian quality.

The Firemen's Strike 1977

In November 1977 a strike of all fire service personnel was called for the fourteenth of the month. At the outset the Home Secretary said that if it became necessary troops would be used, working under the supervision of senior fire officers. It was added that requests for assistance would have to come from local authorities; that men from all three armed services would be made available; and that they would use their own appliances and whatever machines were available. These appliances — quickly dubbed 'Green Goddesses' — were in many cases war vintage civil defence vehicles more primitive and less effective than the modern equipment abandoned in the fire stations by the striking firemen. About this equipment it was alleged, first, that the military fire-fighters were not trained for

[9] House of Commons Debates, 8 Dec. 1970, col. 251.

its use and, secondly, that the dispute might be exacerbated if troops were allowed to cross firemen's picket lines, enter fire stations, and seize the equipment against their will. On 17 November the Prime Minister, Mr James Callaghan, addressing himself to this point, said that he thought it unwise to endanger a possible settlement by 'rushing into the fire stations and dragging out equipment'. Endangering those whose houses were burning down because the equipment was immobilized seemed to have a lower priority. The Minister of Defence supported the Prime Minister. He thought that the specialized equipment could not be used with safety, though what precise forms of disaster the Minister envisaged was not clear.

The question of removing fire equipment from the fire stations remained a major issue. In some areas pickets tried to obstruct the troops or to block supplies to them. It was also suggested that senior fire officers might join the strike if the Government took over the fire station equipment. *The Times*, however, thought that the Government should not have hesitated to use it, the strikers having 'no right to deny it to the community'.[10]

The strike ended on 12 January 1978, having lasted for three months. Subsequently published insurance figures showed that the cost of fire damage to property was roughly twice that of the corresponding period in the previous twelve months (about £117m. as against £52m.). The evident unpopularity of the strike, together with the lack of sympathetic action by other unions or support by the Trades Union Congress were factors that helped to bring about a settlement. But a major part was undoubtedly the size and effectiveness of the effort by which the strikers were replaced. Approximately 30,000 firemen withdrew their services, but there were made available in the end about 20,000 troops whose work was assisted by 4,000 senior fire officers and many thousands of part-time firemen.

[10] *The Times*, 19 Nov. 1977.

Constitutional Implications

Although in the discussion of military aid to the civil power an obvious distinction can be made between the deployment of troops for the purposes of maintaining order and their use to maintain supplies and services, the foregoing recital of cases in which the armed forces have been called upon during industrial disputes shows that the two purposes may be closely connected. Indeed one can see that in a strike involving a number of powerful unions, the use of the army to replace strikers might lead to violent clashes between troops and pickets in which the second purpose would quickly involve the first. In fact nothing of the kind has happened in the United Kingdom since the 1920s and it can hardly be said that British governments have not been alive to the dangers.

From the constitutional point of view there is, however, a significant difference between law enforcement and the maintenance of supplies and services. The maintenance of law and order in Britain is primarily a matter for local police and magistrates, whereas decisions about the deployment of forces in an emergency are in effect the responsibility of the Cabinet and Prime Minister. There remain, therefore, some unresolved questions about the process by which order is maintained if civil resources prove insufficient in industrial or any other forms of disputes.

A decision as to the use of the armed services to maintain essential supplies and services rests undoubtedly in the hands of the government of the day. The Emergency Powers Act of 1964 (which re-enacted a Defence Regulation of 1939) provided that 'the Admiralty, the Army Council or the Air Council may by order authorise officers and men of her Majesty's naval, military and air forces under their respective control to be temporarily employed on agricultural work or such other work as may be approved, as being required work of national importance'. What work is of national importance or necessary to the survival of the community is a matter on which a wide range of political judgment is possible. A great many services are in the long run central or even vital to the survival of organized living, but in recent times the community has been expected to demonstrate its ability to survive without them for lengthy periods. Strikes by railwaymen, gas workers, water workers, refuse collectors, hospital workers, coal-miners, air traffic controllers, telephonists, bakers, and teachers provide familiar and continually extended interruptions to the continuity of life. Perhaps power supplies stand on their own on a higher level of necessity.

In 1977 some doubts were expressed about the use of troops in the firemen's strike on the ground that the Queen's Regulations authorized the use of troops in 'limited or local' emergency situations whereas the firemen's strike was not limited or local. It was also argued that troops could be used in civil situations on a national scale only so long as a state of emergency had been declared and approved by Parliament under the Emergency Powers legislation.

In fact, however, neither a declaration of a state of emergency nor approval by Parliament is necessary to the deployment of troops. Parliamentary approval is necessary for the making of emergency regulations during a state of emergency, but since the 1964 Emergency Powers Act itself provides authority for the employment of servicemen on 'urgent work of national importance' the wording of the Queen's Regulations could not have the effect of narrowing that authority. Requisitioning of vehicles and ships is also possible under statutory and prerogative powers without a state of emergency. (Such requisitioning powers were used without emergency legislation being invoked during the Falkland Islands hostilities in 1982.)

From time to time doubts have also been expressed as to whether orders to troops to perform non-military duties would be lawful orders. But these doubts also seem unfounded. It is true that under the Army Acts lawful orders must relate to military purposes, but what are military purposes is a matter (up to a point) for the Crown to determine. The deployment and use of the armed forces is a prerogative power at the disposal of the Crown[11] and there seems no reason why the Crown should need express authority to order troops to do what it is lawful for anyone to do (to fight fires, for example).

When we turn, however, from the maintenance of supplies

---

[11] *Chandler* v. *D.P.P.*, [1964] A.C. 763.

and services to the maintenance of public order, it is not so clear that the ultimate decision in all matters rests with the government. Here military intervention is to some degree governed by common law principles. The common law imposes on soldiers, as on every citizen, an obligation to come to the aid of the civil power when so required,[12] and even perhaps without being so required.[13] Traditionally the requirement of military assistance was made by the magistrates to the nearest military commander. Today in practice it is local Chief Constables who would be likely to assess the need for military intervention. Such a contingency might conceivably arise in the event of large-scale mass picketing outstripping the resources of the police. In the 1972 coal-miners' strike, police in both Birmingham and Glasgow were in fact outnumbered by pickets with the result that unlawful picketing prevented the removal of fuel to power stations. In Birmingham, 800 police − facing crowds amounting at times to 15,000 people − were unable to enforce the law. A call for military assistance in such a situation might face the government − particularly a Labour government − with a political and constitutional dilemma. It might be their fervent conviction that it would be unwise to allow the army to become involved in a conflict with trade unionists. But would it be proper for them to interfere with the common law obligations of the military? In 1910 the Home Office view had been that the troops must be sent if called for,[14] and there seems no reason to suppose that

---

[12] *R.* v. *Brown* (1841), Car. & M. 314; *Charge to the Bristol Grand Jury* (1932), 5 C. & P.261:3 State Trials (N.S.), 11. In the latter case Tindal CJ said 'The law acknowledges no distinction in this respect between the soldier and the private individual. If the one is bound to attend the call of the civil magistrate so is the other.' Cf. the *Report of the Select Committee on the Featherstone Riots* (Parliamentary Papers 1893-4, c. 7234). 'By the law of this country every one is bound to aid in the suppression of riotous assemblages . . . Officers and soldiers are under no special privileges and subject to no special responsibilities as regards this principle of the law. A soldier for the purpose of establishing civil order is only a citizen armed in a particular manner . . . when the call for help is made and a necessity for assistance from the military has arisen, to refuse such assistance is in law a misdemeanour.'

[13] Tindall CJ (loc. cit.,:above) added: 'The military subjects of the King, like his civil subjects, not only may, but are bound to do their utmost, *of their own authority* to prevent the perpetration of outrage, to put down riot and tumult and to preserve the lives and property of the people.' (Italics added.)

[14] Sir Edward Troup told the Permanent Under-Secretary of State for War

the basic position has changed. Lord Haldane's view as Secretary of State for War may be compared. 'The War Office', he said, 'has no discretion. We are in charge of a number of people who are citizens as well as soldiers and if they are requisitioned to assist the civil authority, then if it is necessary that they should assist and if they are required and if they cannot be done without, then they have to go.'[15]

Since the 1926 General Strike no troops have been employed in England, Scotland or Wales for purposes of maintaining order. In Northern Ireland since 1968, on the other hand, the Army has been constantly used in support of the civil power. These duties raise a further point about the political control of the armed forces in relation to common law obligations. The *Manual of Military Law*, in summarizing the principles involved in suppression of civil disorder, emphasizes the personal responsibility of the soldier, as a citizen in uniform, in preserving the peace. Soldiers as citizens, it rules, are bound to come to the aid of the civil power and to take such action as the circumstances demand 'even though the civil authority should give directions to the contrary'.[16] In an account of events in Belfast and Londonderry between 1969 and 1973, one retired military commander has complained that he and his colleagues were prevented by improper political directions from carrying out their duties to suppress disorder.[17] 'On 3 August 1969 [in Belfast] Mr Wolseley the Police Commissioner for Belfast told Lieutenant-Colonel J. Fletcher, Commanding Officer of the 2nd

(21 May 1910), 'Of course if the Mayor or Magistrates requisition them, they (the troops) must be ready to go.' (Randolph Churchill, *Winston Churchill*, vol. ii, p. 372).

[15] *Report of the Select Committee on the Employment of Military in Cases of Disturbance* (Parliamentary Papers, HC 236 (1908), para. 103). For the practice when military assistance to the police is necessary in emergencies caused by terrorist activities see *Report of the Metropolitan Police Commissioner for 1975* (Cmnd. 6496 (1976)).

[16] See *Manual of Military Law* (1968 edn.), pt. ii, sect. v. Cf. Lord Diplock's description of the common law position of the soldier in *Reference under s. 48A of the Criminal Appeal (Northern Ireland) Act (No. 1 of 1975)*, [1977] AC 105, 136.

[17] Robin Evelegh, *Peacekeeping in a Democracy: The Lessons of Northern Ireland* (1978). The author retired from the army in 1977 after serving as commander of an infantry battalion in Belfast in 1972-3.

Battalion, the Queen's Regiment, that all police reserves had been committed in Belfast and asked him for military assistance. Mr Wolseley received the reply from the Chief of Staff, Army Headquarters Northern Ireland, that the deployment of troops in his aid was a "political decision". No troops were deployed.'[18]

Eventually United Kingdom ministerial approval was given for the use of troops in Belfast on 15 August after two further weeks of mob violence and inter-sectarian rioting. Once the troops were deployed much law breaking was ignored. 'For nearly a year . . . the army accepted orders not to enforce the law in Londonderry . . . acting against the law on the orders of the Cabinet.'[19] Illegal marches, funerals, and no-go areas were ignored. Though Ministers, the author argues, may send troops to the scene of disorder, they have no constitutional power to use the chain of military command to order troops not to suppress civil disorder when they get there. Cabinet orders to the military not to intervene in a disorderly strike or to tolerate illegal processions are of no effect, and not only may but should be disregarded if in the opinion of the military commander at the scene of trouble his orders require him to contravene the general law.

As with the role of the police, there is a conflict here of two theories difficult to reconcile. If the common law position of troops in relation to the civil power is taken seriously it plainly conflicts with the practice of all recent British governments and with the assumption of direct accountability to the House of Commons. Textbook writers, under the rubric of 'Parliamentary Control of the Armed Forces', suggest that 'the tasks which are undertaken by the armed forces, the objectives which they are set and the manner in which they carry out these tasks and fulfil these objectives are matters for which the Government is accountable to Parliament'.[20] In the particular matter of a decision to use troops where a local police force is unable to control civil disturbance, it is now assumed that local magistrates would have no part in any attempt to requisition assistance

[18] Evelegh, p. 6.   [19] Evelegh, p. 17.
[20] E. C. S. Wade and G. Godfrey Phillips, *Constitutional and Administrative Law* (9th edn.), ed. A. W. Bradley, p. 383.

but that a Chief Constable would communicate with the Home Office, and the Home Secretary and the Secretary of State for Defence would take the decision to authorize military assistance.[21] If civil disorder were connected with strike activity or mass picketing the decision would be likely to involve other members of the Cabinet.

Clearly, the assumptions made by Lord Haldane, Sir Edward Troup, and the 1908 Commons Select Committee in its Report on *The Employment of Military in Cases of Disturbance*, are no longer held. Whatever the law is, and whether or not it has changed, the practice and the associated conventions plainly have. If the conventional rules are defensible, however, it may be that a change in the law is needed. This illustrates a point worth noting about the impact on law of convention. For the most part conventional rules modify legal rules by inhibiting in practice the exercise of lawful powers. They cannot, or should not, modify legal rules by permitting in practice the exercise of unlawful powers.

[21] See 909 HC Deb., col. 617 (1976).

X
The Rules of the Commonwealth

Nowhere has the impact of convention on constitutional law been clearer than in the relationships of the United Kingdom with the other member states of the Commonwealth. Though there is a background of statute and common law, many of the rules of the Commonwealth association are conventional in character. The principal convention was established by agreement and set out in the Balfour Declaration of 1926. The Declaration announced the existence of:

> autonomous communities within the British Empire equal in status, in no way subordinate one to another . . . though united by a common allegiance to the Crown and freely associated as members of the British Commonwealth of Nations.

At that time the communities of the Empire were not in law autonomous or equal in status, and were legally subordinate to the Imperial Parliament at Westminster. The nomenclature of the Commonwealth is also in many respects a matter of habit and convention. We are not even sure what to call it or how to name its parts. It is not now, as once it was, the British Commonwealth. Nor do we talk of Dominions, or of the Commonwealth and Empire. When did the British Empire disappear? It was present and voting at the end of the First World War, a member in fact of the League of Nations. Winston Churchill used to speak of the Commonwealth and Empire between 1939 and 1945. In the sense in which it was used in the Balfour Declaration the Empire disappeared between 1926 and 1931 when the newly autonomous parts became the 'Dominions', and the still subordinate parts were left with their various dependent technical labels. Some were 'Colonies'. Others were 'Protectorates', 'Protected States' or 'Trust Territories', though only the first were properly speaking part of the Crown's dominions (in the earlier imperial sense of the term). As a way of describing the fully independent Commonwealth countries the word

'Dominion' disappeared after the Second World War.[1] The equal and independent nation states then became 'member countries' or 'full members of the Commonwealth'. The Dominions Office gave way in 1947 to the Commonwealth Relations Office, and at about the same time it was discovered that the name of the Dominion of Canada was simply 'Canada'.[2]

The United Kingdom and the Commonwealth

Convention again — or something like it — has removed the former unity of the Commonwealth. Until 1947 unity was symbolized by the Crown, or possibly the Queen. The preamble to the Statute of Westminster in 1931 certainly alleged that there was a common allegiance to the Crown. But the supposedly common and undivided Crown raised a number of taxing queries. (Some were unanswerable. At one Dominion Conference in the 1920s, it was said that the lawyers had been asked to settle the question 'what happens to the Royal Prerogative in a Dominion if the king goes mad?') Could the Crown, it was asked, be at peace in one part of the King's realms and at war in another? (The answer in 1939 turned out to be 'yes'.) In any event the unity of common allegiance was broken in 1950 when India became a Republic but remained a member of the Commonwealth. For India's benefit there was conceived a remarkable piece of pragmatic nonsense, the Headship of the Commonwealth. Perhaps 'nonsense' puts the point too strongly; but the sense and meaning of the term is certainly obscure and uncertain. It is a position with no powers, prerogatives, or characteristics except that of being acknowledged by those who acknowledge it. Some Commonwealth countries, of course, retain the Queen as their Head of State and in each country her title is a matter of law. In 1952 the Canadian Government proclaimed Elizabeth II

---

[1] See F. R. Scott, 'The End of Dominion Status', (1945), 23 *Canadian Bar Review* 725 and K. C. Wheare, *The Statute of Westminster and Dominion Status* (5th edn. 1953), chap. 8.

[2] It always had been. S. 3 of the British North America Act, 1867, said that. 'The Provinces . . . shall form and be one Dominion under the name of Canada.'

'Supreme Liege Lady in and over Canada', but in the style and title adopted in 1953 she is simply 'Queen of Canada' as of the United Kingdom and of her other realms and territories in addition to being Head of the Commonwealth and Defender of the Faith. In 1953 South Africa, Pakistan, and Ceylon, not wishing the Queen to defend their faith, or else not thinking her capable of it, dispensed with this element in their acknowledgement of her title.

Perhaps the most striking change in the Commonwealth relationship is the virtual disappearance of the United Kingdom Crown and Parliament's former centrality of status. Though British statutes provided all the Commonwealth countries with the legal foundation for their Constitutions, a number of them preferred to adopt the fiction that their legal systems were home-grown. Where such a theory was contentious — as in Rhodesia — it was dubbed 'UDI'. Where done with Imperial approval and complicity, the more sonorous label 'autochthony' has been attached. Either is a repudiation of the central sovereign authority of Westminster. The other striking manifestation of that rejection is the thesis that membership of the Commonwealth is a matter for decision by all the members and not for the United Kingdom. Commonwealth monarchies that have adopted republican forms of government have applied for continuation of membership and have been given it by the Prime Ministers assembled at Commonwealth Conferences. South Africa followed the precedent of applying for continued membership on becoming a Republic in 1961. The attitudes of the other members, however, persuaded South Africa to withdraw its application. Entry to full membership may be from outside the Queen's realms and territories (as with Cyprus) or from inside, in which case independent status, which is a requirement of full membership, depends upon the action of the United Kingdom. If a newly independent territory were denied full membership, it could of course retain the Queen as its Head of State and maintain allegiance to the Crown. Secession of a member country does not require the assent of the members. Expulsion from membership is theoretically possible; but if the United Kingdom were expelled some amendment of the Royal Titles Act, 1953 would no doubt be necessary.

In the past decade one important convention previously adopted by the Commonwealth Prime Ministers has clearly changed. In 1960 Mr Robert Menzies, the Australian Prime Minister, remarked that 'the Prime Ministers' Conference would break up in disorder if we affected to discuss and decide what we thought to be the proper measure of democracy in our various countries'. The members, he said, were not a tribunal sitting in judgment or publicly ventilating intra-Commonwealth grievances. In recent years, however, this convention seems to have been allowed to lapse by mutual disagreement.

In most respects, therefore, relations between the member countries of the Commonwealth resemble those between independent nation states. But there remain some formal relationships between them, and the Government and Parliament of the United Kingdom. The United Kingdom Parliament provided all of them with their Constitutions and in some cases has had until very recently a part to play in their legal processes. A crucial turning-point was the Statute of Westminster in 1931 which gave legal force to the convention of equal status, empowering Australia, Canada, New Zealand, the Irish Free State, and South Africa to exercise sovereign powers of amendment over their own constitutions. Canada and Australia, however, were federal states with legislatures at the centre and at the state or provincial level. In Canada the British Parliament was retained as part of the constitutional amendment process; and until the passage of the Canada Act in 1982 changes in the structure of the federal system still required an Act of the Westminster Parliament. Some changes affecting the states of the Commonwealth of Australia also still require British legislation as would any alteration of the fundamental federal Commonwealth association (as, for example, by secession of one or more of the states). In theory of course (British theory that is), the United Kingdom Parliament could repeal the entire Constitutions of New Zealand, and Australia, reducing them to colonial status, or legislate for both countries without their consent. There being no legal requirement in the Statute of Westminster that the actual consent of a Dominion should precede the enactment of legislation extending to it, the rule that the United Kingdom Parliament does not exercise its powers in such a fashion is an unstated but fundamental United Kingdom convention.[3]

Two vestigial links between the United Kingdom and the Queen's Commonwealth realms are the Privy Council and the Governors-General. Though the Judicial Committee of the Privy Council hears appeals from the dependent territories, almost all the independent Commonwealth countries have abolished appeals. The Australian states until 1986 enjoyed the right of appeal by special leave, and unlike the Canadian provinces could still be said to be 'self-governing dependencies of the British Crown'.[4] State Governors were thus still appointed by the Queen (of the United Kingdom, not Australia) on the advice of United Kingdom Ministers.

Ministers and Governors-General

As to the position of the Governors-General there remain some uncertainties. By convention a Governor-General is not the representative of the United Kingdom Government but of the Queen. Since 1930 the rule[5] has been that he is appointed on the advice of the Government of the Commonwealth country concerned, but it is not perhaps quite clear whether (in Australia, for example) local Ministers are advising the Queen of Australia or the Queen of the United Kingdom. The Queen referred to in the Federal Constitution is presumably Her Majesty as Queen of Australia and it must be she whose representative the Governor-General is. It would also seem to be in that capacity that she would act if advised by Commonwealth Ministers to remove a Governor-General from office, though the only precedent occurred in 1932 when the Governor-General of the then Irish Free

---

[3] In s. 2 of the Canada Act, 1982, it is provided that no future Act of the Parliament of the United Kingdom shall extend to Canada as part of its law after the coming into force of the Canadian Constitution Act, 1981. This is a purported termination of the British Parliament's power of legislation and similar provisions have been embodied in other independence legislation in the post-war period. (See chap. XII below).

[4] Memorandum by the Foreign and Commonwealth Office to the Foreign Affairs Committee, HC 42 I and II (1981), p. 135. See now Australia Act 1986.

[5] These rules originated in declarations made at the Dominion Conferences of 1926 and 1930 (Cmd. 2768 (1926), p. 16 and Cmd. 3717 (1930), p. 27).

State was removed at the instance of Mr de Valera. The point might have been of some importance in November 1975 when the Governor-General of Australia dismissed Mr Gough Whitlam and his Government in order to resolve a parliamentary deadlock between the two Houses. If Mr Whitlam had thought such a development likely, and anticipated the Governor-General's action by advising the Queen to dismiss Sir John Kerr from his office as Governor-General, the Queen would have faced a difficult decision. It seems to have been thought in 1932 that there was no choice but to comply with the de Valera Government's advice. But on that occasion no significant constitutional disagreement between Ministers and the Governor-General was in issue. It is true that the Queen must behave in relation to her Commonwealth Ministers as she would in relation to her United Kingdom Ministers, acting in general on their advice. But in this case there is no comparable United Kingdom issue. Nor can it be settled by appeal to the principle that there should be no imperial interference in Commonwealth affairs since it is assumed that the Queen's action would not be taken as Queen of the United Kingdom. The conclusion must be that the removal of a Governor-General is a personal prerogative to be exercised on the Queen's responsibility as Queen of the Commonwealth country concerned, and in principle it would seem that she would not in every case be bound to accept advice to dismiss. As with ministerial advice on dissolution, it would be a matter of assessing the issue and the political consequences of a refusal to act. The situation differs from any comparable problem in that a tactical delay to consider the advice would permit the Governor-General to exercise the power of dismissal, and remove the Ministers before their advice could be acted on.

In 1975 a letter was addressed by the Queen's private secretary to the Speaker of the Australian House of Representatives after the Queen's intervention had been sought to restore Mr Whitlam to office. The letter concluded:

As we understand the situation here the Australian constitution firmly places the prerogative power of the Crown in the hands of the Governor General as the representative of the Queen of Australia. The only person competent to commission an Australian Prime Minister is the Governor General and the Queen has no part in the decisions which the Governor-General must take in accordance with the Constitution. Her Majesty as Queen of Australia is watching events in Canberra with close interest and attention, but it would not be proper for her to intervene in person on matters which are so clearly placed within the jurisdiction of the Governor General by the Constitution Act.[6]

Some points of interest appear in this letter. In the first place it appears to be written by command of the Queen as Queen of Australia, and not as Queen of the United Kingdom of Great Britain and Northern Ireland. Secondly, its contents illustrate the necessity of distinguishing clearly between law and convention, and between prerogative and statutory powers. It is asserted, for example, that the Australian Constitution places the prerogative power of the Crown in the hands of the Governor-General. Section 64 of the Constitution certainly makes statutory provision for the appointment of Ministers and states that they shall hold office during the pleasure of the Governor-General. Perhaps therefore these powers are not properly classifiable as prerogative powers (as they would be in the United Kingdom). Section 61 of the Constitution provides that the Queen's powers are 'exercisable' by the Governor-General, but it vests the executive power of the Commonwealth in the Queen (as Queen of Australia) and not in the Governor-General. So when it is asserted that the Queen has 'no part in the decisions that the Governor General must take' and that the Constitution places these powers firmly in his hands, the assertions perhaps must be understood as statements of constitutional convention, not law. 'The executive power of the Commonwealth', in relation to prerogative or executive powers other than appointment and dismissal of Ministers is not by the Constitution conferred on the Governor-General[7] and not all of it is exercisable by the Governor-General as her representative, since it obviously does not include the power of removal and appointment of the Governor-General himself. That power can only be exercised by the Queen, both in law and in practice. But

[6] The text of the letter was released for publication on 24 November 1975. It is reproduced in full in Sir John Kerr, *Matters for Judgment* (1978), at pp. 374-5.

[7] S. 61 reads: 'The executive power of the Commonwealth is vested in the Queen and is exercisable by the Governor-General as the Queen's representative.'

as to the powers of appointment and dismissal of Ministers, the letter sent to the Australian Speaker in 1975 seems accurately to represent the terms of the Constitution Act and also the convention that Governors-General and Governors, once appointed, exercise their powers on their own responsibility. That assumption, however, developed historically on a rather different basis, namely from the cessation of the practice of issuing instructions or advice by *British Ministers* to Dominion Governors and Governors-General.[8] In itself it does not provide an entirely firm basis for the rule that the Queen as Queen of Australia must never exercise any of the powers vested in her by the Constitution; though other grounds of principle or prudence may support such a convention.

In Canada the exercise of the Queen's prerogative powers by the Governor-General rests on law rather than convention. The British North America Act, 1867 (now the Constitution Act, 1867), like the Australian Constitution, vests the executive government of Canada in the Queen, but the office of Governor-General was constituted by letters patent which, as revised in 1947, authorize the Governor-General, either with the advice of the Privy Council for Canada or individually, to exercise all powers and authorities lawfully belonging to the Queen in respect of Canada, and in particular to appoint or remove Ministers and other office-holders; and to exercise the powers of summoning, proroguing and dissolving Parliament. The only power and authority not conferred on the Governor-General in respect of Canada would, therefore, seem to be the Queen's power as Queen of Canada to appoint and remove the Governors-General (together with the power to revoke the letters patent).[9] Even stronger

---

[8] Cf. L. S. Amery, *Thoughts on the Constitution* (2nd edn. 1953), p. 7. 'In the Dominions that authority . . . has in our time ceased to be exercised with reference to advice from a Secretary of State in London and is exercised solely on the personal judgement and discretion of the Governor General or Governor on his ultimate responsibility to the nation or State concerned.' Amery quotes his own statement in the House of Commons as Dominions Secretary (on 15 Mar. 1926) that 'it would not be proper for the Secretary of State to issue instructions to the Governor with regard to the exercise of his constitutional duties'.

[9] The instrument provides that 'We do hereby reserve to ourselves, our heirs and successors, full power and authority from time to time to revoke, alter or amend these Our Letters Patent as to Us or them shall seem meet.' (*Letters Patent constituting the Office of Governor-General of Canada* (1947).

grounds exist, therefore, in Canada than in Australia for resisting any appeal for Royal intervention to reverse a decision of the Governor-General that brings him into conflict with his Ministers.

The Statute of Westminster Conventions

Writing in 1937 Richard Latham said that in each of the Dominions the common law shone separately, but their relations with each other were 'shrouded in a mist of convention'. 'The Statute of Westminster', he added, 'is all that there is of the Commonwealth in law and it is not very much.'[10]

Yet even the central provision of the Statute of 1931 depended curiously in the end on the operation of convention rather than law. The effects of conferring unlimited legislative powers on the Parliaments of each Dominion raised separate problems in each. The agreed aim of the Statute of Westminster was to remove the ties of the Colonial Laws Validity Act, and the subordination of the Dominions as communities to the United Kingdom and to the sovereignty of the Imperial Parliament. It was not intended, nor did any Dominion wish it, to change the internal working of the Dominion Constitutions. In the Federal Dominions of Canada and Australia saving clauses were inserted into the Statute to prevent the Federal Parliaments from acquiring any additional powers to amend the British North America Acts or the Commonwealth of Australia Constitution Act at the expense of the Australian states and Canadian provinces. The Federal Parliaments of each country were restrained by the Statute itself from removing the restraints imposed by their existing internal Constitution Acts; and a similar saving clause protected the Constitution of New Zealand.

In two of the non-federal dominions, however, namely South Africa and the Irish Free State, no saving clauses were requested. Despite misgivings in the British Parliament, it was agreed that the wishes of the Irish and South African

[10] 'The Law and the Commonwealth' (in *Survey of British Commonwealth Affairs*, ed. W. K. Hancock, 1937, at p. 513).

Governments and Parliaments not to have any hindrances placed on the full sovereign legislative power given by the Statute should be complied with. In each case assurances were given that the existing internal constitutional amendment procedures would be respected. In South Africa resolutions of both Houses of Parliament authorized the Government to request British legislation 'on the understanding that the proposed legislation will in no way derogate from the entrenched provisions of the South Africa Act (the constitution act of the Union).' The Hertzog Government stated that there was no question of the entrenched provisions in the Constitution[11] ceasing to constitute a binding obligation on successive Parliaments. In other words the maintenance of the existing constitutional position rested on a convention that the newly agreed sovereign power of Parliament in the Dominion would not be abused. Similar assurances were given by Mr Cosgrave's Government in the Irish Free State that guarantees contained in the Irish Free State Treaty would not be changed. 'The solemnity of this instrument in our eyes' (Mr Cosgrave stated) 'could not derive any additional strength from a Parliamentary law.'[12] In 1935, however, the Irish Treaty was abrogated, and in 1956, after a long constitutional struggle,[13] the South African entrenched clauses were removed and the Constitution changed by a simple majority of the South African Parliament.[14]

[11] The entrenched provisions protected voting rights and required certain franchise disqualifications based on race or colour to be enacted by special two-thirds majorities in a joint session of both Houses.

[12] Letter to Mr Ramsay MacDonald cited by Lord Salisbury in the Lords debate on the Statute of Westminster. 183 HL Deb., cols. 190, 191 (1931).

[13] See 'South Africa: the Courts and the Constitution' in Marshall, *Parliamentary Sovereignty and the Commonwealth* (1957), chap. 11.

[14] The Statute of Westminster (s. 2) empowered Dominion Parliaments to legislate repugnantly to the law of England and to repeal any United Kingdom Act of Parliament in its application to the Dominion. In 1952 the South African courts held that the special majority provisions still bound the Parliament of South Africa when acting to amend the entrenched provisions in the South Africa Act: *Harris v. Minister of the Interior* (1952), (2) SA 428; but the Government outmanoeuvred the entrenchment by enlarging the Senate by a simple majority change in the electoral system, thus producing a two-thirds legislative majority for constitutional amendment. After an enlargement of the Supreme Court the amended legislation was upheld: *Collins v. Minister of the Interior* (1957), (1) S.A. 552 A.D.

Thus the British gift of sovereignty conveyed in s. 2 of the 1931 statute had built into it an inherent and continuing constitutional uncertainty, since the legal instrument by which it was conveyed failed to provide clearly for the manner and form of its exercise.

Despite the attempt to deal in the Statute of Westminster with the federal difficulties of Australia and Canada by specific saving clauses, an uncertainty in the operation of constitutional convention led there also to major political controversy and crisis. The uncertainty in these cases was as to the conditions under which the powers of the United Kingdom Parliament would continue to be used for Dominion purposes. Section 4 of the Statute of Westminster specifically preserved the power to legislate for a Dominion, though declaring that no British Act of Parliament should extend to a Dominion as part of its law unless it should be expressly declared in the Act that the Dominion had requested and consented to its enactment. But the significance of s. 4 of the Statute depended crucially upon convention. In Australia's case the request and consent were defined as meaning the request and consent of the Government and Parliament of the Dominion, but no attempt was made in s. 4 or in the similar declaration in the preamble to the Statute of Westminster to determine the conditions under which such requests should be made in the Dominion or met in the United Kingdom. That remained a complex problem of convention, both within the Commonwealth countries and in their relations with the British Government and Parliament.

XI
The Problem of Patriation

The constitutional struggle to 'patriate' and amend the Constitution of Canada, which came to a head in 1980-2, raised a crucial question of convention for the British Parliament about its role as a Commonwealth legislator. The exercise of such a role by Parliament derived from the fact that major constitutional amendment in Canada required legislation at Westminster, enacted at Canadian request, to amend the British North America Act of 1867 which could not (except in certain ways) be amended in Canada. After 1931 all such requests for further amendments to the British North America Acts had been complied with; and when such amendments took place it could be supposed that, conventionally, if not legally, the members of the United Kingdom Parliament were acting not as the British legislature but as part of the Canadian constitutional process under the form of legislation envisaged in the request and consent provisions of the Statute of Westminster.

The Patriation Problem

The British Parliament's continued role in Canada's constitutional machinery, preserved at Canada's request in the Statute of Westminster, was accepted somewhat reluctantly and as a temporary expedient in 1931, and it was subsequently made clear that Canada could 'patriate' its Constitution at any time by promoting legislation in Britain that would provide for all future constitutional amendment of the British North America Acts to take place in Canada (just as amendments to the Constitution of Australia took place in Australia). The 'patriation' of the Constitution simply meant the passing of a final agreed British North America Act at Westminster, designed to vest future amendment powers in some body of legislators in Canada.

Unhappily, persistent federal–provincial differences after

1931 prevented for fifty years any agreement in Canada on an amendment formula that could be incorporated by agreement in such an Act. So transfer to Canada of full legal control over its Constitution was postponed, and Federal-Provincial conferences or discussions failed to agree on an amending formula in 1927, 1936, 1950, 1961, 1964, 1971, 1976, and 1979. In February of 1980 the Liberal Party regained office in Canada and Mr Pierre Trudeau as Prime Minister indicated that the Government would patriate the Constitution, if necessary without the support of the ten provinces, or an agreed amendment formula; and at the same time would enact a Charter of Rights that would bind both the provinces and the Federal Government. A joint resolution would be placed before each House of the Canadian Parliament incorporating the Charter of Rights and an amendment to the British North America Act that would provide for future constitutional change to take place in Canada. The resolution would then be forwarded to Westminster for enactment as a final British North America Act.

The British Government had already been informed of the Canadian Government's intentions and in October 1980 two of Mr Trudeau's Ministers were sent to London to explain the patriation proposals and to emphasize the need for enactment of the Canadian resolutions by July of 1981 (the fiftieth anniversary of the Statute of Westminster). Meetings were held with the Prime Minister and Foreign Secretary, and the Ministers also had an audience with the Queen. It is not known what precise assurances they were given, but it later became clear that the Canadian Prime Minister had received an undertaking that the British Government would seek to secure the passage of the Canada Bill as soon as it was transmitted from Ottawa.

In Parliament the Lord Chancellor when questioned about the Government's intentions repeated the substance of a reply already given to questioners in the Commons in the previous year, namely that 'if a request to patriate the Canadian Constitution were to be received *from the Parliament of Canada* it would be in accordance with precedent for the Government to introduce into Parliament and for Parliament to enact appropriate legislation complying with that request'.[1]

Neither the Canadian nor the British Government, however, appeared to contemplate any constitutional difficulty in procuring British legislation to enact the patriation proposal and the Charter of Rights. The proposals were introduced into the Canadian House of Commons in October 1980 and committed to a Joint Committee of the House of Commons and Senate. The Federal Government made it plain that when the constitutional package was complete they expected the British Government and Parliament to pass the legislation without question or amendment.[2] It became clear very quickly, however, that provincial opposition in Canada was on a scale unprecedented in the history of amending the British North America Act. Eight of the ten Provinces opposed the Federal Government's proposals and a number of provincial Attorneys-General began legal actions to test their constitutionality.

Proceedings were begun in Manitoba, Quebec, and Newfoundland and it seemed likely that the Supreme Court of Canada would eventually hear appeals from each of the provincial courts. At Westminster the Foreign Affairs Committee of the House of Commons stated its intention to hold an inquiry and report to the House on the constitutional responsibilities of Parliament in relation to the British North America Acts, and a large amount of written evidence was placed before it by the governments of the dissenting provinces. The Canadian Federal Government was invited through the Canadian High Commission to provide evidence for the Committee but declined to do so, considering it 'inappropriate for the executive government of one nation to offer advice to a committee of the Parliament of another nation'.

The Conventions and the Precedents

In their public references to acting in accordance with precedent in complying with a Canadian request for legislation, British Ministers showed no awareness of the possibility that there might be a difference between legislating in

[1] House of Lords Debates, 27 Oct. 1980 (Italics added.)

[2] Mr Trudeau's graphic phrase was that they should, if necessary, hold their noses and enact the Bill.

accordance with the wishes of Canada and legislating in accordance with the wishes of the Federal Government and Parliament of Canada. That difference is easily over-looked in an unitary state with a sovereign Parliament. Subsequently much use was made of the sentiment that the proposals of a sovereign independent nation could not be made the subject of debate at Westminster. But though a national government in a federal state may rep-resent the nation in its external relations and foreign policy, it does not in the same way represent the nation or exercise sovereign authority in relation to the process of internal legislation or constitutional amendment.

This was not a novel point, raised for the first time in 1980. The question whether the British Parliament could properly look behind a request for legislation from the Parliament of a Dominion, and possibly decline to follow it if opposed by the provincial or state authorities had been discussed in the 1930s after the passage of the Statute of Westminster,[3] and been debated both in relation to Canada and other Commonwealth countries.[4] But it was particularly crucial in the Canadian federal system, as was recognized in 1949 when the British North America Act (No. 2) of 1949 was passed to give the Federal Parliament power to amend the BNA Act in matters affecting the federal sphere, but excluding matters assigned by the Constitution to the Provinces. Other reservations were also written into the 1949 Act, including a prohibition on extending the life of Parliament, except by two-thirds vote, in time of war or insurrection. In the Canadian House of Commons the Prime Minister, Mr St-Laurent, was asked whether there might be a danger of suspending this protection by a simple ma-jority address asking for a British amendment. The reply was that it would be legally possible but that the sense of

[3] K. C. Wheare, *The Statute of Westminster and Dominion Status* (5th edn.), p. 180. Wheare's view was that 'although the United Kingdom Parliament was bound by Convention not to alter the (BNA) Act without the request and consent of the Dominion Government and (usually) Parliament, it was not bound by convention to alter the Act if and when the Dominion Government and Parlia-ment requested it'. Cf. W. S. Livingston, *Federalism and Constitutional Change* (1956), chap. 2.

[4] G. Marshall, *Parliamentary Sovereignty and the Commonwealth* (1957), pp. 90-4.

responsibility of the Canadian nation might stand in the way.[5] One of Canada's most eminent constitutional lawyers, Professor Frank Scott, commenting on this episode, said that Mr St-Laurent could have gone further and suggested that the United Kingdom Parliament might well have refused to follow such a joint address.[6]

In 1980, however, the Federal authorities in Canada prepared and published a paper setting out their view of the constitutional position. Its conclusion was that:

The British Parliament or Government may not look behind any federal request for amendment, including a request for patriation of the Canadian Constitution. Whatever role the Canadian provinces might play in constitutional amendments is a matter of no consequence as far as the UK Government and Parliament are concerned.[7]

That view was an understandable one for the Canadian Government to take, since on a number of occasions between 1940 and 1979, British Ministers had made statements in the House of Commons that clearly implied that there was a practice of automatic action at the request of the Federal authorities and both Mrs Thatcher and Lord Carrington and their predecessors in office had probably acted on that belief in the assurances that they had given to Canadian Ministers.

The origins of this ministerial belief, however, were of some interest, as an illustration of the role of precedent in the making of conventions. It had been stated initially in 1940 in relation to a proposed amendment of the British North America Act involving unemployment insurance to which there was no provincial opposition.[8] The question had never been the subject of any detailed Parliamentary consideration or debate, and it could be argued that the

[5] Canada House of Commons Debates, 20 Oct. 1949.
[6] 'The British North America (No. 2) Act, 1949', in F. R. Scott, *Essays on the Constitution* (1977), p. 206.
[7] *Department of External Affairs Memorandum, 2 October 1980.* Repr. in HC 362, xxii (1979–80).
[8] In 1940 the Solicitor-General (Sir William Jowitt) said 'I do not know what the view of the Provincial Parliament is . . . It is a sufficient justification for the Bill that we are morally bound to act on the ground that we have the request of the Dominion Parliament and that we must operate the old machinery which has been left over at their request and in accordance with their interests.' (362 HC Deb. 5s., cols. 1180–1 (10 July 1940).)

early ministerial statements had been simply repeated in much the same form by successive Ministers, who had themselves, understandably enough, not devoted much independent thought to the British North America Act or to the nature of Federal Government.

A contrary view could be stated, therefore, drawing a different conclusion from the series of British amending acts, namely:

1. That objections by one or two Provinces had not been allowed to stand in the way of amendments that did not affect the Federal-Provincial balance of legislative powers or the rights or powers of Provincial Governments or legislatures.
2. That requests for amendment of the BNA Act by Provinces without the support of the Federal Government would not be received.

No series of precedents could therefore be said to have established a convention for acting automatically upon a Federal request for an amendment that clearly *did* affect the Federal-Provincial balance of powers and the legislative powers of the Provinces, when that amendment was opposed by a substantial number of Provinces (and in this case a majority of Provinces). Nor had there been any previous occasion when a statute had been enacted at the request and consent of Canada when a majority of the Provinces of Canada were attempting to establish their rights to object to it in the Canadian courts.

It is worth noting that, although there had not until 1980 been any real consideration in Britain of the problem of disputed amendments to the British North America Act, the issue had in fact been discussed in Canada, and a White Paper[9] tabled in the Canadian House of Commons in 1965 had set out four general principles that it was said 'had come to be recognised and accepted in practice as part of the amendment process in Canada'. Principles (1), (2), and (3) were uncontroversial (namely that British action should be taken only upon formal request from Canada; that the

---

[9] *The Amendment of the Constitution of Canada* (Queen's Printer, Ottawa, 1965). Repr. in HC 42 1 and 11 (1980-1) at pp. 279-300. (Italics added.)

procedure for signifying request should be in the form of a joint address from the Canadian Senate and House of Commons; and that a Province could not secure an amendment merely upon its own request[10]). The fourth principle, however, stated that:

The Canadian Parliament will not request an amendment *directly affecting federal-provincial relationships without prior consultation and agreement* with the provinces.

But what connection, it might be asked, could be held to exist between that Canadian convention (supposing it to be such) and the convention to be followed in Britain when Parliament was faced by a Federal request for legislation affecting provincial rights but lacking provincial approval? Some Canadian constitutional authorities did in fact argue that the two issues were connected on the implicit grounds that in amending the Constitution of Canada, the British Parliament was in effect acting, with Canada's consent, as part of Canada's constitutional amendment mechanism. Professor Paul Gérin-Lajoie, the author of the leading work on Canadian constitutional amendment, held that the Westminster Parliament had an obligation to concern itself with the working of the constitutional amendment process as a whole. ('Sur réception d'une demande d'amendement, Londres doit donc s'assurer avant d'agir que cette demande est faite conformément aux règles constitutionelles du Canada.')[11] Britain, he suggested, should not act on a Canadian request unless it could be seen to represent 'la collectivité canadienne'. Another constitutional authority, Professor W. R. Lederman, had also written that 'I do not think the present convention permits the British Government and British Parliament to override any provincial dissent' (where amendments affect the distribution of powers). 'In the face of any provincial dissent', he went on, 'I think the present convention requires that the British Government and Parliament do nothing, simply regarding the request from the

---

[10] See also Eugene E. Forsey, 'Provincial Requests for Amendments to the BNA Act', (1966-7) 12 *McGill Law Journal* 397.
[11] 'Du Pouvoir d'Amendement Constitutionnel au Canada', 29 *Canadian Bar Review* 1136, at 1156. See the same writer's *Constitutional Amendment in Canada* (1950).

Canadian Parliament in these circumstances as improper.'[12] That was the view now also apparently taken by a majority of Canada's Provincial Governments.

The Statute of Westminster Provisions

The implication of these arguments was that the part played by Britain in Canada's amendment process was not an anachronistic survival of Imperial legislative authority, but a continuing role undertaken at the instance of Canada and given to it of set purpose in 1931 jointly by both provincial and federal authorities. That role flowed from the transactions that preceded the enactment of the Statute of Westminster. The mechanism employed in the Statute to confer legal equality of status on the Dominions took the form of empowering the Parliaments of each Dominion to repeal any existing or future British Act of Parliament in its application to the Dominions. That power (contained in s. 2 of the Statute) would, as we have seen,[13] if inserted without qualification, have given the Federal Parliaments in both Canada and Australia an apparently unrestricted authority to repeal or amend their own Constitution Acts, since these were British Acts of Parliament (the BNA Acts and the Commonwealth of Australia Constitution Act, 1900). Thus the Canadian and Australian Federal Parliaments would have been given *carte blanche* to overturn the federal division of powers. Both the provincial and federal authorities in each country in 1931 did not wish that to be possible and asked for the insertion of the crucial saving clauses in ss. 7-9 of the Statute of Westminster to preserve the Constitution Acts themselves from the scope of the new power to repeal British statutes and to legislate repugnantly to the law of England. At the same time, s. 4 of the Statute retained the mechanism by which a British enactment might extend as part of Dominion law at the request and consent of the Dominion.[14] So the British Parliament's

---

[12] 'The Process of Constitutional Amendment for Canada', 12 *McGill Law Journal* 371 at 379.
[13] Above, chap. X.
[14] Though the enactment of amendments to the BNA Act since 1931 has not

power to amend the BNA Act was retained by consent, to be exercised when Canada should so request.

The procedure adopted for forwarding Canadian requests for British legislation was by resolution of the Federal Parliament. That mechanism was of course familiar in 1931 since it had been established for sixty years. No one at that time supposed that it could properly be used by the Federal authorities to evade the protection that had been inserted in s. 7 of the Statute of Westminster precisely to prevent the Federal Parliament from unilaterally changing the existing constitutional balance and the rights of the Provinces. The British Parliament, in other words, was given a protective role in its amending process by Canada. But Canada would have been wasting its time if it had intended the British Parliament unquestioningly to carry out the requests and resolutions of the Federal Parliament to enact in Britain amendments to the BNA Act that it could not bring about in Canada on its own legislative authority.

A parallel could be drawn with Australia. There also the request and consent of Australia for any British legislation was signified by the Parliament and Government of the Commonwealth. But Australia already had a local constitutional amendment process involving a majority vote of both electors and states in a referendum. Legally speaking the Australian Federal Government and Parliament could request British legislation for Australia. But equally Australia in 1931 could hardly have intended that procedure to give a licence to the Federal authorities to obtain a Constitutional amendment at Westminster that they could not procure through the constitutional referendum mechanism in Australia. In fact the only unilateral request to have come from Australia has been from the side of the Australian states.

been governed by the request and consent requirement of s. 4 of the Statute of Westminster (since by s. 7 nothing in the Statute of Westminster – including the request and consent provisions of s. 4 – is to apply to the amendment of the BNA Acts, 1867 to 1930). So for that purpose the position remained as it was, the request and consent of Canada in relation to BNA Act amendments being enjoined by the convention existing before 1931 (mentioned in the Statute of Westminster preamble), and not by the legal requirement of the Statute itself. The recitals of Westminster BNA Act amendments have not in fact consistently embodied the express recital of Canada's request and consent.

A British Committee of both Houses[15] was set up in 1935 to consider a request for secession legislation for Western Australia, but declined to recommend British action, saying that Parliament should act only at the request of the Dominion 'speaking with the voice that represents it as a whole'.

That principle was a general one that would rule out unilateral requests by either Federal or state authorities for legislation that affected the interests of the other. The Australian states have on more than one occasion complained about Federal approaches to the British Government. In 1973 all the states set out their views in a memorandum asserting that 'the Government and Parliament of the United Kingdom are constitutionally bound to consider the wishes of the Governments of the States when faced with a request by the Commonwealth upon a matter which is primarily one of concern to the States'.[16]

The British North America Act 1949

Some reinforcement of this conclusion could be derived from a consideration of the British North America (No. 2) Act of 1949 and its interpretation by the Canadian courts. The British amendment of 1949 gave to the Federal Parliament the power to amend the Constitution of Canada except in matters falling within the classes of subjects reserved to the Provinces and certain other matters guaranteed in the British North America Act. It was interpreted as a measure to enable the Federal Parliament to make amendments to the Constitution without recourse to the British Parliament in so far as they affected the Federal Government itself.

Subsequently to 1949 the Parliament of Canada enacted the British North America Acts 1952, 1965, No. 2 of 1974, 1975, and No. 2 of 1975. It was acknowledged that none of this legislation affected Federal–Provincial relationships since they all dealt in various ways with the constitution of

[15] HL 75, HC 88 (1935).
[16] Cf. *Ukley* v. *Ukley* [1977] V.R. 121, 129 (Supreme Court of Victoria). 'In our view it cannot be doubted that in these times the Parliament at Westminster would not legislate so as to affect the law in operation in an Australian State except at the request of and with the consent of the State concerned.'

the Canadian Senate and House of Commons. The Supreme Court of Canada described them in 1979 as 'measures which according to the practice existing before 1949 would have been referred to the British Parliament by way of a joint resolution of both Houses and *without the consent of the provinces*'.[17] By contrast, a proposal to abolish the Senate would, in the Court's opinion, affect Federal-Provincial relationships and would have required United Kingdom action. By implication it would not have been under the established practice referred to the British Parliament without the consent of the Provinces. The practice referred to, and set out in the opinion of the court, was that in the 1965 Canadian White Paper, the relevant principle being Principle Four which, as already noted, recited that 'the Federal Parliament will not request an amendment directly affecting . federal-provincial relationships without prior consultation and agreement with the provinces'.

A distinction could be seen, therefore, between the position before and after 1949. Before 1949 some British amendments to the BNA Act did not affect federal-provincial relationships, and did not for that reason fall within the provincial agreement requirement of Principle Four of the 1965 White Paper. After 1949 such amendments did not require British action at all since they could be enacted in Canada by the Federal Parliament. All amendments that did require British action after 1949 could be presumed to affect either reserved matters or Federal-Provincial relationships or provincial rights to which Principle Four related.

The Kershaw Reports

The terms of reference of the House of Commons Foreign Affairs Committee (under the Chairmanship of Sir Anthony Kershaw) drawn up by itself, were to study the role of the United Kingdom Parliament in relation to the British North America Acts. They appointed as special adviser to the

---

[17] *Reference by the Governor in Council concerning the legislative authority of the Parliament of Canada in relation to the Upper House*, [1980] 1 S.C.R. 54 at 65; [1979] 102 D.L.R. (3d) 1 at 8 (italics added).

Committee Dr J. F. Finnis (Reader in the Laws of the British Commonwealth and the United States, and Fellow of University College, Oxford), and they addressed a questionnaire to the Foreign and Commonwealth Office seeking to elicit a view on the conventions governing the British Parliament's role as a Commonwealth legislature. The Foreign Office's answers were carefully drawn and non-committal. Asked if in their view the general principles set out in the Canadian White Paper of 1965 on constitutional amendment accurately represented the constitutional position, they replied that they 'had no reason to question that the statement was a fair reflection of Canadian governmental views at that time'. In the light of the position that British Ministers had implicitly taken, the Foreign Office's caution was comprehensible. The same reticence was maintained by Mr Nicholas Ridley, Minister of State at the Foreign Office, when he appeared before the Committee. He was not willing to say what the Foreign Office thought the conventions were; but the Government's position was that they would act in accordance with them when a request for legislation was received from Canada.

The non-governmental witnesses examined by the Committee, however, all suggested that there was no British convention that required automatic compliance with requests for British legislation that would affect provincial rights and that was not approved by the Provinces. Various suggestions were made as to possible courses of action. One was that the Government should arrange with the Canadian Federal Government to have the issues referred for an advisory opinion to the Supreme Court of Canada.[18] Another was that Parliament should take no action in the face of substantial provincial objection but seek to be guided in formulating the British convention by the constitutional practice of Canada as declared in the forthcoming decisions of the Canadian courts.[19]

[18] See the evidence of Professor H. W. R. Wade: HC 42, 1 and 11 (1980–1) at 113. In December 1980 a senior British Minister was sent to Ottawa to urge this course but without success.
[19] Evidence of Mr G. Marshall. HC 42 1 and 11 (1980–1) at p. 101. Cf. the evidence of Mr E. Lauterpacht QC, ibid., at p. 116. 'The amendment of the Canadian Constitution is a matter in which there are three participants: the Federal Parliament, the Provinces and the United Kingdom Parliament (here acting in effect as an organ of Canadian constitutional machinery).'

The report of the Committee appeared on 30 January 1980. It argued that the central issue of principle was the federal character of Canada's Constitution. The Committee accepted the view that in exercising its responsibilities as part of the process of Canadian constitutional amendment the British Parliament should take account of the federal structure and not accede automatically to a request for amendment or patriation from the Canadian Government and Parliament. For if it were to do so 'it would be treating itself as for all relevant purposes the agent of the Canadian Government and Parliament (and) would thus be treating the Canadian Government and Parliament as having in constitutional reality a substantially unilateral power of amending or abolishing Canada's federal system'.[20]

The Committee's conclusion, therefore, was that though there was no rule requiring unanimity of all the Provinces to constitutional changes affecting their rights, it was the duty of the United Kingdom Parliament to decide whether a request from the Government and Parliament of Canada conveyed 'the clearly expressed wishes of Canada as a federally structured whole'.[21] It would also be in accord with the role of the United Kingdom authorities for them to take into consideration at the time the request was received the existence of court proceedings in Canada testing the constitutionality of the request for amendment or patriation.

The convention recommended by the Kershaw Committee to the British Parliament was admittedly general and imprecise. Its application and what it included might in some cases have been uncertain. But it was clear enough what it excluded. A resolution opposed by eight out of ten Provinces could not be said to express the clearly expressed wishes of Canada as a federally structured whole. So the report's implication for action at Westminster was unequivocal.

The emphatic nature of the report brought a new element into the situation and created a difficulty for the British Government. The representations made at Westminster by the Provincial Governments, together with the publicity

[20] HC 42 (i), *First Report from the Foreign Affairs Committee* (1980-1), at p. xlv.
[21] Ibid., at pp. xii–xiii.

given to the Kershaw Report in both countries, raised a serious doubt whether the British Cabinet could make good the undertakings given to Ottawa. In both the House of Commons and in the Lords there were many who said that they would not vote for the Canada Bill if it continued to be opposed by a substantial number of Provinces and whilst its constitutionality remained in issue before the Canadian courts. So even with the whips on there was no guarantee that the measure would be carried.

In Ottawa the Kershaw Committee and its report were viewed with displeasure. The Federal authorities, like Ministers in Britain, had felt sure that convention and precedent supported the case for an unquestioned passage of the patriation legislation in Britain. In March of 1981 the Government of Canada published a counterblast to the Kershaw Report entitled *The Role of the United Kingdom in the Amendment of the Canadian Constitution.*[22] The White Paper stated that the Kershaw Committee had seriously misconstrued the Canadian Constitution and the fundamental nature of Canada's relationship to the United Kingdom, and that should its advice be followed Canada's relations with the United Kingdom would be severely strained and the future course of Commonwealth relationships seriously affected. Nothing in the patriation proposals, or the Charter of Rights, the Paper went on, would diminish the rights or powers of the Provinces or affect the federal structure to their disadvantage. There was no support in Canadian law or practice for the Kershaw Committee's belief that provincial consent was required for amendments significantly affecting the federal structure. The convention of automatic action at Westminster at the request of the Federal Authorities had always been honoured and any other course would constitute an interference in Canada's internal affairs and a denial of the Federal Government and Parliament's right to exercise the national sovereignty of the nation in its relations with the outside world. Though the Canadian Constitution was in general federal, it departed from the federal model in having made the federal order of government responsible for securing constitutional amendment

[22] Background Paper, Minister of Justice, Ottawa (Mar. 1981).

until an all-Canadian amendment procedure had been devised. The Kershaw Committee had misunderstood the nature of Canadian federalism, and many of the submissions made to it suffered from illogicality and errors of fact.

In April 1981 the Kershaw Committee, risking a further deterioration in Commonwealth relations, published a rejoinder to the Government of Canada's remonstrance, in a further report to the House of Commons. Some acidity of tone was evident. 'Your committee', they said, 'have welcomed the opportunity to learn more directly the views of the Canadian Government.' The view that the Kershaw report had misconstrued the constitutional situation 'did not come as a surprise to your Committee'. Though the Federal Government had declined to offer any evidence, the Committee had been acquainted with its views by studying various documents published by it and by its arguments addressed to the provincial courts in Canada. 'We were thus aware of the degree to which the published opinions of the present Canadian Government diverge from the opinions of former Canadian Governments.' No errors of fact or law had been pointed out in their Report, the Committee stated, and the Federal Government's criticisms all related to the proper inferences to be drawn from the law and historical facts. The major assertions made as to the duties of the British Parliament, the Committee thought, were inherently unreasonable. They implied 'that the U.K. authorities would be bound to accede automatically to a request even if that request were to abolish the Provinces against the protests (formally conveyed to the UK authorities) of all or most Provincial Governments or legislatures, or were found by Canadian courts to be unconstitutional'.[23]

In the meantime the Provinces had been bringing their cases against the Federal proposals in the courts in Manitoba, Quebec, and Newfoundland.

The Canadian Judicial Decisions

The successive actions in the provincial courts were brought

[23] *Supplementary Report on the British North America Acts: the Role of Parliament,* HC 295 (1980–1), p.v.

under provincial statutes that provided for reference to the Provinces' Appeal Courts of questions either of law or fact.[24] In both Manitoba and Newfoundland the courts were asked first, whether the patriation proposals would affect Federal–Provincial relationships; secondly, whether there was a constitutional convention to the effect that the House of Commons and Senate of Canada should not request Her Majesty the Queen to lay such a measure before the British Parliament without first obtaining the agreement of the Provinces; and thirdly, whether the agreement of the Provinces was constitutionally required for such an amendment to the Constitution of Canada.

The meaning of the final question was somewhat unclear. Since amendment of the Constitution took place in Britain it might have been supposed to refer to the constitutional obligations of the United Kingdom Parliament as compared with the constitutional convention governing the making of the request for legislation in Canada. But in both courts the third question about 'constitutionality' was interpreted as being about the *legal* obligation of the Federal Parliament as contrasted with its *conventional* obligation referred to in the second question. In Quebec the second and third questions were fused into a single one, which asked whether the Canadian Constitution empowered the Federal Parliament to cause the Constitution to be amended without the consent of the Provinces in such a way as to affect their legislative competence.

The Provinces pressed their arguments about the illegality of the Federal action in two ways. They urged that it was unlawful, in infringing provincial sovereignty conferred by the British North America Acts and the Statute of Westminster. In addition, and alternatively, they said that the conventions protecting the rights of the Provinces should be held by the courts to have hardened or solidified into law. These arguments failed to carry a majority of the judges in Manitoba and Quebec and perhaps directed attention away

[24] The Newfoundland Judicature Act, 1979, provides for reference by the Lieutenant Governor in Council to the Court of Appeal of 'any matter which he thinks fit to refer'. The Quebec Court of Appeal Reference Act, 1977, similarly authorizes the Government of Quebec to refer to the Court of Appeal for hearing and consideration 'any question which it deems expedient'.

from the question of the conventions. However, in New-foundland, the Provinces carried the day on both law and convention. So, though the legal and conventional issues remained confused, the Provinces had failed to persuade the courts of their case in two of the three judicial appeals.

On 23 and 24 of April 1981, after long debate, the Canadian Senate and House of Commons adopted the Government's proposed amendments to the British North America Act. The resolutions provided for a new Constitution Act containing the Charter of Rights and Freedoms, and a new amendment clause under which the Act could be amended in Canada after the cessation of British authority. Shortly afterwards the appeals from the three provincial courts came before the Supreme Court of Canada, whose judgment was delivered on 28 September 1981.[25]

Its import turned entirely on the complex issue of law and convention. In consolidating the appeals the Court divided the issue of constitutionality clearly into its legal and conventional senses. Their answers to the three major questions submitted to them were:

Question 1 Would the proposals affect Federal–Provincial relationships and the rights and powers of the Provinces?

Answer Yes.

Question 2 Is it a constitutional convention that no measure of such a kind be laid before the British Parliament without first obtaining the agreement of the Provinces?

Answer Yes.

Question 3 Is the agreement of the Provinces constitutionally required to such amendments?

Answer As a matter of constitutional convention 'Yes'. As a matter of law 'No'.

On the first question the Provinces could claim that their argument had been decisively upheld. On the second and third questions a majority of seven judges to two upheld the Federal Government's position on the law and a majority

[25] *Reference Re Amendment of the Constitution of Canada (Nos. 1, 2 and 3)* (1982), 125 D.L.R. (3d.) 1.

of six judges to three upheld the Provinces on the question of convention. At first that sounded like a complex kind of drawn match. But on the issue that mattered the Provinces had won.

The decision as to the law of the Constitution affirmed that nothing restricted the power of the Canadian Senate and House of Commons to pass resolutions or to petition the Crown. Neither did anything limit the legal power of the British Parliament to amend the British North America Acts or require that power to be exercised with the consent of the Provinces. Canada's Federal system, in other words, was legally speaking at the mercy of its central government and Parliament. With the co-operation of the British Parliament they could turn Canada into a unitary state or a republican state, or any kind of state.

But all of that was of a piece with talk of similar legal excesses that might be perpetrated by the legally omnipotent sovereign Parliament of the United Kingdom. The issue before the United Kingdom legislators was not whether they could legally amend the British North America Act without the Provinces' consent. No one doubted that they could. The role of the United Kingdom Parliament, to which the Kershaw Committee had directed its mind, was not its legal role but what its conventional duty might be. The decision of the Supreme Court on the question of convention could be said to have confirmed the view of the Foreign Affairs Committee on almost every major point. The Court's conclusion was that:

The agreement of the Provinces of Canada, no views being expressed as to its quantification, is constitutionally required for the passing of the . . . joint Address . . . and . . . the passing of the Resolution without such agreement would be unconstitutional in the conventional sense.

The purpose of the conventional rule was 'to protect the federal character of the Canadian constitution and prevent the anomaly that the House of Commons and Senate could obtain by simple resolution what they could not validly accomplish by statute'. If the proposed amendments became law 'Canada would remain a federation . . . but it would be a different federation, made different at the instance of a majority in the Houses of the Federal Parliament acting alone'. In the ten Federal-Provincial conferences since 1927 at which unsuccessful attempts had been made to achieve consensus on an amendment formula a major issue had been the quantification of provincial consent. No consensus had been reached. 'But the discussion of this very issue for more than fifty years postulates a clear recognition by all the governments concerned of the principle that a substantial degree of provincial consent is required'. It was, the majority opinion added, sufficient for the court to decide whether the situation before it met with this requirement. Two provinces agreed with the amendments and eight provinces opposed. They concluded that 'By no conceivable standard could this situation be thought to pass muster.'

The Sequel

Though there was some suggestion after the Court's decision that the Government might still consider whether to proceed unilaterally on the basis of its legal entitlement, that course would not have been conceivable in practice. It seems reasonable to suppose that no majority could have been found in either House of the British Parliament to enact a measure declared by the Supreme Court of Canada to be a violation of the constitutional practice of Canada. That at any rate was the conclusion plainly drawn. On 5 November 1981, after further meetings between Federal and Provincial representatives, by offering major concessions on items affecting provincial rights,[26] the Canadian Government secured the agreement of nine of the ten Provinces. It was clear that despite the withholding of Quebec's agreement the support of nine Provinces would secure British Parliamentary approval. The Foreign Affairs Committee's view that unanimity was not required clearly implied that no one Province — even Quebec — was entitled to exercise a veto. The Third Report of the Committee noted that the revised

[26] Including legislative veto or override powers under which a Province can enact that its laws shall operate notwithstanding the provisions of the Charter of Rights (with the exception of voting rights, language rights, and mobility rights). Constitution Act, s. 33. For the provisions and implications of the Charter see the special issue of the *Canadian Bar Review* March 1983 (vol. 61).

post-patriation amendment procedure requires amendments affecting provincial powers to be supported by the legislators of not less than seven Provinces with at least 50 per cent of the population; that Provinces can in effect opt out of the consequences of particular amendments and that future changes to the amendment procedure will require the concurrence of every provincial legislature.[27] The Canada Bill therefore, in its view now conveyed the clearly-expressed wishes of Canada as a federally structured whole.[28] That view was accepted by the British Government. After the final debate in the Canadian House of Commons had approved the resolution embodying the patriation proposals the Prime Minister of Quebec addressed a letter to Downing Street requesting rejection of the Federal proposals. The Leader of the House of Commons in his reply stated that the Government regretted that these proposals did not enjoy unanimous support, but added:

We have given weight to the decision of the Supreme Court of Canada of 28 September 1981. We believe that the agreement of nine out of the ten provinces constitutes a substantial measure of support for the proposals and we therefore feel we would not be justified in declining to act upon the request by the Federal Government and Parliament. Similarly our view is that it would not be proper for the United Kingdom Parliament to amend the Canada Bill because to do so would introduce an element which had not been requested by the Parliament of Canada and would thus be inconsistent with the convention recited in the Statute of Westminster.[29]

[27] See ss. 38-49 of the Constitution Act, 1982.
[28] *Third Report on the British North America Acts: The Role of Parliament,* HC 128 (1981-2), pp. vi-vii. The Committee also concluded that the treaty rights of the Indian and other native peoples were rights against the Canadian and not the British Government. See *R. v. Secretary of State for Foreign and Commonwealth Affairs, ex p. Indian Association of Alberta,* [1982] 2 W.L.R. 641, [1982] 2 All E.R. 143; holding that any liability of the Crown for the Indian peoples of Canada arising out of the British North America Acts was not a liability in respect of Her Majesty's Government in the United Kingdom within the meaning of s. 40 of the Crown Proceedings Act, 1947, and was not justiciable in the United Kingdom Courts. Also *Manuel v. Attorney-General,* [1982] 3 All E.R. 822.
[29] *Canada Today* (Canada High Commission, Sept. 1982), p. 12. The Government of Quebec thereafter asserted its right to veto the Federal proposals and made a further reference to the Quebec Court of Appeal. The convention of provincial support upheld by the Supreme Court either required provincial unanimity (it was argued) or Quebec had a right of veto under the principle of duality in the federal system. The Quebec Court of Appeal held that Quebec had

That was the view also taken by both Houses when the Queen (in right of the United Kingdom) laid the measure before them. The Bill received a third reading by 177 votes to 33 on Commonwealth Day, 8 March, and received the Royal assent on 29 March as the Canada Act, 1982. The Constitution Act contained in it was proclaimed by the Queen (in right of Canada) in Ottawa on 17 April 1982 and has been in force since that date.

The decision of the Canadian Supreme Court in the Patriation Reference case was a landmark in Commonwealth constitutional history. It provided a solution to the patriation problem. It also suggested some general principles that are of relevance to the British Parliament's surviving role as a Commonwealth legislator. In addition it raised and helped to clarify some long-standing issues of constitutional theory, both about the character of conventions and about their relationship to the exercise of legal authority.

no conventional right of veto and its decision was upheld by the Supreme Court on 6 December 1982 in a second Patriation Reference judgment. *Re Attorney-General of Quebec and Attorney General of Canada* (1982) 140 D.L.R. (3d) 385.

XII
The Limitation of Sovereignty

Since the passage of the Canada Act, questions have been raised about its character and consequences that may remind us that one function for convention has always been that of controlling the impact of the traditional legal doctrine of the supremacy of Parliament. That doctrine provides an obvious meeting-point between law and convention. Though it is hardly ever remarked upon in discussions of the role of conventions, any listing of conventional rules in the United Kingdom would have to include the most basic — though imprecise — rule of the governmental system, namely the rule that the legally unlimited power of the legislature is not used to its limits, but is exercised in accordance with broad principles described in such terms as constitutionalism, the rule of law and toleration of minority rights. It is a good example of a convention that is both general in its formulation and founded on principle rather than precedent. That the Queen in Parliament's powers are not used (as Leslie Stephen said that they lawfully might be) to provide for the execution of all blue-eyed babies, or in pursuance of policies of an equally immoderate character, is not a notion derived from previous instances. It plainly does not rest upon any series of unsuccessful arbitrary legislative attempts on the lives of helpless infants or randomly chosen minorities. That the powers of the Canadian, Australian, or Indian Parliaments may be similarly limited by broadly defined general principles drawn from constitutionalism or federalism in addition to any legal inhibitions specified in their constituent instruments, also illustrates this primary and patent use of convention as a restraining and modifying influence on legal power.

A particular application of the use of convention can be seen wherever the United Kingdom Parliament has acted so as to create independent legislative bodies with technically devolved or subordinate powers, such for example as those conferred on the Parliament of Northern Ireland between

1920 and the resumption of direct rule in 1972. A scheme similar in principle, though more complex in design, would have operated under the Scotland Act of 1978 if it had survived. An independent sphere of legislative authority was given to the Scottish Parliament but it would have been an ineffective measure unless it had been supported by a convention that the Westminster Parliament was not to use its power to legislate within the sphere reserved to the legislature of Scotland.

Similar conventions exist in relation to the powers exercised by the legislatures of the Channel Islands and the Isle of Man. In 1967 a special committee appointed by the States of Jersey reported that the legislative supremacy of the United Kingdom Parliament was considered to be limited in relation to the island by constitutional usage in respect of matters of purely domestic concern and in particular in respect of taxation. There is by implication a further convention that would operate here, as also if a Scottish Parliament were to be set up, namely that besides not legislating within the devolved legislature's reserved sphere, the Westminster Parliament would not use its undoubted power to change the existing distribution of power unilaterally or to abolish it altogether. A guarantee of that kind was indeed placed in the Northern Ireland Constitution Act of 1973 (modifying a similar declaration in the Ireland Act of 1949). It provided that 'in no event will Northern Ireland or any part of it cease to be part of Her Majesty's dominions and of the United Kingdom without the consent of the majority of the people of Northern Ireland voting in a poll for the purposes of the section . . . '.

The *Manuel* Case

The convention that the United Kingdom Parliament would not legislate for a Dominion without its request and consent clearly existed from 1926 and possibly earlier. Since conventions of this type are of fundamental importance, we have seen that some have wished to argue for one of two propositions (though they are distinguishable and indeed inconsistent), namely that conventional rules are not fundamentally different from laws, or alternatively that at some point in time conventions may become laws by a process that may be dubbed 'crystallization', 'concretization', 'hardening', or 'ripening'. That view was advanced in 1982 as part of the argument put forward, after the enactment of the Canada Act, on behalf of Indian minorities in Canada. In *Manuel and Others* v. *Attorney-General*,[1] a declaration was sought in Britain to establish that Parliament had no power to amend the Constitution of Canada so as to prejudice the Indians without their consent and that the Canada Act was *ultra vires*.

The basis for this assertion was an argument requiring several steps. The first was that the Canada Act was not (or not merely) an Act dealing with the repeal, amendment or alteration of the British North America Acts 1867 to 1930. Consequently s.7 (i) of the Statute of Westminster, which excluded from the operation of the Act any such amendment, had no application. Section 4 of the Statute of Westminster therefore applied to the Canada Act and in consequence of this it could be asserted that Parliament could not legislate for Canada without the request and consent of Canada. Since (it was argued) the Dominion meant not the Federal Parliament but all the constituent fractions including the Provinces and the Indian minorities, the Canada Act had been passed in violation of the legal principles established in 1931. For this argument to succeed, however, it was necessary to meet the argument that s.4 of the Statute of Westminster enacted only that the legislative power of the United Kingdom Parliament could be exercised so as to have effect in a Dominion if the British Act contained a *recital* of the Dominion's request and consent. In other words, the law itself as set out in the Statute of Westminster did not require the actual consent of a Dominion at all, and if such consent were to be recited (rightly or wrongly) as having been given it would under the terms of the statute change the law of the Dominion with or without its consent. The plaintiffs in *Manuel* however surmounted this difficulty by claiming that the convention or tradition that the United Kingdom could not legislate for Canada *had ripened into*

[1] [1982] 3 All E.R. 822.

law by 1931, and s. 4 of the Statute of Westminster despite its wording was merely declaratory of the existing law. The Court of Appeal, however, rejected this claim and held that even if it were to be assumed that Parliament was bound by the terms of s. 4, that section required only a recital of Canada's consent and since it contained such a recital the Act must be valid. The conclusion that no convention limiting the British Parliament's powers had ripened or hardened into law is one that is also accepted by the Supreme Court of Canada, since in the Constitution Reference case of 1981 it was concluded that no provincial consents were necessary in law to the passage of the Canada Act, and that the powers of the United Kingdom Parliament (until the passage of the Canada Act) were legally untrammelled. Though the point was not discussed, it was not suggested that in reaching that conclusion the Canadian Supreme Court was merely enunciating a proposition about the law of the United Kingdom. The implication was that up to the enactment of the Canada Act, any Act of the United Kingdom Parliament changing the law of Canada was part of the law of Canada and would be applied in Canadian courts notwithstanding any contrary conventions. That proposition might have been tested in relation to the Canada Act itself if events had turned out in such a way that the Trudeau Government had been able to procure a British patriation statute without provincial consent before the issue had been referred to the courts in Canada. Suppose that the British Government and Parliament had immediately acquiesced in the federal request and that the patriation legislation had received the Royal Assent. If the Act had then been challenged in Canada, would the Canadian courts have upheld it even if they had also then concluded that it violated a convention requiring provincial consent? The assumptions made in the early stages of the patriation argument by the Federal Government's legal advisers were in fact that early enactment by the Westminster Parliament would settle the legal issue and that is the implication of the Supreme Court's majority view on the relation of the law and the conventions.

Those who support the 'concretization of convention' theory may then pose a harder question. Suppose that the

British Parliament at any time before 1982 had purported
to legislate for Canada without any request and consent
at all, either federal or provincial, and in blatant disregard
of the convention requiring Dominion consent, referred to
in the Balfour Declaration and the preamble to the Statute
of Westminster. Would the courts in Canada not then have
given effect to the convention and treated it as having hardened into a rule of law? If this were indeed the only way
in which Canadian or any other Commonwealth courts
could avoid giving effect to hypothetical imperial legislation
of this extreme character it might certainly provide evidence
that in at least one instance convention could be transmuted
into law. But it is not the only conceivable way of explaining
the undoubtedly reasonable supposition that Commonwealth
courts would never have felt compelled to give effect to such
imagined exercises of sovereignty. The problem is akin to
that raised by all the post-war Commonwealth Independence
Acts by which the United Kingdom Parliament legislated not,
as in the Statute of Westminster, to preserve its authority
to legislate for a Commonwealth country with its consent
and on its request, but so as to terminate its authority
altogether. In the Nigeria Independence Act of 1960, for
example, it was provided that 'no Act of the Parliament
of the United Kingdom passed on or after the appointed
date shall extend or be deemed to extend to Nigeria or any
part thereof as part of the law thereof'. This, of course, was
the emphatic form of words adopted in the Canada Act.
'No Act of the Parliament of the United Kingdom passed
after the Constitution Act 1982 comes into force shall extend
to Canada as part of its law.'

As far as the law of the United Kingdom goes, however,
such legislation might in theory be repealed. Here again convention (as well as common sense and every other consideration) suggests that no such legislation should be enacted. We
know that Commonwealth courts would ignore any such
repeal. Could it not be said here also then that in doing so
they would be prepared to give legal effect to a conventional
rule? This is one suggestion that certainly might be made in
considering the consequences of the patriation legislation.
So have the events of 1982, it may be asked, finally accom-
plished the patriation of Canada's Constitution?

Convention and Autochthony

It can be agreed that the answer must be that they have not, if patriation is equated with the idea of 'autochthony'. Canada's new Constitution is not (in the term popularized by Sir Kenneth Wheare) 'autochthonous'.[2] That idea was explained by him in the following way. Some members of the Commonwealth, he said, wished to establish not merely that their systems of government were no longer subordinate to that of the United Kingdom, but that their Constitutions had the force of law within their territory through their own native authority and not because they were enacted or authorized in the United Kingdom. They wished to be something more than autonomous. They wanted to be constitutionally rooted in their own soil.[3] This ambition was graphically described for Canada some years ago by Professor F. R. Scott. Long before the terms 'patriation' or 'autochthony' had come into currency he wrote that:

Until now all legal rules in Canada . . . have derived their validity from the elephant of the B.N.A. Act which stood firmly upon the turtle of the sovereignty of the United Kingdom Parliament. Beneath the turtle nothing further has existed to support a stable universe. Now . . . we are looking for a Canadian turtle.[4]

It is not entirely clear whether in the sense intended by Professor Scott Canada now has its own turtle. In one sense it clearly does not, since the Canada Act has the force of law in Canada because it was enacted by the United Kingdom Parliament. In that sense the Canadian Constitution has not been severed from its imperial root as it might have been if by an agreement in Canada some constituent body of legislators had been assembled and endorsed a new constitutional instrument without recourse to Westminster.[5] One

---

[2] See Peter W. Hogg, 'Patriation of the Canadian Constitution: Has it been achieved?', (1983) 8 *Queen's University Law Journal*, 123.
[3] See *The Constitutional Structure of the Commonwealth* (1960), p. 89.
[4] 'The Redistribution of Imperial Sovereignty' (1950), repr. in *Essays on the Constitution* (1977), p. 244.
[5] Some Canadians (but not Mr Trudeau) favoured this in preference to the 'Westminster route'. See Edward McWhinney, *Canada and the Constitution 1979-1982.*

good reason for not severing it is that any such unilateral declaration of independence would have put the Canadian judges in considerable difficulty if the autochthonous consensus had not been complete, and any group or Province had attempted to dispute the validity of the purportedly home-grown constitutional enactment in the courts. That the root has not been severed is also shown by the fact that the Canada Act has not been endorsed or re-enacted by any Canadian process, an implied recognition that any such re-enactment would be legally redundant. But what needs to be asked is whether lack of autochthony or a native root in this sense matters. The answer ought to be that constitutionally − as distinct from emotionally − speaking it does not matter at all, since preservation of the British historical and legal root is compatible with its being the case that the Westminster Parliament is no longer able to legislate for Canada or to reverse the process by which its former authority was terminated.

At this point, therefore, it is necessary to enquire whether the termination of United Kingdom authority by s.2 of the Canada Act *is* irreversible. In that Canadian courts would disregard any United Kingdom law enacted for Canada after 1982 it clearly is so; and since they would treat as a nullity any United Kingdom repeal of the Canada Act, the patriation of unrestricted constituent authority to Canada can be considered complete, effective, and irreversible. None the less there may be some disagreement about the means by which this has come to be so. Some Canadian authorities have argued that s.2 of the Canada Act was not the reason for the termination of the authority over Canada of the United Kingdom Parliament, but that the United Kingdom Parliament had lost much of its authority over Canada before 1982 and retained only what was necessary to fill the gaps in domestic legislative power.[6]

If indeed it was the fact of Canada's non-colonial status and not the Act of the British Parliament that terminated the United Kingdom Parliament's authority over Canada, s.2 of the 1982 Canada Act would be redundant, and it would indeed seem that the conventions of Commonwealth

---

[6] See Brian Slattery, 'The Independence of Canada', (1983) *Supreme Court Law Review*, p. 369.

equality and independence had ripened or hardened into law that could at any time have been recognized by the Canadian courts. It can be argued, however, that this conclusion is not a necessary one. Certainly there seem to be some arguments against it. If s.2 of the Canada Act is redundant, perhaps also s.2 and s.4 of the Statute of Westminster were redundant or became so at some point. If the convention of independent status in the Balfour Declaration crystallized or ripened into law, it may be necessary to ask whether it did so in 1926 or in 1935 or in 1949; and there is no clear answer.

Moreover, it is difficult to rely without circularity upon the facts of Canada's independent or non-colonial status as a ground for the inability of the United Kingdom Parliament to legislate for Canada. Whatever the facts of diplomatic practice or international law, the question whether there is for constitutional purposes an independent system of legal authority in Canada depends, for the British and Canadian courts, upon the answer to the question: Who in the domestic law of Canada and the United Kingdom is entitled to legislate for Canada? There is good reason to suppose that the Canadian courts did not regard the general authority of the United Kingdom Parliament as having been terminated at any point before 1982. How unlimited they would have allowed that power to be, and what they would have done in the face of extreme or hypothetical cases (such as repeal of the Statute of Westminster or a purported abolition of the Province of Quebec) is a question that cannot now be answered, and may perhaps be treated as an unprofitable one. It would be equally impossible to say what the British courts would do about the unlimited authority of the British Parliament if one were to envisage equally unlikely exercises of sovereign authority, such as legislative abolition of General Elections, or imprisonment without trial of all members of the parliamentary opposition.

If the question is pressed as to the future repealability of the Canada Act or of any independence legislation either as a question of British or Commonwealth law, it is better to suppose that the United Kingdom Parliament is capable of making a legally effective abdication of its authority to legislate for particular territories and that it has done so. It is true that the traditional theory of parliamentary sovereignty presents difficulties for the contention that the Westminster Parliament can irreversibly terminate its authority in this fashion. As set out by Dicey, the doctrine of parliamentary sovereignty professes the view that Parliament can divest itself of authority in only two ways: by abdication and self-dissolution, leaving no successor, or by transfer of its authority to a new legislative body.[7] Dicey's concession about transfer of authority clearly implies that the transfer in question can be only of the entire existing legislative power to some new authority. It does not envisage transfer of jurisdiction over a particular area by a legislative sovereign that itself remains in existence. Nevertheless we are operating here at the untested limits of the traditional doctrine. Developments since Dicey suggest that there are ways of accommodating within the doctrine, the notion of an extinction of Westminster authority over a particular area. One way is to suppose that for British courts independence legislation is an extreme case of a manner and form provision that changes the way in which legislative authority can be exercised for particular purposes.[8] A simpler expedient, though it would modify the traditional theory, is to extend Dicey's cases of sovereign divestment of authority to include territorial abdication so that 'freedom once conferred cannot be revoked'. There are some judicial dicta to this effect,[9] and they would quickly be added to if any attempt were made in the United Kingdom to enact post-independence legislation for Commonwealth countries. That territorial abdication of power by the British Parliament can be legally effective is certainly the view that would be adopted by Commonwealth courts.[10] On that view patriation and autonomy are both complete and irreversible. They have, however, been brought about by legal enactment and they lend no weight to the hypothesis that law has been fashioned from convention.

[7] A. V. Dicey, *Introduction to the Study of the Law of the Constitution* (10th edn.), p. 69.
[8] Cf. G. Marshall, *Parliamentary Sovereignty and the Commonwealth* (1957), chaps. 4 and 7. *Constitutional Theory* (1971), pp. 43-53. De Smith, *Constitutional and Administrative Law* (4th edn.), pp. 97-101.
[9] e.g. *Blackburn* v. *Attorney-General* [1971] 1 W.L.R. 1037, 1041 (per Lord Denning); *Ndlwana* v. *Hofmeyr*, [1937] A.D. 229, 237 (South Africa).
[10] See P. W. Hogg, *Constitutional Law of Canada* (1977), p. 12 and *Canada Act 1982 Annotated* (1982), p. 6.

XIII
The Character of Convention

It cannot be denied that there remain some puzzles about the general nature of conventions. They were aptly illustrated by the sharply expressed differences of political and judicial opinion in Canada between 1979 and 1982. In Chapter I we reached some initial conclusions that can now be reviewed in the light of what we have seen of attempts to formulate and apply conventions in particular areas of government in Britain and the Commonwealth. The conclusions were that:

1. Conventions are rules that define major non-legal rights, powers and obligations of office-holders in the three branches of government, or the relations between governments or organs of government. (It being often useful to distinguish duty-imposing from right-conferring conventions.)

2. Conventions have as their main general aim the effective working of the machinery of political accountability.

3. Conventions can in most cases be stated only in general terms, their applicability in some circumstances being clear, but in other circumstances uncertain and debatable.

4. No general reason needs to be advanced to account for compliance with duty-imposing conventions beyond the fact that when they are obeyed (rather than disobeyed, rejected or changed), they are believed to formulate valid rules of obligation.

5. Conventions are distinguishable from rules of law, though they may be equally important, or more important than rules of law.

6. Conventions may modify in practice the application or enforcement of rules of law.

7. Conventions are not direct sources of legal rights and duties, but they may be used or invoked by courts in the application or interpretation of existing rules of law.

8. Conventions may be incorporated by reference or specification into newly-enacted constitutional instruments or rules of law.

9. In some cases law may provide for the existence of conventions to be certified or declared by judicial declaration.

But as the events narrated in the preceding chapters show, not all of these proposals are uncontroversial. Three particular points of difficulty can be identified. They involve first, the vagueness of convention; secondly, the justiciability of convention; and thirdly, the type of obligation imposed (or right created) by convention.

The Vagueness of Conventions

If a convention is to be a guide to conduct it must be known what course of action it prescribes. But if an alleged rule is vague it cannot be known with certainty what it prescribes. Thus its existence as a convention may be put in question. The convention about the need for a substantial measure of provincial support for constitutional amendment in Canada was, for example, a vague convention and a minority of Supreme Court Judges rejected it as being a convention, on the ground that it could not be known with sufficient clarity what the content of the convention was and what was required to conform to it.[1] There is a difficulty here that turns on what is meant by knowing the content of a convention and what is required to conform with it. If this were to imply a knowledge of what would be required by the convention in all possible cases and fact situations, it would be too severe a test of the existence of convention. All conventions and many other rules of behaviour share this characteristic, namely that what they require in some central and clear cases is known but what they require in more marginal or arguable cases cannot be stated in advance. A moral rule, such as 'Eating people is wrong', may be thought of as existing and having clear and uncontested

---

[1] Cf. Dr Eugene Forsey's view of the convention (in a letter to *The Times*, 2 November 1981) as a 'gulf profound as that Serbonian bog . . . where armies whole have sunk'.

applications, but there may be situations, not yet enumerated or agreed, in which eating people is not wrong; and there may be doubts also as to the meaning of the term 'person'. Uncertainty of this kind is inherent in legal rules as well as in conventional rules. It is of course a matter of degree. Some legal rules are fairly vague and some conventional rules are fairly precise. (Compare 'The legislature shall have power to make laws for peace, order and good government' and 'The Queen must assent to a Bill that has received the approval of a majority in each House of the legislature'.) Most of the major conventions of parliamentary government, such as those of collective and individual ministerial responsibility, suffer from vagueness as to their application, although they undoubtedly exist. Defenders of the majority opinion on convention in the 1981 Canadian Supreme Court decision could say that the Court did not profess to be spelling out even the main applications of the disputed convention, but simply deciding that the facts presented were a clear case that fell within the rule. This, indeed, was said, and it was added that the application of the rule remained to be worked out by the political actors.

Nevertheless, if an alleged convention embraces few clear cases, and many disputed situations need to be confronted, the difference between saying that a general conventional rule exists and saying that no conventional rule clearly exists may be a fine one.[2]

The Justiciability of Conventions

In what sense are conventions justiciable? In recent times some have argued that conventions are justiciable and others

---

[2] If the undisputed applications of a convention are few, there will be many practices or usages that will not be certainly identifiable as being required by convention. Since there are clear applications of convention, however, it is misleading to say that 'conventions' cannot be clearly distinguished from 'practices'. (Marshall, *Constitutional Theory* (1971), p. 12.) That was a clumsy way of suggesting that the boundaries of even the best-established conventions are too uncertain for constitutional *law* to be equated with what is regarded by officials as conventionally obligatory — a suggestion made by Professor A. L. Goodhart (see 'An Apology for Jurisprudence' in *Interpretations of Modern Legal Philosophers*, ed. P. Sayre, 1947).

that they are not. Each view needs clarification. One sense in which a question may be said to be justiciable raises merely factual issues. In this sense a question is justiciable if it has been given to a court for decision by a competent authority and can be made the subject of litigation. Another sense of justiciability raises an issue for judgment and evaluation. In this sense a question is justiciable if it is a suitable or proper issue to be made the subject of legal decision.

Some Canadian judges, and critics who were opposed to the making of a declaration as to the conventions of the Constitution, have called it an unwise excursion into the realm of political science, on the ground that conventions raise political or non-justiciable issues. The meaning of this is unclear. If 'non-justiciable' is being used in the first sense the assertion would be false, if the reference statutes had (rightly or wrongly) provided for questions about political or conventional matters to be placed before the courts. Of course there might be a doubt about the proper interpretation of the reference legislation or about whether conventions were amongst the matters that could properly be made the subject of a governmental referral.

If, on the other hand, 'non-justiciable' is to be understood in the second (evaluative or policy) sense, then justiciability would not itself seem a proper issue for court decision. Legislators often give to courts decisions that are thought by some to be unsuited to their role. Decisions about industrial relations or restrictive trade practices are examples. In particular jurisdictions (as in Canada) there may in the case-law concerning advisory opinions be principles that permit the courts to decline to answer what they judge to be unsuitable questions;[3] that is simply a matter of interpretation of what the scope of a particular reference statute happens to be. But in a system based upon the supremacy of Parliament the duty of courts to carry out the clearly expressed intention of the legislature is normally accepted. So, in principle, issues about justiciability in the evaluative sense should be for legislators rather than judges to determine.

---

[3] See P. W. Hogg, 60 *Canadian Bar Review* 307 at 322. The reference statutes, however, are drawn in wide terms. That in Manitoba, for example, allows the Lieutenant-Governor to submit for consideration or hearing 'any matter which he thinks fit to refer'. (c.f. p. 195 above)

Whether conventions are (properly) justiciable is therefore a question of legislative policy. There are some advantages, certainly, in the existence of a facility for seeking judicial clarification of conventions, since one of the characteristic disadvantages of a conventional rule is that when disputes arise about its meaning or application there is no one capable of settling it. In some cases, grave questions of political behaviour turn on disputes about convention, and an impartial arbitration may sometimes be as important as it typically is in disputes about legal rules. But a query remains. In what sense does the decision of a court on a non-legal question *settle* the question? On an issue of law a critic who disagrees with the reasoning or conclusion of a court is none the less bound by it. But an opinion on a question of fact or a judgment of a non-legal issue seems to be different. If I as a critic or a politician disagree with a court's opinion either about the existence or application of a convention, in what sense can it be said that I am not free to do so? What would being bound by the court's decision mean? In what sense are critics, politicians, or citizens entitled to take their own view of the existence or meaning of rules that by definition do not create legal rights or impose legal duties?

The Obligation of Conventions

A different but equally obscure question arises even when a convention is acknowledged by all to exist and when its meaning is clear. If it is a duty-imposing convention, what kind of duty does it impose? Obedience to convention is assumed to be something more than a matter of political judgment or prudence. Conventions, in the words of Sir Ivor Jennings, are rules that 'not only are followed but . . . have to be followed'.[4] But is this obligation something distinct from both legal and moral obligation? Can there be a conflict between what is constitutionally required and what is morally justified or permitted? Or is it that the obligations imposed by conventions are in a straightforward sense moral

---

[4] *Cabinet Government* (3rd edn.), p. 2.

obligations operating on those who work the machinery of government (just as 'political obligation' does not name a distinct kind of obligation, but is ordinary moral obligation operating in the political sphere)?

On the first hypothesis it would be possible for a government to say that although it was aware of what constitutional convention required, it nevertheless felt that there were overriding moral reasons related to the general welfare or national interest which justified ignoring the convention. On the alternative supposition (that the obligation to obey conventions is ordinary moral obligation), there would be no such move available to governments or office-holders who wished to ignore or override the conventions of the Constitution.

A similar query could be posed in relation to right-conferring conventions. Can it be supposed, for example, in relation to the constitutional rights of the Crown that it is possible to distinguish between what the Queen is constitutionally (in the conventional, not legal sense) entitled to do and, what she is morally entitled to do? In 1951, for example, King George VI's legal entitlement to refuse a dissolution of Parliament to his Prime Minister was, of course, not in doubt and what was in question was his constitutional right. But he was advised that though he was constitutionally entitled to refuse, the arguments were against doing it in this particular case. If that is to be understood as meaning that refusal would be in some sense unjustified, it sounds like a juxtaposition of a narrow constitutional right with a wider moral or political consideration. But that again would make no sense if constitutional rights or entitlements are ordinary moral rights. (Though, of course, it would make sense to say what can be said of any ordinary moral right — that the outcome would be better or happier if it were not exercised or that the bearer of the right or others would benefit from its not being exercised, or that it would be expedient not to exercise it.)

What may confuse the issue in the case both of right-conferring and duty-imposing conventions is that situations may arise in which politicians do contrast conventional and moral considerations and imply that one can override the other because they wish to disregard, or feel it expedient to 'suspend', a constitutional rule. The Labour Party in 1975 stated, for example, that they would for good reasons suspend the rule of collective cabinet unanimity during the EEC referendum campaign. Such a policy may of course have been justified (as suggested earlier) on the ground that the supposed duty-imposing convention did not in fact exist. It might also be justified by showing that the convention when properly considered allowed disagreement in circumstances of a special kind. That might infringe or offend against a putative rule of absolute and invariant unanimity. But it would not (if the exception could be justified in terms of precedent or principle) be to *suspend* the convention. It would merely be to apply the convention correctly to the particular case. But if a duty-imposing convention really existed and no such principled exception could be suggested, then the proper conclusion might simply be that infringing the convention could not be morally justified. Similar arguments could be applied to right-conferring conventions. When the convention governing refusal of dissolution had been correctly applied to the party situation facing George VI in 1951, it would not have been the case that his morally correct course of action could have conflicted with his constitutional or conventional entitlement. On this view constitutional conventions simply spell out the moral duties, rights, and powers of office-holders in relation to the machinery of government in particular areas. The last proviso seems necessary since not all the moral rights and duties of politicians or office-holders are necessarily governed by convention, if only because moral issues can arise in government in areas where no conventions have developed.

The Changing of Conventions

If conventions are rules that politicians are bound to follow, how can they ever be changed? The practice of revising or changing conventions suggests that conventions are in a number of ways unlike both legal rules and ordinary moral rules. They are unlike legal rules because they are not the product of a legislative or of a judicial process. They differ from ordinary moral rules because their content is determined partly by special agreement, and many of them govern matters that apart from such agreed arrangements would be morally neutral. Some moral obligations can, of course, have the same special character. The obligation to do what one has promised, for example, is a special obligation created by an agreed institutional arrangement. One form of conventional change is then the deliberate abrogation of an old convention or creation of a new one by agreement, if the old rule is felt to be outdated or inconvenient. In this sense, of course, conventions are not rules that have to be followed unconditionally and permanently. It will always be possible for governments or politicians to propose a change of convention. They must be followed only in the sense that they cannot be changed unilaterally and must be complied with if in force until changed by agreement.

But conventions can also develop or extend in new directions by being applied to fresh political circumstances. In this process agreed precedents are the stepping-stones, and arguments about what the conventions are will in principle always be about the existence and implications of existing rules. Like rules of linguistic usage, it will be the case that the rules ultimately reflect what people do. In that sense conventions will become in the end whatever politicians think it right to do. But at any one time what politicians in fact do may conflict with and infringe a rule based on existing precedents or agreements.

Why, it may be asked, should we study convention? Is it not an arid and formal task? In reply it may be said that an examination of the rules of constitutional behaviour can have many purposes. It is not now perhaps as necessary as it once was to rebut the idea that any study of constitutional rules must have conservative implications or be a job too formal to deserve the energies of full-blooded twentieth-century political scientists. The effective analysis of constitutional usage has always involved both factual and historical investigation of political behaviour; and it need not be divorced from appraisal of policy. Indeed its traditional practitioners never separated it from criticism of existing ideas, or proposals for improving the machinery of government or the practices of politics. Nor should we.

XIV
The Conventions of Accountability:
Recent Developments

The clarification and development of conventions is a continuous process. Fresh events and episodes are always of interest. Sometimes they modify or suggest modification of a previous generalization; sometimes they help to make clear a rule or practice that may have been vaguely or tentatively formulated; sometimes again they may confirm a line of precedents or underline an existing rule with fresh examples. Since 1984 a number of episodes and events have occurred that bear in one or other of these ways on the conventions of political accountability.

The Queen and Ministerial Advice

In 1986 the Australia Act changed the relationship between the Crown and the Australian states that had obtained since 1931. By agreement between the States and the Commonwealth, legislation was promoted in Australia and at Westminster to sever the last vestiges of colonial dependence, including the remaining right of appeal by special leave in certain cases from the states to the Judicial Committee of the Privy Council. These legal changes involve some change in the existing conventions. State Governors are no longer appointed by the Queen as Queen of the United Kingdom on the advice of United Kingdom Ministers. The Act provides that advice to the Queen in respect of any powers and functions in relation to a state shall be tendered by the Premier of that state. Australia's Constitution has now, like Canada's, been 'patriated'.

The tendering of advice to the Queen as Head of the Commonwealth has also been the subject of some recent disagreement. Is she, for example, personally responsible for the way in which she carries out the role? It seems doubtful whether the Queen ever gets advice in her capacity as Head of the Commonwealth since there are no Ministers exclusively entitled to give it. When the Commonwealth Ministers meet together at Commonwealth Conferences their conclusions are usually issued in the form of Commonwealth Prime Ministers' statements and do not take the form of advice to Her Majesty — though perhaps if all the Premiers were in agreement they might offer advice on some matter of common concern.

One act that the Queen appears to carry out in her capacity as Head of the Commonwealth is the Christmas Day broadcast. In 1984 Mr Enoch Powell criticized the content of the Christmas broadcast as conveying the impression that the Queen 'had the interests of other countries more at heart than those of her own people'. He insisted that in mounting such criticism he was imputing blame to the Queen's Ministers and not to her, since on his view all the Queen's public statements must be made on ministerial advice. This assertion was disputed by the Prime Minister, who in reply to questions in the House of Commons said that the Queen's Christmas message was a personal one, and that 'The Queen makes her Christmas broadcast as head of the Commonwealth. She does not make it on the advice of United Kingdom Ministers.' A spirited exchange of views followed in *The Times*. Lord Blake stated that speeches made by the Queen when visiting a Commonwealth republic were made by her on the advice of United Kingdom Ministers, and when visiting a Commonwealth monarchy on the advice of the Prime Minister of the country concerned. But, he added, it had always been the convention that the Christmas broadcast was made without ministerial advice and responsibility.[1]

Mr Powell did not apparently accept the existence of this last convention. At least he wished to know when it had been declared. Lord Blake replied that conventions were not always declared but sometimes grew, as this had. Which Ministers then, asked Mr Powell, now accepted responsibility for the convention that advice was not tendered on this matter. 'Advice that advice is not requisite', he said, 'is also advice.' To this shaft Lord Blake replied with another — 'If advice is not needed, advice that it is not needed, is not needed.'

---

[1] *The Times*, 20 February 1984.

Conventions for Hung Parliaments

Since 1983 there has been fairly continuous discussion amongst political commentators of the constitutional ethics of a hung (or hanging) Parliament if an election returns no clear single-party majority. One point on which some political differences of view have been expressed is whether a sitting Prime Minister who after an election has lost an overall majority is in a different position if he or she leads the largest party group as against a position in which the major opposition party has gained a larger number of seats, though not an absolute majority. It is clear that in either event no immediate action by the Crown is called for, since the government and Prime Minister remain in office until defeated under appropriate circumstances in the House of Commons. Some feel that a Prime Minister who continues in office, perhaps negotiating for support in the House from the third or minor parties (as Mr Edward Heath did in 1974), is improperly frustrating the wishes of the electorate. But it seems clear that as a matter of constitutional convention a government, whatever its numbers, is entitled after an election to test the opinion of the House and to remain in office until defeated on a confidence motion.

The existence of three or more party groups in the House poses a further question about potential changes of party leadership. It might be that a third party was unwilling to support the government in office after an election under the government's existing leader but made it known that it would do so under an alternative leader. If the leader of the incumbent party were to resign, should the Queen — it has been asked — send for the leader of the next largest opposition party, or should she co-operate in the formation of a coalition government by acting on advice that an alternative incumbent party leader would in the event be likely to attract the support of two of the party groupings? In this situation the Queen might seem to be called upon to balance a speculative alternative leader of the incumbent party against the leader of the next largest party. Perhaps an incumbent Prime Minister would be wise to delay any planned resignation and only to offer her (or his) resignation after her (or his) party had set its leadership election machinery in motion and elected a successor. A party in office and undefeated in the House has normally been supposed entitled to elect a new leader on the death or resignation of an existing leader without a change of government. The new leader, if he were acceptable to the third party as head of a government that they were willing to support or join by way of coalition, would presumably remain undefeated in the House. If on the other hand he was not acceptable then he would resign whenever that refusal of support led to his defeat in the House, and only at that point could the leader of the second largest opposition party expect to be sent for. If a party in office after an election, but without an overall majority, changes its leader after an election and the new leader is defeated more or less immediately he clearly could not expect to be given a dissolution of Parliament in order to hold a fresh general election.

A future regime of coalition or minority governments clearly poses fresh questions about the right of any incumbent Prime Minister to a dissolution of Parliament on defeat in the House. Existing principles, we have seen, suggest that this is not automatic. However, if a Prime Minister has been summoned to office because the incumbent government after an election has been defeated in the House there will, if he has held office for any significant period, usually seem no practical alternative to a further election.

Under the present electoral system there is at least the prospect that a general election will produce an overall majority. If, however, proportional representation were to be introduced, that expectation might be absent and new conventions might have to be developed — for example that no party leader should be appointed Prime Minister until he has discovered whether he can form a majority government.[2]

It may be, of course, that new conventions cannot easily be introduced whilst the issues at stake are controversial. The Crown would presumably have to decide what the conventions were, and since party agreement is only one element in the make-up of conventions such agreement might not be

---

[2] See for a discussion of new conventions appropriate to a proportional electoral system Vernon Bogdanor, *No Overall Majority: Forming a Government in a Multi-party Parliament* (Constitutional Reform Centre 1986).

conclusive but merely be one — though perhaps major — element to be placed alongside the existing precedents and arguments of principle that determine the convention. Given what conventions are they cannot simply be invented.

Individual Ministerial Responsibility

Two ministerial departures, those of Mr Cecil Parkinson in 1985 and of Mr Leon Brittan in 1986, illustrate different facets of the convention of individual ministerial responsibility. Mr Parkinson resigned from his position as Secretary of State for Trade and Industry after publicity had been given to a long-standing affair with his secretary Miss Sarah Keays and after making a statement that he had decided not to marry Miss Keays, who had become pregnant by him, but to remain with his wife and family. Mr Parkinson's case raises at least one point of interest about the morality of political office. A number of ministerial resignations have been the result of personal faults or sexual irregularities. Earlier cases, however, such as those of John Profumo in 1963 and Lords Lambton and Jellicoe in 1973, were linked, whether plausibly or not, with possible security dangers and the need to avoid the possibility of blackmail arising from the activities of call girls, the presence of Russian agents, and the dangers potentially arising from drug-consumption or sexual deviance. In the first of these cases there was the additional element of Parliamentary affront arising from the Minister's misleading of the House of Commons. These factors were set out at some length in the Denning Report of 1963 and in the reports of the Security Commission. Lord Denning was willing to specify at least some types of sexual misdemeanour that did not call for dismissal of public servants on security grounds. One of them was 'adultery committed clandestinely with a person not likely to resort to blackmail'. That description fits more or less exactly the situation of Mr Cecil Parkinson. Lord Denning's report, however, was not concerned with the political impact of clandestine relationships becoming publicly known. It might perhaps be inferred that Mr Parkinson's departure from office supports the conclusion that a constitutional convention or usage is emerging that Ministers are not to be allowed to treat deviation from conventional sexual morality as a private matter that need not impinge upon their continuance and effectiveness in public office.

On the other hand, the Prime Minister's first conclusion when Mr Parkinson's predicament became public knowledge was that no question of resignation arose. Several days later she apparently relinquished that belief. It is not entirely clear whether she changed her mind when a letter to *The Times* from Miss Keays gave further publicity to the affair. We do not know whether she then required Mr Parkinson to resign, or whether she failed to convey her own firm convictions to the Secretary of State and he insisted on leaving office despite being urged to remain.

So perhaps no new constitutional norm can be inferred from the episode. Past practice suggests that in the certain absence of any security danger the rules of comportment for Ministers of the Crown are a matter in which each Prime Minister and Cabinet are entitled to set their own standards, however conventional or peculiar. If it were to be decreed that all Cabinet Ministers were to wear red spotted handkerchieves on their heads at all times, no one's constitutional rights would be infringed, there being no entitlement to Cabinet membership. Ministerial chastity, we must conclude, is like the conventions of Cabinet secrecy and collective responsibility. It is a rule that can be suspended or breached except in circumstances when the Prime Minister, having considered the immediate and long-term political implications, feels it to be more honoured in the observance.

Mr Leon Brittan's resignation in January 1986 (also from the office of Secretary of State for Trade and Industry) adds to the small collection of post-war examples in which ministers have accepted responsibility for political or administrative misjudgment as distinct from private or personal misdemeanours. The only other clear instances are the resignations of Sir Thomas Dugdale as Minister of Agriculture after the Crichel Down affair in 1954 and Lord Carrington's resignation from the Foreign Secretaryship after the Falkland Islands invasion in 1982.

Mr Brittan's resignation was one of the consequences of a number of misunderstandings and failures of communication that occurred in the government's handling of the Westland

Helicopter Company affair in January 1986. The exact reason for Mr Brittan's resignation is not easy to state but perhaps it could be said to have arisen from an accumulation of misfortunes or misjudgments. The first was his failure to explain clearly to the House of Commons the facts about a confidential letter that had been received from British Aerospace PLC. For this he apologized to the House – a matter that might have been excused under the well-known doctrine of excusable ministerial error laid down by Mr Herbert Morrison in the Crichel Down debate in 1954. Mr Brittan's second misfortune was his authorization of the leaking by his press office of a critical letter written to the Secretary of State for Defence, Mr Michael Heseltine, by the Solicitor General. Mr Brittan believed that his civil servants had obtained the agreement of the Prime Minister's office (and presumably the Prime Minister) to the disclosure made by his office. The Prime Minister's office and the Prime Minister claimed, however, that they had misunderstood what was being proposed, and the Prime Minister stated in the House that she had known nothing of Mr Brittan's role in the disclosure until she saw the results of an inquiry by the Cabinet Secretary sixteen days later. As with Mr Parkinson, we do not know exactly whether Mr Brittan insisted on resigning or was told to do so. But like Mr Parkinson he seems to have been abandoned when political and Parliamentary criticism of his action persisted. His resignation adds a useful precedent to what previously looked a rather thin parade of examples that provide the evidence for the existence of a resigning convention for political error. The evidence now seems convincing.

Collective Responsibility

Mr Michael Heseltine's resignation from his office of Secretary of State for Defence at the time of the Westland affair falls into the different category of collective responsibility policy resignations rather than individual fault resignations. The grounds of resignation, however, though emphatically stated, were not articulated with complete clarity or consistency. Mr Heseltine had over some considerable period seemed to be pursuing a policy different from that of some of his ministerial colleagues, preferring a European solution to the problem of helicopter supply whereas the Prime Minister persistently claimed that the Cabinet's policy was one of neutrality as to the commerical future of Westland Helicopters.

The interest of Mr Heseltine's position was that he claimed that his apparent differences from his colleagues' policy were not inconsistent with respect for collective responsibility since there had been no opportunity for the Cabinet to debate and form a collective view on the policy in question. On this view, however, there would seem to have been no need for his resignation. The actual occasion for it was on a point of little substantive importance about the clearing of departmental statements by the Cabinet office, a procedure to which Mr Heseltine could mount no convincing objection. The continuance for so long of an open difference of view between different members of the Cabinet might well help to persuade us that Cabinet unanimity is not a constitutional obligation or a segment of the convention of collective responsibility, and that a Cabinet may have a policy, if it wishes, of permitting public disagreements between Ministers even on matters of major policy without endangering constitutional principles.

Ministers, Civil Servants, and the State

The trial of Mr Clive Ponting under the Official Secrets legislation in 1985 raised an issue both of law and convention about the relationship of civil servants to Ministers, to the Crown, and to Parliament. Mr Ponting, a senior civil servant in the Ministry of Defence, believed that Ministers in his department had misled the House of Commons in answering questions about the sinking of the Argentine cruiser *General Belgrano* during the Falklands War. Mr Ponting passed certain confidential documents to a Member of Parliament, Mr Tam Dalyell. At his trial on a charge of disclosing information to an unauthorized person he called expert evidence as to the implications of ministerial responsibility to Parliament and claimed that he was authorized and under a duty to communicate with Members of Parliament in the circumstances of the case. Mr Justice McCowan instructed the jury that the interests of the state could in this instance be interpreted as those of the government of the day. The jury, however, acquitted Mr Ponting, perhaps feeling some dissatisfaction with the equation. Legally speaking, civil servants clearly serve the Crown, and it is difficult to maintain that they have any legal duties to Parliament. In a memorandum of guidance written after the Ponting case Sir Robert Armstrong,[3] head of the Home Civil Service, stated that 'The Civil Service as such has no constitutional personality or responsibility separate from the duly elected government.' As a constitutional proposition (if not as a legal one) this might be disputed. Conventional rules of practice within the civil service do at present place certain limitations on the duties carried out by civil servants on behalf of ministers. Though there is no formal relationship between civil servants and Parliament, it is possible that the rights of the House through its select committees to obtain evidence by sending for persons and papers may test the limits of the civil servant's duty to maintain the confidences of his ministerial employers and that a duty to serve the state or the public interest might require civil service witnesses to answer truthfully or to give evidence which their political superiors would wish to withold. In the 1985-6 session the Select Committee on the Treasury and Civil Service took evidence from a number of governmental and non-governmental witnesses on the duties and responsibilities of civil servants and Ministers.

Ministers and Select Committees

The Westland affair and the resignation of Mr Leon Brittan provided further evidence of the prevailing uncertainty about the limits posed to select committee inquiries by the rights or prerogatives of ministers. The Select Committee on Defence in January 1986 wished to take evidence from some of the officials who had been involved in the leaking of information to the press in the course of the Westland affair. The Cabinet Secretary, Sir Robert Armstrong, appeared and gave evidence both to the Defence Committee and to the Treasury and Civil

---

[3] See HC Deb. 130 (1985) and 84 HC Deb. 663 (1985).

Service Select Committee. He informed them that the Government was unwilling to allow the officials concerned to give evidence, and neither Select Committee in the end pressed the matter.

The Select Committee on Defence also wished the Solicitor-General to appear before them. He declined the invitation on the ground that the Law Officers are not answerable to Parliament for the legal advice that they give to the Government. The Attorney General in a written answer to a Parliamentary question also referred to the convention of non-disclosure of such advice. The unwillingness to permit cross-examination of the Law Officers rests of course on different grounds from the withholding of junior civil servants' evidence. But perhaps in both cases the Government's position rests more on the convenience of past practice than on constitutional principle. The Law Officers of the Crown are after all Ministers, and in the words of Sir William Anson they are 'members of the House of Commons and responsible to Parliament for the advice given to the Crown and its servants'.[4] It is true that the opinions of the Law Officers have generally (though not invariably) been withheld from Parliament and treated as confidential. But so have a great many other matters for which Ministers are undoubtedly answerable to Parliament. In 'relation to select committees, Governments have claimed the privilege of deciding that particular Ministers or officials are not to be permitted to give evidence and the immunity of the Law Officers seems to rest more on this – possibly weakening – practice than on any special constitutional principle or convention. No such principle seems to preclude the Law Officers from giving evidence. The official memorandum of guidance for officials appearing before Select Committees indeed seems to envisage it, noting that 'It is only when Law Officers expressly authorise the disclosure of (their) advice or themselves report to or advise Parliament or a Committee that such advice is revealed.'[5]

---

[4] *Law and Custom of the Constitution* (10th edn. 1935), vol. 2, pt. 1, pp. 221–2.
[5] HC 588-1 (1977–8), p. 44.

Ministers and Prosecutions

The Ponting case raised strong feelings about the decision to prosecute under the Official Secrets Act in a case that involved a breach of ministerial confidentiality, but no danger to national security. In the Commons on 12 February 1985 the Leader of the Opposition, Mr Neil Kinnock, asked the Prime Minister what her involvement had been in the decision to prosecute. Mrs Thatcher replied that Ministers 'have no role in deciding whether or not to prosecute' (and that she had been on holiday at the time). Mr Kinnock replied that he did not believe her assurance and a series of letters passed between them about the Attorney-General's decision. Both Sir Michael Havers and the Prime Minister denied that there had been any ministerial involvement. Sir Michael stated that the facts reported by the Ministry of Defence to the Director of Public Prosecutions had been conveyed to him by the Director and by the Solicitor-General. Both of them advised prosecution. He then decided that the case fell within his published guidelines and agreed to the prosecution. Neither he, nor the Solicitor-General, nor any of his officials sought the views of, or consulted, any other ministers. Nor was the view of any other minister communicated to them before the decision.

In his correspondence with the Prime Minister, Mr Kinnock quoted the words of Mr Sam Silkin, former Attorney-General, in a letter to *The Times* on 26 September 1984, to the effect that whilst the Law Officers must take instructions from nobody, they are free to consult colleagues, particularly those with a departmental concern, and there would be times when they would be fools not to do so.

In her reply, Mrs Thatcher stated that there was no such long-established convention and that the Law Officers considered each case on its merits.

Consultation is not of course inconsistent with consideration of each case on its merits, and precedent seems to support Mr Silkin's view, with, however, a necessary clarification. The Law Officers are entitled to consult ministers, but should maintain the distinction between consultation as to the desirability of prosecution and consultation as to the effects of a prosecution on departmental interests or on ministerial views of the public interest. The balancing of the latter against all other matters in issue and the decision to prosecute itself is not one that Ministers are equipped to consider or advise upon. Ministers who make representations should by implication confine themselves to factual matters. Seemingly they are entitled to make representations of this kind even if not consulted, and even if on holiday at the time.

Appendix A: Extract from *Attorney-General v. Jonathan Cape Ltd.* (1976)

[1976] Q.B. 752

Lord Widgery CJ:

It has always been assumed by lawyers and, I suspect, by politicians, and the Civil Service, that Cabinet proceedings and Cabinet papers are secret, and cannot be publicly disclosed until they have passed into history. It is quite clear that no court will compel the production of Cabinet papers in the course of discovery in an action, and the Attorney-General contends that not only will the court refuse to compel the production of such matters, but it will go further and positively forbid the disclosure of such papers and proceedings if publication will be contrary to the public interest.

The basis of this contention is the confidential character of these papers and proceedings, derived from the convention of joint Cabinet responsibility whereby any policy decision reached by the Cabinet has to be supported thereafter by all members of the Cabinet whether they approve of it or not, unless they feel compelled to resign. It is contended that Cabinet decisions and papers are confidential for a period to the extent at least that they must not be referred to outside the Cabinet in such a way as to disclose the attitude of individual Ministers in the argument which preceded the decision. Thus, there may be no objection to a Minister disclosing (or leaking, as it was called) the fact that a Cabinet meeting has taken place, or, indeed, the decision taken, so long as the individual views of Ministers are not identified.

There is no doubt that Mr. Crossman's manuscripts contain frequent references to individual opinions of Cabinet Ministers, and this is not surprising because it was his avowed object to obtain a relaxation of the convention regarding memoirs of ex-Ministers to which Sir John Hunt referred. There have, as far as I know, been no previous attempts in any court to define the extent to which Cabinet proceedings should be treated as secret or confidential, and it is not surprising that different views on this subject are contained in the evidence before me. The Attorney-General does not attempt a final definition but his contention is that such proceedings are confidential and their publication is capable of control by the courts at least as far as they include (a) disclosure of Cabinet documents or proceedings in such a way as to reveal the individual views or attitudes of Ministers; (b) disclosure of confidential advice from civil servants, whether contained in Cabinet papers or not; (c) disclosure of confidential discussions affecting the appointment or transfer of such senior civil servants.

The Attorney-General contends that all Cabinet papers and discussions are prima facie confidential, and that the court should restrain any disclosure thereof if the public interest in concealment outweighs the public interest in a right to free publication. The Attorney-General further contends that, if it is shown that the public interest is involved, he has the right and duty to bring the matter before the court. In this contention he is well supported by Lord Salmon in *Reg.* v. *Lewes Justices, Ex parte Secretary of State for the Home Department* [1973] A.C. 388, 412, where Lord Salmon said:

when it is in the public interest that confidentiality shall be safeguarded, then the party from whom the confidential document or the confidential information is being sought may lawfully refuse it. In such a case the Crown may also intervene to prevent production or disclosure of that which in the public interest ought to be protected.

I do not understand Lord Salmon to be saying, or the Attorney-General to be contending, that it is only necessary for him to evoke the public interest to obtain an order of the court. On the contrary, it must be for the court in every case to be satisfied that the public interest is involved, and that, after balancing all the factors which tell for or against publication, to decide whether suppression is necessary.

The defendants' main contention is that whatever the limits of the convention of joint Cabinet responsibility may be, there is no obligation enforceable at law to prevent the publication of Cabinet papers and proceedings, except in extreme cases where national security is involved. In other words, the defendants submit that the confidential character of Cabinet papers and discussions is based on a true convention as defined in the evidence of Professor Henry Wade, namely, an obligation founded in conscience only. Accordingly the defendants contend that publication of these Diaries is not capable of control by any order of this court.

If the Attorney-General were restricted in his argument to the general proposition that Cabinet papers and discussion are all under the seal of secrecy at all times, he would be in difficulty. It is true that he has called evidence from eminent former holders of office to the effect that the public interest requires a continuing secrecy, and he cites a powerful passage from the late Viscount Hailsham to this effect. The extract comes from a copy of the Official Report (House of Lords) for December 21, 1932, in the course of a debate on Cabinet secrecy. Lord Hailsham said; col. 527:

But, my Lords, I am very glad that the question has been raised because it has seemed to me that there is a tendency in some quarters at least to ignore or to forget the nature and extent of the obligation of secrecy and the limitations which rigidly hedge round the position of a Cabinet Minister. My noble friend has read to your Lordships what in fact I was proposing to read — that is, the oath which every Privy Councillor takes when he is sworn of His Majesty's Privy Council. Your Lordships will remember that one reason at least why a Cabinet Minister must of necessity be a member of the Privy Council is that it involves the taking of that oath. Having heard that oath read your Lordships will appreciate what a complete misconception it is to suppose, as some people seem inclined to suppose, that the only obligation that rests upon a Cabinet Minister is not to disclose what are described as the Cabinet's minutes. He is sworn to keep secret all matters committed and revealed unto him or that shall be treated secretly in Council.

Lord Hailsham then goes on to point out that there are three distinct classes to which the obligation of secrecy applies. He describes them as so-called Cabinet minutes; secondly, a series of documents, memoranda telegrams and despatches and documents circulated from one Cabinet Minister to his colleagues to bring before them a particular problem and to discuss the arguments for and against a particular course of conduct; and thirdly, apart from those two classes of documents, he says there is the recollection of the individual Minister of what happens in the Cabinet. Then the extract from Lord Hailsham's speech in the House of Lords report continues in these words:

I have stressed that because, as my noble and learned friend Lord Halsbury suggested and the noble Marquis, Lord Salisbury, confirmed Cabinet conclusions did not exist until 16 years ago. The old practice is set out in a book which bears the name of the noble Earl's father, Halsbury's Laws of England, with which I have had the honour to be associated in the present edition.

Then the last extract from Lord Hailsham's speech is found in col. 532, and is in these words:

It is absolutely essential in the public interest that discussions which take place between Cabinet Ministers shall take place in the full certainty of all of them that they are speaking their minds with absolute freedom to colleagues on whom they can explicitly rely, upon matters on which it is their sworn duty to express their opinions with complete frankness and to give all information, without any haunting fear that what happens may hereafter by publication create difficulties for themselves or, what is far more grave, may create complications for the King and country that they are trying to serve. For those reasons I hope that the inflexible rule which has hitherto prevailed will be maintained in its integrity, and that if there has been any relaxation or misunderstanding, of which I say nothing, the debate in this House will have done something to clarify the position and restate the old rule in all its rigour and all its inflexibility.

The defendants, however, in the present action, have also called distinguished former Cabinet Ministers who do not support this view of Lord Hailsham, and it seems to me that the degree of protection afforded to Cabinet papers and discussion cannot be determined by a single rule of thumb. Some secrets require a high standard of protection for a short time. Others require protection until a new political generation has taken over. In the present action against the literary executors, the Attorney-General asks for a perpetual injunction to restrain further publication of the Diaries in whole or in part. I am far from convinced that he has made out a case that the public interest requires such a Draconian remedy when due regard is had to other public interests, such as the freedom of speech: see Lord Denning M.R. in *In re X (A Minor) (Wardship: Jurisdiction)* [1975] 2 W.L.R. 335, 343.

Some attempt has been made to say that the publication of these

Diaries by Mr. Crossman would have been a breach of his oath as a Privy Councillor, and an echo of this argument is, of course, to be found in Lord Hailsham's words recently quoted. This is, however, not seriously relied upon in the two actions now before me, and the Attorney-General concedes that the present defendants are not in breach of the Official Secrets Acts. It seems to me, therefore, that the Attorney-General must first show that whatever obligation of secrecy or discretion attaches to former Cabinet Ministers, that obligation is binding in law and not merely in morals.

I have read affidavits from a large number of leading politicians, and the facts, so far as relevant, appear to be these. In 1964, 1966 and 1969 the Prime Minister (who was in each case Mr. Harold Wilson) issued a confidential document to Cabinet ministers containing guidance on certain questions of procedure. Paragraph 72 of the 1969 edition provides:

The principle of collective responsibility and the obligation not to disclose information acquired whilst holding Ministerial office apply to former Ministers who are contemplating the publication of material based upon their recollections of the conduct of Cabinet and Cabinet committee business in which they took part.

The general understanding of Ministers while in office was that information obtained from Cabinet sources was secret and not to be disclosed to outsiders.

There is not much evidence of the understanding of Ministers as to the protection of such information after the Minister retires. It seems probable to me that those not desirous of publishing memoirs assumed that the protection went on until the incident was 30 years old, whereas those interested in memoirs would discover on inquiry at the Cabinet Office that draft memoirs were normally submitted to the Secretary of the Cabinet for his advice on their contents before publication. Manuscripts were almost always submitted to the Secretary of the Cabinet in accordance with the last-mentioned procedure. Sir Winston Churchill submitted the whole of his manuscripts concerned with the war years, and accepted the advice given by the Secretary of the Cabinet as to publication.

In recent years, successive Secretaries of the Cabinet, when giving advice on the publication of a Minister's memoirs, were much concerned about (a) disclosure of individual views of Members of the Cabinet in defiance of the principle of joint responsibility; (b) disclosure of advice given by civil servants still in office; (c) disclosure of discussions relating to the promotion or transfer of senior civil servants.

Mr. Crossman, as appears from the introduction to volume one of his Diaries, disapproved of the submission of manuscripts to the Secretary of the Cabinet. He made no attempt to admit the three categories of information just referred to, and expressed the intention to obtain publication whilst memories were green.

Mr. Crossman made no secret of the fact that he kept a diary which he intended to use for the writing of his memoirs. It was contended on behalf of the literary executors that any bond of confidence or secrecy normally attending upon Cabinet material had been lifted in Mr. Crossman's case by consent of his colleagues. Even if, as a matter of law, a Minister can release himself from a bond of secrecy in this way, I do not find that Mr. Crossman effectively did so. It is not enough to show that his colleagues accepted the keeping of the diary. It was vital to show that they accepted Mr. Crossman's intention to use the diary whether it passed the scrutiny of the Secretary of the Cabinet or not. The strongest evidence in support of this is in Lord Gordon-Walker's affidavit sworn on July 27, 1975, when he said:

It was obvious to, and accepted by Mr. Crossman's Cabinet colleagues, that Mr. Crossman intended publication; that his publication would include detailed accounts of Cabinet committee meetings including the direct attribution to members of views which they expressed there.

I would have welcomed the opportunity to discuss this more fully with Lord Gordon-Walker because he disclaims any knowledge of Sir John Hunt's parameters, and says that his understanding of the procedure of submitting manuscripts to the Secretary of the Cabinet was to avoid 'inadvertent breaches of national security,' rather than to protect the doctrine of joint responsibility.

The main framework of the defence is to be found in eight submissions from Mr. Comyn. The first two have already been referred to, the allegation being that there is no power in law for the court to interfere with publication of these diaries or extracts, and that the Attorney-General's proper remedy lies in obtaining a change of the statute law.

I have already indicated some of the difficulties which face the Attorney-General when he relied simply on the public interest as a ground for his actions. That such ground is enough in extreme cases is shown by the universal agreement that publication affecting national security can be restrained in this way. It may be that in the short run (for example, over a period of weeks or months) the public interest is equally compelling to maintain joint Cabinet responsibility and the protection of advice given by civil servants, but I would not accept without close investigation that such matters must, as a matter of course, retain protection after a period of years.

However, the Attorney-General has a powerful reinforcement for his argument in the developing equitable doctrine that a man shall not profit from the wrongful publication of information received by him in confidence. This doctrine, said to have its origin in *Prince Albert* v. *Strange* (1849) 1 H. & T. 1, has been frequently recognised as a ground for restraining the unfair use of commercial secrets transmitted in confidence. Sometimes in these cases there is a contract which may be said to have been breached by the breach of confidence, but it is clear that the doctrine applies independently of contract: see *Saltman Engineering Co. Ltd.* v. *Campbell Engineering Co. Ltd.* (1948) 65 R.P.C. 203. Again in *Coco* v. *A. N. Clark (Engineers) Ltd.* [1969]

R.P.C. 41 Megarry J., reviewing the authorities, set out the requirements necessary for an action based on breach of confidence to succeed.
He said, at p. 47:

> In my judgment three elements are normally required if, apart from contract, a
> case of breach of confidence is to succeed. First, the information itself, in the
> words of Lord Greene M.R. . . . must 'have the necessary quality of confidence
> about it.' Secondly, that information must have been imparted in circumstances
> importing an obligation of confidence. Thirdly, there must be an unauthorised
> use of that information to the detriment of the party communicating it.

It is not until the decision in *Duchess of Argyll* v. *Duke of Argyll*
[1967] Ch. 302, that the same principle was applied to domestic
secrets such as those passing between husband and wife during the
marriage. It was there held by Ungoed-Thomas J. that the plaintiff
wife could obtain an order to restrain the defendant husband from
communicating such secrets, and the principle is well expressed in the
headnote in these terms, at p. 304:

> A contract or obligation of confidence need not be expressed but could be
> implied, and a breach of contract or trust or faith could arise independently
> of any right of property or contract . . . and that the court, in the exercise of its
> equitable jurisdiction, would restrain a breach of confidence independently of
> any right at law.

This extension of the doctrine of confidence beyond commercial
secrets has never been directly challenged, and was noted without
criticism by Lord Denning M.R. in *Fraser* v. *Evans* [1969] 1 Q.B.
349, 361. I am sure that I ought to regard myself, sitting here, as bound
by the decision of Ungoed-Thomas J.

Even so, these defendants argue that an extension of the principle
of the *Argyll* case to the present dispute involves another large and
unjustified leap forward, because in the present case the Attorney-
General is seeking to apply the principle to public secrets made confidential in the interests of good government. I cannot see why the
courts should be powerless to restrain the publication of public secrets,
while enjoying the *Argyll* powers in regard to domestic secrets. Indeed,
as already pointed out, the court must have power to deal with publication which threatens national security, and the difference between
such a case and the present case is one of degree rather than kind. I
conclude, therefore, that when a Cabinet Minister receives information
in confidence the improper publication of such information can be
restrained by the court, and his obligation is not merely to observe
a gentleman's agreement to refrain from publication.

It is convenient next to deal with Mr. Comyn's third submission,
namely, that the evidence does not prove the existence of a convention
as to collective responsibility, or adequately define a sphere of secrecy.
I find overwhelming evidence that the doctrine of joint responsibility
is generally understood and practised and equally strong evidence
that it is on occasion ignored. The general effect of the evidence is
that the doctrine is an established feature of the English form of
government, and it follows that some matters leading up to a Cabinet

decision may be regarded as confidential. Furthermore, I am persuaded that the nature of the confidence is that spoken for by the Attorney-General, namely, that since the confidence is imposed to enable the efficient conduct of the Queen's business, the confidence is owed to the Queen and cannot be released by the members of Cabinet themselves. I have been told that a resigning Minister who wishes to make a personal statement in the House, and to disclose matters which are confidential under the doctrine obtains the consent of the Queen for this purpose. Such consent is obtained through the Prime Minister. I have not been told what happened when the Cabinet disclosed divided opinions during the European Economic Community referendum. But even if there was here a breach of confidence (which I doubt) this is no ground for denying the existence of the general rule. I cannot accept the suggestion that a Minister owes no duty of confidence in respect of his own views expressed in Cabinet. It would only need one or two Ministers to describe their own views to enable experienced observers to identify the views of others.

The other defence submissions are either variants of those dealt with or submissions with regard to relief.

The Cabinet is at the very centre of national affairs, and must be in possession at all times of information which is secret or confidential. Secrets relating to national security may require to be preserved indefinitely. Secrets relating to new taxation proposals may be of the highest importance until Budget day, but public knowledge thereafter. To leak a Cabinet decision a day or so before it is officially announced is an accepted exercise in public relations, but to identify the Ministers who voted one way or another is objectionable because it undermines the doctrine of joint responsibility.

It is evident that there cannot be a single rule governing the publication of such a variety of matters. In these actions we are concerned with the publication of diaries at a time when 11 years have expired since the first recorded events. The Attorney-General must show (a) that such publication would be a breach of confidence; (b) that the public interest requires that the publication be restrained, and (c) that there are no other facts of the public interest contradictory of and more compelling than that relied upon. Moreover, the court, when asked to restrain such a publication, must closely examine the extent to which relief is necessary to ensure that restrictions are not imposed beyond the strict requirement of public need.

Applying those principles to the present case, what do we find? In my judgment, the Attorney-General has made out his claim that the expression of individual opinions by Cabinet Ministers in the course of Cabinet discussion are matters of confidence, the publication of which can be restrained by the court when this is clearly necessary in the public interest.

The maintenance of the doctrine of joint responsibility within the Cabinet is in the public interest, and the application of that doctrine might be prejudiced by premature disclosure of the views of individual Ministers.

There must, however, be a limit in time after which the confidential character of the information, and the duty of the court to restrain publication, will lapse. Since the conclusion of the hearing in this case I have had the opportunity to read the whole of volume one of the Diaries, and my considered view is that I cannot believe that the publication at this interval of anything in volume one would inhibit free discussion in the Cabinet of today, even though the individuals involved are the same, and the national problems have a distressing similarity with those of a decade ago. It is unnecessary to elaborate the evils which might flow if at the close of a Cabinet meeting a Minister proceeded to give the press an analysis of the voting, but we are dealing in this case with a disclosure of information nearly 10 years later.

It may, of course, be intensely difficult in a particular case, to say at what point the material loses its confidential character, on the ground that publication will no longer undermine the doctrine of joint Cabinet responsibility. It is this difficulty which prompts some to argue that Cabinet discussions should retain their confidential character for a longer and arbitrary period such as 30 years, or even for all time, but this seems to me to be excessively restrictive. The court should intervene only in the clearest of cases where the continuing confidentiality of the material can be demonstrated. In less clear cases — and this, in my view, is certainly one — reliance must be placed on the good sense and good taste of the Minister or ex-Minister concerned.

In the present case there is nothing in Mr. Crossman's work to suggest that he did not support the doctrine of joint Cabinet responsibility. The question for the court is whether it is shown that publication now might damage the doctrine notwithstanding that much of the action is up to 10 years old and three general elections have been held meanwhile. So far as the Attorney-General relies in his argument on the disclosure of individual ministerial opinions, he has not satisfied me that publication would in any way inhibit free and open discussion in Cabinet hereafter.

It remains to deal with the Attorney-General's two further arguments, namely, (a) that the Diaries disclose advice given by senior civil servants who cannot be expected to advise frankly if their advice is not treated as confidential; (b) the Diaries disclose observations made by Ministers on the capacity of individual senior civil servants and their suitability for specific appointments. I can see no ground in law which entitle the court to restrain publication of these matters. A Minister is, no doubt, responsible for his department and accountable for its errors even though the individual fault is to be found in his subordinates. In these circumstances, to disclose the fault of the subordinate may amount to cowardice or bad taste, but I can find no ground for saying that either the Crown or the individual civil servant has an enforceable right to have the advice which he gives treated as confidential for all time.

For these reasons I do not think that the court should interfere with the publication of volume one of the Diaries, and I propose, therefore, to refuse the injunction sought but to grant liberty to apply in regard to material other than volume one if it is alleged that different considerations may there have to be applied.

Appendix B: Extract from *Reference re Amendment of the Constitution of Canada* (1981)[1]

(1982) 125 D.L.R. (3d.) 1

1 *The Nature of Constitutional Conventions*

It was apparently Dicey who, in the first edition of his *Law of the Constitution*, in 1885 referred to 'the conventions of the constitution',[2] an expression which quickly became current. What Dicey described under these terms are the principles and rules of responsible government, several of which are stated above and which regulate the relations between the Crown, the Prime Minister, the Cabinet and the two Houses of Parliament. These rules developed in Great Britain by way of custom and precedent during the nineteenth century and were exported to such British colonies as were granted self-government.

Dicey first gave the impression that constitutional conventions are a peculiarly British and modern phenomenon. But he recognized in later editions that different conventions are found in other constitutions. As Sir William Holdsworth wrote:

In fact conventions must grow up at all times and in all places where the powers of government are vested in different persons or bodies — where in other words there is a mixed constitution. 'The constituent parts of a state,' said Burke, [French Revolution, 28] 'are we obliged to hold their public faith with each other, and with all those who derive any serious interest under their engagements, as much as the whole state is bound to keep its faith with separate communities.' Necessarily conventional rules spring up to regulate the working of the various parts of the constitution, their relations to one another, and to the subject.[3]

Within the British Empire, powers of government were vested in different bodies which provided a fertile ground for the growth of new constitutional conventions unknown to Dicey whereby self-governing colonies acquired equal and independent status within the Commonwealth. Many of these culminated in the Statute of Westminster, 1931.[4]

A federal constitution provides for the distribution of powers between various legislatures and governments and may also constitute a fertile ground for the growth of constitutional conventions between those legislatures and governments. It is conceivable for instance that usage and practice might give birth to conventions in Canada relating to the holding of federal–provincial conferences, the appointment of

---

[1] Majority opinion of Ritchie, Dickson, Beetz, Chouinard, and Lamer JJ.
[2] W. S. Holdsworth, 'The conventions of the eighteenth century constitution', (1932), 17 *Iowa Law Rev.* 161.
[3] W. S. Holdsworth, op. cit., p. 162.
[4] 22 Geo. V, c.4.

lieutenant-governors, the reservation and disallowance of provincial legislation. It was to this possibility that Duff C.J.C. alluded when he referred to 'constitutional usage or constitutional practice' in *Reference re The Power of the Governor-General in Council to disallow provincial legislation and the Power of Reservation of the Lieutenant-Governor of a Province.*[5] He had previously called them 'recognized constitutional conventions' in *Wilson v. Esquimalt and Nanaimo Ry. Co.*[6]

The main purpose of constitutional conventions is to ensure that the legal framework of the Constitution will be operated in accordance with the prevailing constitutional values or principles of the period. For example, the constitutional value which is the pivot of the conventions stated above and relating to responsible government is the democratic principle: the powers of the state must be exercised in accordance with the wishes of the electorate; and the constitutional value or principle which anchors the conventions regulating the relationship between the members of the Commonwealth is the independence of the former British colonies.

Being based on custom and precedent, constitutional conventions are usually unwritten rules. Some of them however may be reduced to writing and expressed in the proceedings and documents of imperial conferences, or in the preamble of statutes such as the Statute of Westminster, 1931, or in the proceedings and documents of federal-provincial conferences. They are often referred to and recognized in statements made by members of governments.

The conventional rules of the Constitution present one striking peculiarity. In contradistinction to the laws of the Constitution, they are not enforced by the courts. One reason for this situation is that, unlike common law rules, conventions are not judge-made rules. They are not based on judicial precedents but on precedents established by the institutions of government themselves. Nor are they in the nature of statutory commands which it is the function and duty of the courts to obey and enforce. Furthermore, to enforce them would mean to administer some formal sanction when they are breached. But the legal system from which they are distinct does not contemplate formal sanctions for their breach.

Perhaps the main reason why conventional rules cannot be enforced by the courts is that they are generally in conflict with the legal rules which they postulate and the courts are bound to enforce the legal rules. The conflict is not of a type which would entail the commission of any illegality. It results from the fact that legal rules create wide powers, discretions, and rights which conventions prescribe should be exercised only in a certain limited manner, if at all.

Some examples will illustrate this point.

As a matter of law, the Queen, or the Governor-General or the Lieutenant-Governor could refuse assent to every bill passed by both Houses of Parliament or by a Legislative Assembly as the case may be.

[5] [1938] S.C.R. 71 at p. 78   [6] [1922] 1 A.C. 202 at p. 210.

But by convention they cannot of their own motion refuse to assent to any such bill on any ground, for instance because they disapprove of the policy of the bill. We have here a conflict between a legal rule which creates a complete discretion and a conventional rule which completely neutralizes it. But conventions, like laws, are sometimes violated. And if this particular convention were violated and assent were improperly withheld, the courts would be bound to enforce the law, not the convention. They would refuse to recognize the validity of a vetoed bill. This is what happened in *Gallant* v. *R*.,[7] a case in keeping with the classic case of *Stockdale* v. *Hansard*[8] where the English Court of Queen's Bench held that only the Queen and both Houses of Parliament could make or unmake laws. The Lieutenant-Governor who had withheld assent in *Gallant* apparently did so towards the end of his term of office. Had it been otherwise, it is not inconceivable that his withholding of assent might have produced a political crisis leading to his removal from office which shows that if the remedy for a breach of a convention does not lie with the courts, still the breach is not necessarily without a remedy. The remedy lies with some other institutions of government; furthermore it is not a formal remedy and it may be administered with less certainty or regularity than it would be by a court.

Another example of the conflict between law and convention is provided by a fundamental convention already stated above: if after a general election where the Opposition obtained the majority at the polls the Government refused to resign and clung to office, it would thereby commit a fundamental breach of conventions, one so serious indeed that it could be regarded as tantamount to a coup d'état. The remedy in this case would lie with the Governor-General or the Lieutenant-Governor as the case might be who would be justified in dismissing the Ministry and in calling on the Opposition to form the Government. But should the Crown be slow in taking this course, there is nothing the courts could do about it except at the risk of creating a state of legal discontinuity, that is a form of revolution. An order or a regulation passed by a Minister under statutory authority and otherwise valid could not be invalidated on the ground that, by convention, the Minister ought no longer to be a Minister. A writ of *quo warranto* aimed at Ministers, assuming that *quo warranto* lies against a Minister of the Crown, which is very doubtful, would be of no avail to remove them from office. Required to say by what warrant they occupy their ministerial office, they would answer that they occupy it by the pleasure of the Crown under a commission issued by the Crown and this answer would be a complete one at law for at law, the Government is in office by the pleasure of the Crown although by convention it is there by the will of the people.

This conflict between convention and law which prevents the courts

---

[7] [1949] 2 D.L.R. 425; [1949] 23 M.P.R. 48. See also for a comment on the situation by K. M. Martin in (1946) 24 *Can. Bar Rev.* 434.

[8] [1839] 9 Ad. and E. 1.

from enforcing conventions also prevents conventions from crystallizing into laws, unless it be by statutory adoption.

It is because the sanctions of convention rest with institutions of government other than courts, such as the Governor-General or the Lieutenant-Governor, or the Houses of Parliament, or with public opinion and ultimately, with the electorate that it is generally said that they are political.

We respectfully adopt the definition of a convention given by the learned Chief Justice of Manitoba, Freedman C.J.M. in the Manitoba Reference at pp. 13 and 14:

> What is a constitutional convention? There is a fairly lengthy literature on the subject. Although there may be shades of difference among the constitutional lawyers, political scientists, and judges who have contributed to that literature, the essential features of a convention may be set forth with some degree of confidence. Thus there is general agreement that a convention occupies a position somewhere in between a usage or custom on the one hand and a constitutional law on the other. There is general agreement that if one sought to fix that position with greater precision he would place convention nearer to law than to usage or custom. There is also general agreement that 'a convention is a rule which is regarded as obligatory by the officials to whom it applies'. Hogg, *Constitutional Law of Canada* (1977), p. 9. There is, if not general agreement, at least weighty authority, that the sanction for breach of a convention will be political rather than legal.

It should be borne in mind however that, while they are not laws, some conventions may be more important than some laws. Their importance depends on that of the value or principle which they are meant to safeguard. Also they form an integral part of the Constitution and of the constitutional system. They come within the meaning of the word 'Constitution' in the preamble of the British North America Act, 1867:

> Whereas the Provinces of Canada, Nova Scotia and New Brunswick have expressed their Desire to be federally united . . . with a Constitution similar in principle to that of the United Kingdom:

That is why it is perfectly appropriate to say that to violate a convention is to do something which is unconstitutional although it entails no direct legal consequence. But the words 'constitutional' and 'unconstitutional' may also be used in a strict legal sense, for instance with respect to a statute which is found *ultra vires* or unconstitutional. The foregoing may perhaps be summarized in an equation: constitutional conventions plus constitutional law equal the total Constitution of the country.

2 *Whether the Questions should be Answered*

It was submitted by counsel for Canada and for Ontario that the second question in the Manitoba and Newfoundland References and the conventional part of question B in the Quebec Reference ought not be answered because they do not raise a justiciable issue and are accordingly not appropriate for a court. It was contended that the issue whether a particular convention exists or not is a purely political one. The existence of a definite convention is always unclear and a matter of debate. Furthermore conventions are flexible, somewhat imprecise and unsuitable for judicial determination.

The same submission was made in substance to the three courts below and, in our respectful opinion, rightfully dismissed by all three of them, Hall J.A. dissenting in the Manitoba Court of Appeal.

We agree with what Freedman C.J.M. wrote on this subject in the Manitoba Reference at p. 13:

In my view this submission goes too far. Its characterization of Question 2 as 'purely political' overstates the case. That there is a political element embodied in the question, arising from the contents of the Joint Address, may well be the case. But that does not end the matter. If Question 2, even if in part political, possesses a constitutional feature, it would legitimately call for our reply.

In my view the request for a decision by this Court on whether there is a constitutional convention, in the circumstances described, that the Dominion will not act without the agreement of the Provinces poses a question that is, at least in part, constitutional in character. It therefore calls for an answer, and I propose to answer it.

Question 2 is not confined to an issue of pure legality but it has to do with a fundamental issue of constitutionality and legitimacy. Given the broad statutory basis upon which the Governments of Manitoba, Newfoundland and Quebec are empowered to put questions to their three respective Courts of Appeal, they are in our view entitled to an answer to a question of this type.

Furthermore, one of the main points made by Manitoba with respect to question 3 was that the constitutional convention referred to in question 2 had become crystallized into a rule of law. Question 3 is admitted by all to raise a question of law. We agree with Matas J.A. of the Manitoba Court of Appeal that it would be difficult to answer question 3 without an analysis of the points raised in question 2. It is accordingly incumbent on us to answer question 2.

Finally, we are not asked to hold that a convention has in effect repealed a provision of the B.N.A. Act, as was the case in the *Reference re Disallowance* (supra). Nor are we asked to enforce a convention. We are asked to recognize it if it exists. Courts have done this very thing many times in England and the Commonwealth to provide aid for and background to constitutional or statutory construction. Several such cases are mentioned in the reasons of the majority of this Court relating to the question whether constitutional conventions are capable of crystallizing into law. There are many others among them *Commonwealth* v. *Kreglinger*,[9] *Liversidge* v. *Anderson*,[10] *Carltona Ltd.* v. *Commissioners of Works*,[11] *Adegbenro* v. *Akintola*,[12] *Ibralebbe* v. *R.*[13] This

[9] [1925] 37 C.L.R. 393.   [10] [1942] A.C. 206.
[11] [1943] 2 All E.R. 560.   [12] [1963] A.C. 614.
[13] [1964] A.C. 900.

Court did the same in the recent case of *Arseneau* v. *R.*[14] and in the still unreported judgment rendered on April 6, 1981 after the re-hearing of *Attorney-General of Quebec* v. *Peter Blaikie et al.*

In so recognizing conventional rules, the Courts have described them, sometimes commented upon them and given them such precision as is derived from the written form of a judgment. They did not shrink from doing so on account of the political aspects of conventions, nor because of their supposed vagueness, uncertainty or flexibility.

In our view, we should not, in a constitutional reference, decline to accomplish a type of exercise that courts have been doing of their own motion for years.

[14] [1979] 2 S.C.R. 136 at p. 149.

Appendix C: Jennings and Dicey on Law and Convention

In the later editions of *The Law and the Constitution* Sir Ivor Jennings made some changes in his chapter on Convention. In the second edition (p. 113) he says that a Frenchman, M. Paul Léon, has made 'an unusual accusation' against him of a Diceyite heresy, and that he does 'not deny that conventions are *droit*, only that they are common law' (see also his article in *Politica*, vol. 2, pp. 398-402).

Many of the views expressed in *The Law and the Constitution* were reactions against views or supposed views of Dicey. Jennings somewhat misrepresents Dicey; — for example, on obedience to conventions by stating his (Dicey's) view baldly as being that obedience rests on the possibility of collision with law and legal tribunals (1st edn., p. 99). He mentions some breaches of convention that would not entail collision with courts of law. But Dicey did not say that all conventions were obeyed for this reason, and himself gives examples similar to Jennings's of breaches of convention that would not involve breaches of law (see the note at p. 26 of Dicey's *Law of the Constitution*, 8th edn.).

In comparing law and convention, however, Jennings is usually thinking about their similarity from the point of view of the *reasons for obedience* or their *binding force* (see the caption at p. 90 of 1st edn. of *The Law and The Constitution* removed in 2nd), and also making the point that the *enforceability* of each rests on acquiescence and *not force or enforcement* (see 1st edn., section heading: 'Neither laws or conventions are "enforced"'). This stems from his view about law in general as not resting on force or being enforced (see 3rd edn., Appendix, 'Note on the Theory of Law').

This is connected in turn with his view about the political nature of English law and its variability in response to political needs (as against being a supposedly fixed and clear body of principles). It is in this context that he introduces the sentence in the third edition (in the chapter on 'English Constitutional Law') that 'All Law and government are politics' so that the conventions 'are rules whose nature does not differ fundamentally from that of the positive law of England' (3rd edn., p. 73).

It is in pursuance of *this* theme that in the chapter on 'Conventions' in the first and third editions he includes a section headed 'No Fundamental Distinction between Law and Convention' (in 3rd edn., 'No Distinction of Substance'). Nevertheless, in the third edition he later includes a section headed 'Real Differences', in which he indicates three differences between law and convention. The differences are that a law has greater sanctity from a 'psychological' point of view; that a law is formally expressed in a decision by a court; and that it is the courts which declare when a breach of law takes place (whereas conventions arise from practice and it is never quite certain at what point they cease to be or become conventions). All this sounds remarkably similar to what Dicey was saying. And Jennings indeed says (3rd edn., p. 113) that 'There is a formal distinction of the kind recognised by Dicey' and that it is important (p. 127) "from the technical angle" whether a rule is law or convention'; but the differences are 'of some, though not fundamental importance'.

So it seems clear that what Jennings means is that Dicey's differences exist, but are not fundamentally important from the point of view of the concerns expressed above about the general character of all socially coercive norms. It is his concern with what he sees as over-narrow definitions of law and over-emphasis on court enforcement of law that leads him to want to analogize law to convention (and to politics).

In the chapter in which he attacks Dicey's distinction, it is primarily on the ground that Dicey says that laws are rules enforced by courts. Against this he argues that the meaning of 'court' is vague and that some rules of law may be enforced by bodies that are not courts. This may show that some law is sometimes not enforced by courts and that some law is sometimes enforced by non- or quasi-courts; but it does not show that it is wrong to say that what distinguishes convention is that it is never enforced by courts. This point which seemed clear and even fundamental to Dicey, may have seemed technical or formal to Jennings and not fundamental from the point of view of his other concerns with the nature of social behaviour generally. So perhaps it is only in that way that Jennings urges that no 'fundamental' distinction between law and convention exists, and his position is not therefore inconsistent with admitting that, for those who think it to have importance, Dicey's differentiation between the two exists (or formally, or technically, exists).

Bibliography

CONSTITUTIONAL CONVENTION (Chapters I and XIII)

W. S. Holdsworth, 'The Conventions of the Eighteenth Century Constitution', (1932) 17 *Iowa Law Review* 101.

O. Hood Phillips, 'Dicey's Predecessors', (1966) 29 *Modern Law Review* 137.

E. A. Freeman, *The Growth of the English Constitution* (3rd edn. 1876), chap. 3.

A. V. Dicey, *Introduction to the Study of the Law of the Constitution* (10th Edn., ed. E. C. S. Wade), chaps. 14 and 15.

Sir I. Jennings, *Cabinet Government* (3rd edn. 1959), chap. 1 and App. 3.

—— *The Law and the Constitution* (5th edn. 1959), chap. 3.

Sir Kenneth Wheare, *Modern Constitutions*, chapter 8.

—— *The Statute of Westminster and Dominion Status* (5th edn. 1952), chap. 1.

O. Hood Phillips, 'Constitutional Conventions: a Conventional Reply', (1964-5) *Journal of the Society of Public Teachers of Law*, NS vii, p. 60.

E. M. McWhinney, 'Constitutional Conventions', (1957) 35 *Canadian Bar Review* 92.

K. J. Keith, 'The Courts and the Conventions of the Constitution', (1967) 16 *International and Comparative Law Quarterly* 542.

C. R. Munro, 'Laws and Conventions Distinguished', (1975) *Law Quarterly Review* 218.

R. Brazier and St. John Robilliard, 'Constitutional Convention: The Canadian Supreme Court's Views Reviewed', (1982) *Public Law* 28.

S. A. de Smith, *Constitutional and Administrative Law* (4th edn., ed. H. Street and R. Brazier), pp. 39-57.

THE QUEEN (Chapters II and III)

G. H. L. LeMay, *The Victorian Constitution: Conventions, Usages and Contingencies* (1979), chaps. 3 and 7.

A. Berriedale Keith, *The King and the Imperial Crown: the Powers and Duties of His Majesty* (1936).

Sir Ivor Jennings, *Cabinet Government* (3rd edn.), chaps. 12-14.

Sir Harold Nicolson, *King George V: His Life and Reign* (1952), chap. VIII.

Sir John Wheeler-Bennett, *George VI: His Life and Reign* (1958).

Lord Blake, 'The Queen and the Constitution' in *The Queen: a Penguin Special* (1977).
G. C. Moodie, 'The Crown and Parliament', (1957) *Parliamentary Affairs* 256.
E. A. Forsey, *The Royal Power of Dissolution of Parliament in the British Commonwealth* (1943).
B. S. Markesinis, *The Theory and Practice of Dissolution of Parliament* (1972).
E. Campbell, 'The Prerogative Power of Dissolution: some recent Tasmanian Precedents', (1961) *Public Law* 165.
D. J. Heasman, 'The Monarch, the Prime Minister and the Dissolution of Parliament', (1960-1) *Parliamentary Affairs* 94.
D. E. Butler, *Governing without a Majority: Dilemmas for Hung Parliaments in Britain* (1983).
R. Brazier, 'Appointing a Prime Minister', (1982) *Public Law* 395.
V. Bogdanor, *Multi-party Politics and the Constitution* (1983).

CABINET AND PRIME MINISTER (Chapter III)

J. Morley, *Life of Walpole* (1889), chap. 7, 'The Cabinet'.
A. G. Gardiner, *The Life of Sir William Harcourt* (1923), vol. ii, App. II.
G. H. L. LeMay, *The Victorian Constitution* (1979), chap. 4, 'Cabinet and Prime Minister'.
H. H. Asquith, 'Prime Minister and Cabinet' in *Fifty Years of Parliament* (1922), vol. ii.
Harold Laski, *Reflections on the Constitution* (1951), chap. 8.
Byrum E. Carter, *The Office of Prime Minister* (1956).
John Mackintosh, *The British Cabinet* (3rd edn. 1977).
P. Gordon Walker, *The Cabinet* (2nd edn. 1972).
G. W. Jones, 'The Prime Minister's Powers', (1965) *Parliamentary Affairs* 167.
A. H. Brown, 'Prime Ministerial Power', (1968) *Public Law* 28, 96.
Harold Wilson, *The Governance of Britain* (1976), chap. 1.
Lord Blake, *The Office of Prime Minister* (1975).

MINISTERIAL RESPONSIBILITY (Chapter IV)

C. B. Anderson, 'Ministerial Responsibility in the 1620s', 34 *Journal of Modern History* 381.
Anson, *Law and Custom of the Constitution* (5th edn.), vol. i, chap. 9. (Particularly section on history of Committees of Inquiry and views of Gladstone and Asquith.)
P. Norton, 'Government Defeats in the House of Commons. Myth and Reality', (1978) *Public Law* 360.
Arthur Silkin, 'The Agreement to Differ of 1975 and its Effect on Ministerial Responsibility', (1977) *Political Quarterly* 65.

David L. Ellis, 'Collective Ministerial Responsibility and Solidarity', (1980) *Public Law* 367.

Report of Select Committee on Parliamentary Questions, HC 393 (1971-2), esp. pp. 114-17.

Report of Tribunal of Inquiry into the Vehicle and General Insurance Co., HC 133 (1971-2), (on position of civil servants and Minsters).

Herbert Morrison and Sir D. Maxwell-Fyfe's speeches in the Crichel Down Debate (20 July 1954), 530 HC Deb. 5s., cols. 1286-7, 1278-87.

Herbert Morrison, *Government and Parliament* (1954), chaps. 3, 8 and 14.

S. E. Finer, 'The Individual Responsibility of Ministers', (1956) *Public Administration* 377.

Report of the Fulton Committee on the Civil Service, Cmnd. 3638 (1968), paras. 281-6.

Report from the Select Committee on Procedure 1977-8, HC 558-1 (1978), App. C. on Select Committee Powers.

K. C. Wheare, *Maladministration and its Remedies*, (chap. 3 on Ministers).

— 'Crichel Down Re-visited', (1975) *Political Studies* 268.

G. K. Fry, 'Thoughts on the Present State of the Convention of Ministerial Responsibility', (1969-70) *Parlt Affairs*, p. 10.

— 'The Sachsenhausen Case and the Convention of Ministerial Responsibility', (1970) *Public Law* 336.

G. Marshall, 'Ministerial Responsibility', (1965) *Political Quarterly*, p. 256.

Lewis Gunn, 'Politicians and Officials: Who is Answerable?', (1972) *Political Quarterly*, p. 253.

Lord Hunt of Tamworth, 'Access to a Previous Government's Papers', (1982) *Public Law* 514.

Report of Select Committee on Nationalised Industries, HC 371 (1967-8), (on Ministerial Control). Also *Government's Observations*, Cmnd. 4027 (1969).

Nevil Johnson, 'Select Committees and Administration' in S. A. Walkland (ed.), *The House of Commons in the Twentieth Century* (1977).

G. Ganz, 'Parliamentary Accountability of the Crown Agents', (1980) *Public Law* 454.

David Butler, 'Ministerial Responsibility in England and Australia', (1974) *Parliamentary Affairs*.

THE OMBUDSMAN'S ROLE *(Chapter V)*

K. C. Wheare, *Maladministration and its Remedies* (1973).

R. Gregory and P. G. Hutcheson, *The Parliamentary Ombudsman* (1975).

Frank Stacey, *Ombudsmen Compared* (1978).

Justice, *Our Fettered Ombudsman* (1977).
R. Gregory, 'The Select Committee on the Parliamentary Commissioner for Administration, 1967-1980', (1982) *Public Law* 49.
—— 'Court Line, Mr Benn and the Ombudsman', (1977) *Parliamentary Affairs* 269.
Sir Idwal Pugh, 'The Ombudsman's Jurisdictional Powers in Practice', (1978) *Public Administration*.
W. B. Gwyn, 'The Ombudsman in Britain', (1982) *Public Administration* 177.
A. W. Bradley, 'The Role of the Ombudsman in Relation to Citizens' Rights', (1980) 39 *Cambridge Law Journal* 304.
Sir Cecil Clothier, 'The Efficacy of the Ombudsman' (in *Parliament and the Executive* R.I.P.A., 1983).
Second Report of the Select Committee on the Parliamentary Commissioner 1979-80 (The System of Ombudsman in the United Kingdom), HC 254 (1980).
Fourth Report of the Select Committee on the Parliamentary Commissioner 1979-80 (The Jurisdiction of the Parliamentary Commissioner), HC 593 (1980).

MORALITY AND SECURITY (Chapters VI and VII)

Lord Denning's Report, Cmnd. 2152 (1963).
Chapman Pincher, *Their Trade is Treachery* (1981), chap. 9.
Positive Vetting Procedures in HM Services and the Ministry of Defence HC 242 (1982-83).
Report of the Security Commission, Cmnd. 5367 (1973) and Cmnd. 8876 (1983).
Report by Lord Radcliffe: Security Procedures in the Public Service, Cmnd. 1681 (1962).
Harry Street, *Freedom, the Individual and the Law* (4th edn.), chap. 8.
Second Report of the Commission of Inquiry concerning Certain Activities of the Royal Canadian Mounted Police (Ottawa, 1981).
J. Ll. J. Edwards, *Ministerial Responsibility for National Security*, Commission of Inquiry Study, Ottawa, 1980.
J. Michael, *The Politics of Secrecy* (1982).
T. Emerson, 'The Control of Intelligence Agencies: the American Experience', (1982) *Political Quarterly* 233.

PROSECUTION AND MACHINERY OF JUSTICE (Chapter VII)

J. Ll. Edwards, *The Law Officers of the Crown* (1964).
—— 'Politics and the Integrity of Criminal Prosecutions', in P. R. Glazebrook (ed.), *Reshaping the Criminal Law* (1978).
B. M. Dickens, 'The Prosecuting Roles of the Attorney-General and Director of Public Prosecutions', (1974) *Public Law* 50.
R. F. Wilcox, *The Decision to Prosecute* (1972), chaps. 4 and 12.

Report of the Royal Commission on Criminal Procedure, Cmnd. 8092 (1981), chaps. 6 and 7.
The Investigation and Prosecution of Criminal Offences in England and Wales: The Law and Procedure (Royal Commission on Criminal Procedure Research Report) Cmnd. 8092-1 (1981).
G. Zellick, 'The Attorney-General's Prosecution Criteria', (1983) *Public Law* 165.

POLICE ACCOUNTABILITY (*Chapter VIII*)

Report of the Royal Commission on the Police, Cmnd. 1728 (1962).
D. G. T. Williams, 'Prosecution, Discretion and the Accountability of the Police' in R. Hood (ed.), *Crime, Criminology and Public Policy* (1974).
G. Marshall, *Police and Government* (1965), chaps. 1-7.
R. Plehwe, 'Police and Government: the Commissioner of Police for the Metropolis', (1974) *Public Law* 316.
Sir Robert Mark, *In the Office of Constable* (1978), chaps. 19 and 24.
S. Morris, 'British Chief Constables: the Americanization of a Role', (1981) *Political Studies* 352.
House of Commons Debates (5 April 1982), 21 H.C. Deb., col. 802 (Police Accountability).
House of Commons Debates (21 April 1982), 22 H.C. Deb., col. 395 (Powers of Chief Constables).
Barry Loveday, 'The Role of the Police Committee', (1983) *Local Government Studies* 39.
Philip C. Stenning, 'Legal Status of the Police' (Law Reform Commission of Canada, 1983).
House of Commons Home Affairs Committee Report (on Police Complaints Procedures), H.C. 98 (1981-2).
Police Complaints Board: Triennial Reports 1980 and 1983.
— – Annual Report 1981.
Home Office Circular No. 54/1982 (*Local Consultative Arrangements Between the Community and the Police*).
Police Complaints Procedures, Cmnd. 8681 (1982).

CIVIL ROLE OF THE ARMY (*Chapter IX*)

Manual of Military Law, pt. ii, sec. v (Employment of troops in aid of the civil power).
A. V. Dicey, *Introduction to the Study of the Law of the Constitution* (10th edn., ed. E. C. S. Wade) chap. 9 'The Army'.
Report of the House of Commons Select Committee on the Employment of Military in Cases of Disturbance HC 236 (1908).
R. F. V. Heuston, *Essays in Constitutional Law* (2nd edn. 1964), chap. 6.

Report of the Metropolitan Police Commissioner for 1975, Cmnd. 6496 (1976), App. 9.
A. F. Wilcox, 'Military Aid to the Civil Power', (1976) *New Law Journal* 404.
R. Evelegh, *Peace-Keeping in a Democratic Society* (1978).
C. Whelan, 'The Law and the Use of Troops in Industrial Disputes' (SSRC Working Paper, 1979).
G. S. Morris, 'The Emergency Powers Act 1920', (1979) *Public Law* 317.
M. Supperstone, *Brownlie's Law of Public Order and National Security* (2nd edn. 1981), chap. 10.
James B. Jacobs, 'The Role of Military Forces in Public Sector Labor Relations', (1982) 35 *Industrial and Labour Relations Review* 163 (United States).
K. Jeffery and P. Hennessy, *States of Emergency: British Governments and Strikebreaking since 1919*.

COMMONWEALTH CONVENTIONS (*Chapter X*)

R. T. E. Latham, *The Law and the Commonwealth* (1949), Repr. from W. K. Hancock, *Survey of British Commonwealth Affairs* (1937).
N. Mansergh, *The Name and Nature of the British Commonwealth* (1954).
K. C. Wheare, *The Constitutional Structure of the Commonwealth* (1960).
S. A. de Smith, *The Vocabulary of Commonwealth Relations* (1954).
—— *The New Commonwealth and its Constitutions* (1964).
F. R. Scott, 'The End of Dominion Status', (1945), 23 *Canadian Bar Review* 23.
—— 'The Redistribution of Imperial Sovereignty', (1950), 44 *Transactions of the Royal Society of Canada Series III* 27.
H. V. Evatt, *The King and His Dominion Governors* (1936).
B. Foott, *Dismissal of a Premier (the Philip Game Papers)* (1968).
Sir John Kerr, *Matters for Judgment* (1978).
Gough Whitlam, *The Truth of the Matter* (1979).
G. Evans (ed.), *Labour and the Constitution 1972-1975* (1977), (Australia).
Geoffrey Sawer, *Federation under Strain* (1972).
J. R. Mallory, 'Politics by Other Means: the Courts and the Westminster Model in Australia', (1979) *Journal of Commonwealth and Comparative Politics* 5.
—— 'Recollected, but not in Tranquillity: the Australian Constitutional Crisis of 1975 in Retrospect', (1980) *Politics* 105.
E. A. Forsey, 'The Role and Position of the Monarch in Canada', (1983) *The Parliamentarian* vol. lxiv, p. 6.
Sir Z. Cowan, 'The Monarch and Her Personal Representative in Australia', *The Parliamentarian* vol. lxiv, p. 1.

PARLIAMENT, PATRIATION AND CONSTITUTIONAL CHANGE
(*Chapter XI*)

K. C. Wheare, *The Statute of Westminster and Dominion Status* (1953), chaps. 5, 7, and 8.

P. Gérin-Lajoie, *Constitutional Amendment in Canada* (1950).

P. W. Hogg, *The Constitutional Law of Canada* (1977).

House of Commons Foreign Affairs Committee Reports:

British North America Acts: The Role of Parliament, HC 362-xxii (1979-80);

British North America Acts: The Role of Parliament, HC 42 I (1980-81), (and Minutes of evidence HC 42 II);

Supplementary Report on the British North America Acts: the Role of Parliament, HC 295 (1980-81);

Third Report on the British North America Acts: the Role of Parliament, HC 128 (1981-82).

S. A. Scott, 'Law and Convention in the Patriation of the Canadian Constitution', 62 *The Parliamentarian* 183.

G. Marshall, P. W. Hogg, and W. R. Lederman, 'Amendment and Patriation', (1981) XIX *Alberta Law Review* 363.

R. Knopff, 'Legal Theory and the Patriation Debate', (1981) 7 *Queen's University Law Journal* 41.

P. W. Hogg, 'Comment on *Reference re Amendment of the Constitution of Canada*', (1982) 60 *Canadian Bar Review* 307.

I. Dickinson, 'Severing the Legislative Link: some Reflections on the Canada Act 1982', (1982) 132 *New Law Journal* 777.

Report by the Joint Committee of the House of Lords and the House of Commons on the Petition of the State of Western Australia HL 75, HC 88 (1935).

E. McWhinney, *Canada and the Constitution 1979-82* (1982).

P. Russell, R. Décary, W. Lederman, N. Lyon, and D. Soberman, *The Court and the Constitution* (1982) (Institute of Governmental Relations, Queens University, Kingston, Ontario, Canada).

B. Slattery, 'The Independence of Canada, (1983) 5 *Supreme Court Law Review*.

The Operation of the Statute of Westminster: memorandum presenting the views of the Australian States (June 1973), Queensland Parliamentary Papers, Minister for Justice and Attorney-General (1973).

R. D. Lumb, 'Fundamental Law and the Process of Constitutional Change' in A. Tay and E. Kamenka (eds.), *Law Making in Australia* (1980).

P. W. Hogg, Patriation and the Canadian Constitution: Has it been achieved? (1983) 8 *Queen's University Law Journal* 123.

Additions to Bibliography

CONSTITUTIONAL CONVENTION

Colin Munro, 'Dicey on Constitutional Conventions', (1985) *Public Law* 637.

THE QUEEN

Vernon Bogdanor, *No Overall Majority: Forming a Government in a Multi-party Parliament* (1986).
R. W. Blackburn, 'The Queen and Ministerial Responsibility', (1985) *Public Law* 361.

MINISTERIAL RESPONSIBILITY

Gavin Drewry (ed.), *The New Select Committees* (1985).

PROSECUTION AND MACHINERY OF JUSTICE

J. Ll. J. Edwards, *The Attorney-General, Politics, and the Public Interest* (1984).

POLICE ACCOUNTABILITY

Laurence Lustgarten, *The Governance of Police* (1986).
T. Jefferson and R. Grimshaw, *Controlling the Constable: Police Accountability in England and Wales* (1984).
G. Marshall, 'The Police Complaints Authority', (1985) *Public Law* 448.
Robert Reiner, *The Politics of the Police* (1985).

CIVIL ROLE OF THE ARMY

S. C. Greer, 'Military Intervention in Civil Disturbances: the Legal Basis Reconsidered', (1985) *Public Law* 573.
P. J. Rowe and C. J. Whelan (eds.), *Military Intervention in Democratic Societies* (1985).
S. Peak, *Troops in Strikes: Military Intervention in Industrial Disputes* (1984).

Index

Printed in the United Kingdom
by Lightning Source UK Ltd.
124604UK00001B/126/A